AN INTRODUCTION TO
THE STUDY OF THE BIBLE

JOHN ROBERT VAN PELT, Ph. D.

AN INTRODUCTION TO THE STUDY OF THE BIBLE

BY

JOHN ROBERT VAN PELT, PH. D.

Professor in Gammon Theological Seminary

Bill Toeepo

NEW YORK
GEORGE H. DORAN COMPANY

An Introduction to the Study of the Bible. III.

———

Printed in the United States of America

TO

WILLIAM FAIRFIELD WARREN

IN IMPERISHABLE AFFECTION
AND GRATITUDE

CONTENTS

PART I: A GENERAL SURVEY

PART II: THE BIBLE IN THE MAKING

vii

PART III: HOW WE GOT OUR BIBLE

PART IV: THE BIBLE IN THE CHURCH

PART V: THE BIBLE IN THE WORLD

PART VI: HOW TO READ THE BIBLE

PART I: A GENERAL SURVEY

An Introduction to the Study of the Bible

PART I: A GENERAL SURVEY

Chapter I

WHAT IS THE BIBLE?

Whatever else it may be, the collection of writings called the Bible is without question the most influential book in the history of the human race. Regarded simply as a book and quite apart from every question of the intrinsic value of its contents, its successes are incomparable.

No other ancient book was so often copied, no modern book has been half so often printed as the Bible. Its countless printed editions exhibit the utmost range of the bookmaker's art, from the most inexpensive to the most sumptuous style. The first complete book to be printed in Europe was a Latin Bible; the earliest decades of the new art of printing saw more copies of the Bible issued than of all other books put together; and in the centuries that have followed no literary sensation has ever, even for its brief day, rivaled the Bible in popular demand.

No other book has been translated into half so many languages as the Bible. Even from ancient times it has been so. But the Bible has not merely been translated

11

into these many tongues, it has infused itself, as no other book, into the very life of the nations. In many nations it has become the one preëminent book of the people. Though sprung from one of the very least of the peoples and lands of the older world, it is to-day the book above all other books for the leading nations of the world; and more and more it seems to be winning its way to a like position with the remotest and most diverse races of mankind. It knows no barrier in racial idiosyncrasy; moreover, in every nation it appeals with power to all sorts and conditions of men. Thus it is the book of mankind.

More than any other book, the Bible has furnished theme and inspiration for poet, painter and musical composer. It has lent a peculiar charm to the land from which it sprung: names, places and incidents connected with Bible history are lifted by this association into a sphere of imperishable interest. No other book has been the object of so much study and research and none has provoked so much controversy. Countless multitudes have sought in all sincerity to be guided by its teachings, and yet no other book has so often been perverted or so needlessly misunderstood. The Bible is an ancient book, yet it, above all other relics of ancient literature, retains the undiminished freshness of perpetual youth.

Such is the book which lies invitingly before us. As we enter upon a systematic study of it, the question at once presents itself: What is this book called the Bible? This is, however, not merely our first question, but also our last. It is the one main question that must accompany us throughout all our researches. Evidently the full answer to the question is not to be thought of at the very threshold of our study; that can come only as the crowning result of all our explorations in the Bible's

broad fields and deep mines. And indeed, since the Bible
is a realm of inexhaustible richness and variety, a complete answer no man will ever be able to give. To the
very last all our observations and discoveries in the way
of Bible study will be but contributions toward a fuller
and clearer answer to the question, What is the Bible?
What is here required is simply the normal first step in
scientific inquiry. At the beginning of any systematic
study it is essential that we fix the place of the object of
our research; that is to say, we need to mark its bounds
and note its broad general relations. In its first general
intention, then, our question has not to do with what the
Bible may be in the last analysis but with what it shows
itself to be in a first broad survey. We do not first inquire what the Bible is for the Christian believer, but
what it is for all observers. "First that which is natural,
and afterward that which is spiritual."

1. The simplest and broadest inquiry as to the place
of the Bible in the world's literature yields at once this
answer: *The Bible is the sacred book of the Christian
religion.* There are in the world other religions besides
Christianity, and some of these have their sacred books.
In the book before us we have the acknowledged sacred
writings of one particular religion. Indeed, the Bible is
the sole collection of writings universally acknowledged
by the Christian Church as sacred and authoritative.
While two great branches of the Christian Church—the
Roman and the Greek Catholics—include in their Bibles
certain writings (known as Apocrypha) not acknowledged by Protestants, they exclude nothing from the Bible
as accepted by Protestants. We must not omit to notice
further, that the portion of the Bible known as the Old
Testament was "Holy Scripture" for the ancient Jews

and is still so regarded by their descendants, while they generally reject the New Testament. These are the most obvious general historical facts pertaining to the Bible; as such they are universally accessible; moreover, one may know them without having the least acquaintance with the inner structure and contents of the book.

2. We may now proceed—just as though it were a book hitherto quite unknown to us—to open the Bible in order to orient ourselves in it. We then immediately observe that *the Bible is not one book but a library*. We may surmise that some unifying principle runs through the books composing the Bible; at all events it is an historical fact that the Church has ever held that the books taken together do present a certain higher unity. But after all they are, strictly speaking, not one book but many. They spring manifestly from many different authors and from widely separated times. Furthermore, as even a very cursory examination will show, this collection of writings presents to us a great variety of literary forms: poetry of many sorts, stories, histories, proverbs, prophecies, biographical sketches, letters, and still other kinds. These and other obvious facts imply an historical process in the production of the books and in their collection and use. All these suggest a multitude of interesting questions, concerning which there will be something to say in due time. Just now, however, one thing before everything else in the matter of the structure of the Bible commands our notice. It is the fact that the Bible shows two grand divisions known as the Old and the New Testament. So striking a fact cannot be without special significance. A little examination will show us that the Old Testament represents the religion of the ancient Hebrews on the background of their history, while

the New Testament represents the early phases of the faith in Jesus of Nazareth as the fulfilment of the Old Testament hope of a Messiah.

3. That the Bible is made up of two parts, the "Old" and the "New," is presumably a fact of real significance and it demands some explanation. The question inevitably occurs to every real student of the Bible: Why is the New Testament perpetually linked with the Old? Is not the New Testament quite sufficient in itself? To this question history itself gives the answer: *The whole Bible is the source-book of the Christian religion.* At first glance it may seem as if only the New Testament could be regarded as the source-book of the Christian religion; yet the statement holds also, though less directly and less completely, in relation to the Old. It was the persuasion that Jesus was the Messiah, risen from the dead, that engendered the historical movement called Christianity. The Bible as a whole is the literary monument of the beginnings of that movement. The New Testament is the direct outgrowth of the movement in its first stages, while the Old Testament shows us its special historical preparation. Some further observations may serve to make clear the truth of this statement.

The New Testament writings are the literary documents of the faith and life of the primitive Christian community. They are the immediate literary outgrowth and expression of the thought and activity of the first propagators of the Christian religion. As such they constitute a sort of autobiography of Christianity in its beginnings and earliest development and expansion. The New Testament Epistles, it will be observed, are documents of the apostolic missionary labors and pastoral care, while the Gospels show us how the life of Jesus was recounted and interpreted in the first age of the Church.

But also the Old Testament is a document bearing upon the founding of Christianity. If we view it apart from every direct relation to the new movement that sprang from Jesus of Nazareth, the Old Testament appears simply as the literary document of the life, especially the religious life, of ancient Israel. As it was complete long before the Christian era, the Old Testament cannot be a *direct* document of the beginnings of Christianity. Yet in another way it is a very real and even indispensable document of Christian origins.

The Old Testament was in the first instance the Bible of Judaism. It was also the Bible of Jesus. It furnished the soil and atmosphere of his personal development and formed a very large part of the background of his work. He himself recognized in it the eternal truth of God and upon it he firmly stood. At the same time he found imperfection and incompleteness in it. His attitude toward it is significantly expressed in his declarations that he came "not to destroy but to fulfill"—to fill up what was lacking in the law and the prophets and to bring the divine intention that was in them to full expression and realization. Except upon the background of the Old Testament, Jesus would be an inexplicable if not an inconceivable phenomenon. Furthermore, the Old Testament was also the Bible of Jesus' apostles and of the churches which they founded. Jesus had recognized an indissoluble relation between his work and the Old Testament, and his disciples instinctively did the same. And the Church has never departed from this view. However imperfect the Old Testament may be in comparison with the New,

Christianity is not to be understood except in relation to it.

Our observations have already made it plain that the center of interest in the Bible is the figure of Jesus. He is manifestly the theme, directly or indirectly, of the writings of the New Testament. And as for the Old Testament, it is the spontaneous recognition of the essential relation of Jesus to it that has linked it inseparably with the word of the New Testament. But it is clear that, in the union of the two, it is the New Testament that dominates. The Old Testament is read and used in the Christian Church in subordination to the New. The reason for this subordination is for Christianity nothing arbitrary, it lies in the manifest historical relation of the "New" to the "Old."

These facts, which seem to be clearly established by history, show why and how the whole Bible, the Old Testament linked with the New, is to be regarded as a document of Christian origins, the perpetual monument of the primitive faith of Christianity.

The three primary observations which we have made may serve for a first orientation in our study of the Bible. We have noted that the Bible is the acknowledged sacred book of the Christian religion; that it is not really a single book but a library, and as such appears to be the outgrowth of a long religious history; and that it is the source-book of the Christian religion. The facts which we have observed are for the most part too obvious to be questioned. Nevertheless, their significance for the understanding of the Bible is not always duly regarded. It is absolutely essential that the student of the Bible should learn to view it historically as well as in its present-day religious significance. Indeed, wherever the Bible is read with disregard of its fundamental historical relations, it is sure to be more or less seriously misread. From the point which we have now reached we may proceed first to a more particular description of the Bible, then to an account of its growth and its historical relations, and finally to inquire into its practical value and use.

Chapter II

OUTWARD ASPECTS OF THE BIBLE

1. Compass, Divisions, and Arrangement.

The Bible, in its compass as accepted by Protestants, contains 66 books. These fall into two grand divisions, the Old and the New Testament. The former is composed of 39 books, the latter of 27. An ancient Greek version of the Old Testament, called the Septuagint, included a number of books—commonly called Apocrypha—not accepted by the Palestinian Jews and not included in their Hebrew Bible. The Old Testament of the Roman and Greek Churches corresponds in the main to the compass of the Septuagint, while the Protestant Churches have adhered to the Palestinian tradition, excluding the Apocrypha. The compass of the New Testament is the same for all branches of the Christian Church.

The 39 books of the Old Testament as we know it in our Bible appear in the Hebrew Bible as 24. This reckoning the ancient scribes effected by means of certain combinations in order to make the number of books coincide with the number of letters in the Hebrew alphabet. Naturally, 1 and 2 Samuel, 1 and 2 Kings, and 1 and 2 Chronicles there appear respectively as undivided books, for such they were originally, while Ezra and Nehemiah are regarded as one book, and the 12 Minor Prophets as one, called "The Book of the Twelve."

At present it is usual to classify the 39 books of our

Old Testament in four main groups: (1) The Law (Pentateuch), 5 books; (2) Historical Books, 12, namely, Joshua, Judges, Ruth, 1 and 2 Samuel, 1 and 2 Kings, 1 and 2 Chronicles, Ezra, Nehemiah, Esther; (3) Poetical Books, 5, namely, Job, Psalms, Proverbs, Ecclesiastes, Song of Solomon; (4) Prophetical Books, 17, namely, Isaiah, Jeremiah, Lamentations, Ezekiel, Daniel, Hosea, Joel, Amos, Obadiah, Jonah, Micah, Nahum, Habakkuk, Zephaniah, Haggai, Zechariah, Malachi. The last group is subdivided into the Major and the Minor Prophets, the former comprising the first five books in this list and the latter the remaining twelve. This classification corresponds to the order of the books in the Christian Bible, and the arrangement is obviously based upon a certain logical principle. The Jews, however, have from the beginning had a different arrangement and a different classification of the books, which likewise are controlled by a certain, though different, idea. They have recognized three groups of sacred writings corresponding at once to a threefold distinction as to the general nature of the several groups and to the three stages in which they obtained recognition as sacred scripture. These three groups are as follows: (1) the Torah (Law); (2) the Nebiim (Prophets); (3) the Kethubim (Writings). Now, it is a very interesting and significant fact, as we shall see more particularly hereafter, that the Law was recognized as sacred and authoritative a considerable time before the Prophets, and the Prophets some time before the Writings. The Torah includes the five books commonly ascribed to Moses (called in Greek usage Pentateuchos, that is, "The Fivefold Book"). The Nebiim the Jews divided into the "Former" and the "Latter" Prophets. The Former Prophets are the books of Joshua,

Judges, Samuel, and Kings. These books, which we classify as "historical," the ancient Jews called "Prophets," because it was supposed they had been written by certain of the prophets. The Latter Prophets are the prophets in the stricter sense of the term; in this group the Jews reckoned four books: Isaiah, Jeremiah, Ezekiel, and the Book of the Twelve, i.e., the twelve "Minor" Prophets (it will be observed that Lamentations and Daniel fall into the next group). The Kethubim (or Writings—a rather vague term suggesting the miscellaneous character of the group) include: (a) The Poetical Books, namely, Psalms, Proverbs, Job; (b) the five Megilloth or Rolls, namely, Song of Solomon, Ruth, Lamentations, Ecclesiastes, Esther; (c) the Remaining Books, namely, Daniel, Ezra-Nehemiah, Chronicles.

Interesting attempts have been made to assign the books of the Old Testament to appropriate literary categories. A literary species is distinguished by two marks: the nature of its contents and especially the form and method of treatment. From this point of view the following classification of the books of the Old Testament will be found useful, though it must be understood that the diversified character of several of the books makes a strict classification impossible. (1) The Pentateuch taken as a whole is a combination of the legal and the narrative species of literature. Genesis is almost purely narrative and it embodies the traditions of the Hebrews concerning the origin of the world, of the human race and its divisions of the same, and especially of Israel. Leviticus is almost wholly a book of Laws, Numbers a book of narration, while Exodus and Deuteronomy are partly legal writing and partly narration. (2) The books from Joshua to Nehemiah inclusive may, with one or two exceptions, be fairly classified as belonging to the category of historical writings. The book of Ruth is probably to be excepted, perhaps also Chronicles, for reasons that will appear hereafter. (3) Poetical books: (a) lyrical—Psalms, Lamentations, Song of Solomon; (b) dramatic (in a qualified sense)—Job. (4) Prophetical books: Isaiah, Jeremiah, Ezekiel and the 12 Minor Prophets with the exception of Jonah. (5) Apocalyptic books: Daniel (also portions of Ezekiel and Zechariah). (6) Midrashic books: i.e., books in which narrative (not necessarily based upon historical facts) is used primarily as a vehicle of moral or religious lessons; Ruth, Jonah, Esther, perhaps also Chronicles. (7) Wisdom books: Proverbs (gnomic), Ecclesiastes (speculative).

The 27 New Testament books fall easily into a fourfold division: (1) Gospels, 4; (2) Apostolic history ("Acts of the Apostles"), 1; (3) Epistles, 21, of which 14 are traditionally called "Pauline" and 7 "General"; (4) Apocalyptic, 1 (the "Apocalypse" or "Revelation"). For convenience' sake a twofold division has had a certain recognition in ecclesiastical prayer-books and lectionaries: "Gospel" and "Epistle"—everything but the four Gospels falling under the second head.

Thus far we have confined our attention to the list of books which Protestants recognize as "canonical" (canon is a Greek word meaning "rule" or "pattern," and hence, in a technical sense, "a list of standard or authoritative writings"). But also those other books called Apocrypha require some notice. The term Apocrypha means "hidden," and is applied to writings which, being "of doubtful origin," were supposed to be unworthy of admission to the canon. The Old Testament Apocrypha comprise the chief remains of literature from Jewish sources not in

the old Hebrew canon, in so far as the writings were
analogous in purpose and style to the undisputed books.
Concerning them the Church of England in the sixth
Article of Religion made this pronouncement: "And the
other books (as Jerome saith) the church doth read for
example of life and instruction of manners: but yet doth
it not apply to them to establish any doctrine." The
Article then proceeds to give a list of the books:

> The Third (now called the First) Book of
> Esdras.
> The Fourth (now called the Second) Book of
> Esdras.
> The Book of Tobias.
> The Book of Judith.
> The Rest of the Book of Esther.
> The Book of Wisdom.
> Jesus the Son of Sirach.
> Baruch the Prophet.
> The Song of the Three Children.
> The Story of Susanna.
> Of Bel and the Dragon.
> The First Book of the Maccabees.
> The Second Book of the Maccabees.

With the exception of 2 Esdras all these are preserved
to us in the Greek version of the Old Testament called
the Septuagint. Several of them were originally written
in Hebrew, but the majority seem to have been written
in Greek. In Alexandria they were highly esteemed, but
the Palestinian rabbis rejected them. Most of them are
included in Luther's Bible as "books which, though not
esteemed equal to the Holy Scriptures, are yet useful and
good to read." The Calvinistic churches in the age of
the Reformation specifically rejected them. The Roman

Church, however, by the Council of Trent in 1546 declared the equal inspiration of all books contained in the Vulgate version of the Bible, in which the list of Old Testament books is almost the same as that of the Septuagint. To the traditional list of Apocrypha as given above might be added a considerable number of other writings belonging to the same period, which for convenience' sake may be called "additional Apocrypha." These, however, are writings that never were canonical. In respect of literary form the apocryphal writings fall into the following classes: historical pieces, romances, additions to canonical books, and apocalyptic literature. All these writings throw much light upon the religious history of the Jews, both in Palestine and in the Dispersion, in the period between the Old Testament and the New.

There are also the New Testament Apocrypha. For a time, especially in the second century, a few of these were so highly esteemed as to be read in the churches along with the canonical books of the New Testament. As these particular writings only narrowly missed being accepted as canonical, they may be called "secondary books" of primitive Christianity. We possess four writings of this class: the Epistle of Clement, the Epistle of Barnabas, the Shepherd of Hermas, and the Teaching of the Twelve Apostles. But there grew up also a large body of apocryphal writings that never found any considerable acceptance in representative churches. These represented for the most part heretical tendencies and special types of unorthodox teaching. They fall into four classes after the manner of the canonical books of the New Testament: "Gospels," "Acts of Apostles," "Epistles," "Apocalypses." They are all of much interest to scholars, as shedding light upon the problems of early Christian history. In intrinsic value, however, they are strikingly inferior to the canonical Scriptures of the New Testament.

All modern Bibles exhibit a peculiar feature which was entirely wanting in the original manuscripts, namely, the division of books into chapters and of chapters into verses. Slight movements in this direction, however, began very early. Jewish rabbis even before the time of Christ marked out portions of the Scriptures, especially of the Pentateuch, for public reading in the synagogues. In the Christian church as early as the fourth century something of the same sort was done for portions of the New Testament. The completion of the movement to divide the whole Bible into chapters is ascribed to Stephen Langton, Archbishop of Canterbury (died 1227). It is universally recognized as a work in many instances ill done. The very first chapter of Genesis, for example, would properly end with the third verse of the second chapter. The division of the New Testament text into verses was the work—based on earlier models—of Robert Stephens in his Greek Testament of 1551. The work was done hurriedly on a journey between Paris and Lyons—*"inter equitandum,"* as he said; which probably means "while resting at inns in the intervals of his journey." Someone, however, suggested that it might mean that Stephens did the work on horseback, pencil in hand, and whenever he received a decided jolt he involuntarily made a mark with his pencil—and the mark fixed the end of a verse! At all events the division of the text into verses, however convenient it may be for reference, was in every other regard anything but a happy stroke. The modern revisers of the English Bible have given us relief by printing the translation in paragraph form, setting the numbers of the verses in the margin.

2. Languages.

By far the greater part of the Old Testament is written in Hebrew; the portions not in Hebrew are written in the kindred Aramaic (mentioned in 2 Kings 18:26 as the "Syrian" or Aramæan language). The Aramaic portions are Ezra 4:8—6:18 and 7:12; Daniel 2:4—7:28; and Jeremiah 10:11. Hebrew was the language of the people of Israel as developed after the Conquest under the powerful influence of the surrounding and intermingling Canaanitish tribes. Like all other languages it passed through various phases in the course of its development, but, once formed, it fairly maintained its integrity as the speech of the people until after the Babylonian Exile, which came to an end about 538 B. C. In the period of the Exile the Jews that were left behind in the homeland were too weak to resist the flood of Syrians that swept over the land. Nor were the returning exiles numerous and strong enough to stem the tide of the Syrian language. The Hebrew was, indeed, still long maintained as the classical or standard language of the nation; in it even the later books of the Old Testament were for the most part written. But eventually it was quite displaced for ordinary uses by the Aramaic. The change came about all the more naturally because of the close kinship between the two languages. Aramaic was the language of Palestine in the time of Christ, the language of Jesus and his hearers. It is referred to several times in the New Testament (John 5:2; 19:13, 17, 20; Acts 21:40; 22:2; 26:14), where, however, it is simply called Hebrew. The Hebrew is a branch of the

Semitic family of languages ("Semitic" from Shem,
eldest son of Noah).   Its most important cognates are
the Assyrian, the Phœnician, the Aramaic, the Syriac,
the Arabic, and the Ethiopic.   These languages show a
strong family resemblance among themselves, and they all
differ in idiom very widely from the Indo-European
family, which includes Sanscrit, Greek, Latin, and the
languages of modern Europe.   The Hebrew is characterized by a certain massive simplicity of structure, and is
therefore an admirable instrument for narration, bold
description, and the expression of emotion.   In case, however, a writer is wanting in fire and imagination, the idiom
of the language appears rather formal and dull.   At its
best the Hebrew is a language of great force and charm.

The language of the New Testament is Greek.   Not
the Greek of the classic writers nor the standard form of
the Attic speech, but the *Koine,* or "common speech,"
which had been formed by the merging of the dialects,
which accompanied the diffusion of the Greek tongue following the conquests of Alexander the Great.   Until
within a few decades "Biblical Greek" was commonly
regarded as virtually a dialect by itself, or rather a corrupt
form of Greek as used by Jews who had never mastered
its idiom.   Yet even as early as 1824 a beginning had been
made in the correction of the traditional misconception.
In that year Winer published his Grammar of New Testament Greek in which he showed that the Greek of the New
Testament was not the unregulated, ungrammatical speech
of aliens, but an established form of the Greek tongue.
It remained for more recent research to show that the
language of the New Testament was not only (as Winer
had shown) the established form of Greek "as used by
the Hellenists," i.e., the Greek-speaking Jews, but that

this "Hellenistic Greek" was just the Koine. Naturally this Koine when used by Jewish writers had a flavor of the Hebrew (or Aramaic) idiom, since all the New Testament authors except Luke were Jews. The fact, however, that there are Hebraisms in the New Testament does not in the least invalidate the statement: the New Testament writers used the Koine, the vernacular of the Mediterranean lands. But it was the vernacular "raised to the level of literature."

This new knowledge we owe, above all, to Adolf Deissmann and the late J. H. Moulton. Their researches are based upon a multitude of Greek papyri discovered— chiefly by Grenfell and Hunt—in old Egyptian rubbish heaps. All of these papyri are examples of the Koine. Many of them date from the time of the New Testament. They relate, in the main, to all sorts of matters of everyday life. Some are private letters, some are memoranda of business transactions, such as bills of sale, receipts, contracts, deeds, wills, and what not. A few—these are of a date later than New Testament times—purport to give sayings of Jesus, some of which are not recorded in our Gospels, while others contain fragments of genuine New Testament writings. All in all, the papyri show the same linguistic usage as that of the New Testament. Now it is a matter of no small historical interest that there *was* a "common speech" (Koine) and that the apostles and evangelists of Christianity were able to use it freely. If the question occurs to us why the New Testament authors did not write in their native tongue (Aramaic), we have but to reflect that, before there was time or occasion for the development of much of a Christian literature, the church's great missionary activities had passed from Jewish to Gentile soil, where Greek was the common tongue.   It is very probable that in the early period while Christianity was still predominantly Jewish, there were some small beginnings of a Christian literature in the Aramaic tongue.   Indeed, there is a definite ancient tradition that Matthew "wrote a Gospel in Hebrew" (Aramaic). This little book seems to have become— probably in a Greek version—the chief basis of our "Matthew" and an important source also for Luke and— in a much smaller measure—even for Mark.   But neither this nor any other primitive Christian writing in Aramaic or in any other language than Greek has been directly preserved.

The Greek has been universally admired for its copious‧ ness, its flexibility, its subtlety, its strength joined with delicacy, and its power of self-development.   When the apostles were moved to go forth to proclaim their message to the whole world, there stood the Greek language, an apt and ready instrument, like a steed saddled and bridled, strong and swift to bear the word to many peoples.

3. Writing and Bookmaking.

The early history of the art of writing is very interest- ing, but there is no space to sketch it here.   For our present purpose it will be enough to indicate a few of the principal stages of the development that lay back of Hebrew literature.   In Egypt, picture-writing, which everywhere has been the first stage of the art, had become highly developed and conventionalized many centuries before the Hebrew people appeared in history.   This mode of Egyptian writing (that is, writing by means of ideograms) is called hieroglyphic.   Here and there it showed some approaches to alphabetic writing.   A later Egyptian mode of writing, called hieratic, was semi-alphabetic; even this was in use more than a thousand years before the time of Moses. It is probable that alphabetic writing, which seems to have been invented by the Phœnicians, was largely based upon the hieratic mode. Meanwhile in the Tigris-Euphrates valley a semi-alphabetic mode of writing was developed, from which nearly all traces of the original pictographic mode have been obliterated. This is the cuneiform system of writing; it was developed chiefly by the Assyrians. Modern archæological research has recovered great numbers of cuneiform inscriptions and tablets, which disclose much of the history and mythology of ancient Assyria and Babylonia and of surrounding lands, including Palestine. As for alphabetic writing, the Phœnicians (a most enterprising maritime people) taught it to neighboring peoples, including the Hebrews and the Greeks, who, of course, introduced some modifications. All modern European alphabets are based, in turn, upon that of the Greeks.

The antiquity of writing cannot be determined. It is, however, certain that the earliest known Egyptian inscriptions reach back to about 5000 B. C. There are many Babylonian inscriptions from about 3750 or even 4000 B. C. The earliest known remains of Palestinian writing are the Tel el-Amarna tablets, which were vehicles of letters written probably in the 14th century B. C. (i.e., before the Hebrew conquest of the land), by governors of Palestinian cities to their masters, Pharaohs of Egypt. It is clear that the art of writing was known in the countries surrounding Palestine and in Palestine itself long before the Israelites entered the land. Moses, having been brought up in the Egyptian court, must have understood the art of writing. (This fact, however, proves nothing as to whether he actually wrote the books traditionally ascribed to him.) As to the question of the antiquity of alphabetic writing, researches have shown that it made its first appearance not later than the 17th century B. C. How early the Hebrews began to write, either pictographically or alphabetically, has not been determined. The earliest extant specimens of Hebrew writing are alphabetic and consist of inscriptions on pottery; they date from about 1000 B. C. But Hebrew inscriptions, of whatever age, are strangely few. We have little to show us how the original manuscripts of the Hebrew Scriptures must have looked. We do, however, know that the characters of the oldest extant Hebrew manuscript differ much from those found in the far more ancient inscriptions.

The earliest material for the reception of writing was stone. The Old Testament affords a number of interesting references to the practice of making inscriptions on stone. The law given at Sinai was "graven on tablets of stone"; and Moses commanded the people that, when they passed over the Jordan, they should set up stones with the law graven thereon (Deut. 27 : 2f; Josh. 8 : 30ff). The earliest portable vehicle of writing was either the wooden or the clay tablet. The latter was used very extensively in Babylonia and Assyria. The use of skins as a vehicle of writing, though it reaches back to a great antiquity, was for the most part a later development. In Palestine it had become prevalent before the date of the earliest books of our Hebrew Bible. In Old Testament times a book was a leather roll, the writing, of course, being only on the inner side. A greatly improved preparation of skins, especially those of sheep and goats, is known as parchment (so named from Pergamos, where it was extensively produced). Parchment began to be widely used in the second century B. C. For many centuries thereafter it continued to be a much-cherished vehicle for the preservation and transmission of the Sacred Scriptures, first of the Old Testament, then also of the New. Somewhat later, however, papyrus became much the commonest vehicle of writing, being preferred both for its cheapness and its convenience. It is a preparation from the papyrus plant, which in ancient times grew in great abundance on the banks of the Nile and elsewhere in regions about the Mediterranean Sea. Egypt's dry climate has made possible the preservation, in the debris of ruined cities, of many fragments of ancient writings on papyrus. As to the form of books, a change gradually took place in Greek and Latin countries from the roll to the tablet (or codex) form. The change was consummated before the close of the first century of the Christian era. The Hebrews, however, clung to the roll form; it is used in their synagogues even yet. In our modern usage the technical description of an ancient manuscript begins with the notation that it is a "roll" or a "codex," as the case may be.

CHAPTER III

NAMING THE SCRIPTURES

The word "Bible" is derived from the Greek *biblia,*
which means "books." The base of this Greek word is
byblos or *biblos,* meaning papyrus, or a scroll made from
papyrus. So biblos came to mean "book" (as in Matt.
1 : 1) ; though the diminutive form, *biblion,* whose plural
is *biblia,* was more common. Greek-speaking Christians,
in applying the term "biblia" to the books recognized as
Holy Scriptures, at first generally used a qualifying
adjective, such as "holy," "divine," "canonical"; later,
however, the usual designation was simply *ta biblia,* that
is, "the books" *par excellence.* In the course of time the
word passed into Latin usage, where "by a happy sole-
cism" the original neuter plural (genitive *bibliorum*) was
soon taken to be a feminine singular (genitive *bibliae*) ;
"biblia" came to mean "the book" rather than "the
books."

Another designation of the Bible that was in frequent
use throughout the Middle Ages is *bibliotheca,* "library."
This term was in vogue even before biblia. Jerome, who
lived in the fourth century, and made the Latin version
of the Bible which became the basis of the Vulgate,
habitually used the term Bibliotheca. For a considerable
period the adjective "divina" or "sacra" was generally
associated with it; later it most frequently stood alone—
Bibliotheca, "the Library." The word was used to designate a complete manuscript of the Holy Scriptures.

In English usage the word "Bible" occurs as the title of the collective book of Holy Scriptures as early as the beginning of the fourteenth century. We may, however, surely infer a much earlier date for the first establishment of this usage of the word in English. In the Durham library catalogue, written in Latin in 1266, we find the following entry: "Unam bibliam in iv magnis voluminibus . . . aliam bibliam in duobus voluminibus" (one Bible in four large volumes . . . another Bible in two volumes). It can hardly be doubted that the vernacular usage of the time was in agreement with the Latin usage.

In New Testament times the Old Testament writings were generally called "the scriptures" or "the holy scriptures" (Greek *graphai, graphai hagiai,* Latin *scripturae, scripturae sacrae*). This usage was naturally continued in the Christian church; later the term was applied as a matter of course also to the New Testament writings. In the New Testament itself, however, only once are any of the writings included in it referred to as being of the same order as "the other scriptures," i.e., the Old Testament writings; and this reference occurs in the latest of its writings (see 2 Peter 3: 16). When the whole body of the then acknowledged sacred writings (that is, the Old Testament) is referred to in the New Testament, the plural, "the scriptures," is regularly used; occasionally, however, the singular, "the scripture," seems to be used in the collective sense as so often by us (see Jn. 10: 35; Acts 8: 32; 1 Peter 2: 6; 2 Peter 1: 20). But ordinarily such a phrase as "the scripture saith" refers not to the whole body of the Scriptures, but to a particular passage or book. The Latin authors of the Middle Ages generally used the singular (*scriptura*) as a collective term rather than the plural (*scripturae*). The reason for the change of usage from the plural to the singular was the same as in the case of *biblia:* it was evidently the growing sense of the unity of the whole body of writings that brought it about.

Far less simple and sure is the explanation of the term "Testament." The word is derived from the Latin *testamentum,* which means "will" (compare our legal formula: "this last will and testament"). Testamentum is the constant Latin rendering of the Greek word *diatheke* as found both in the New Testament and in the Septuagint (the Greek version of the Old Testament). In the latter *diatheke* is the regular rendering of the Hebrew *b'rith,* which means "covenant." Now covenant in the Old Testament sense means ordinarily a compact between two parties, as between God and Israel. Sometimes, however, it means a gracious or promissive decree or dispensation by one party in relation to a second party, as when God solemnly declares his gracious purpose respecting Israel. Obviously this use of the term looks in the direction of the sense of *testamentum* (will), for of course a "will" is a promissive decree or dispensation, and not a compact between two parties. Most modern scholars recognize that in the New Testament usage *diatheke* is not just the same as *diatheke* in the Septuagint and *b'rith* in the Hebrew Scriptures, where the usual meaning is a covenant between two. But neither is *diatheke* in the New Testament "will" or "testament" in the technical sense. Rather it is *God's revelation and confirmation of his gracious purpose for the world.* When Jesus at the last supper declares: "This cup is the new testament in my blood," he is virtually saying: Take this cup as a symbol that in my life and death the Father gives a new and a richer pledge of his love. The fuller revelation of

the love of God in Jesus Christ is the "new testament,"
just as the revelation of his gracious purpose toward
Israel was God's testament or covenant, now become
"old." Of course the expression "old testament" arose
only when it was believed that a *new* testament had been
given. The glory of the old is eclipsed by the excelling
glory of the new (2 Cor. 3 : 10). The usage of the New
Testament writings is not fixed or uniform; what has
been stated is, however, the fundamental conception.
An examination of all the English New Testament passages containing the word "testament" or "covenant"
will reward one; the following are of special interest:
Matt. 26 : 28 and parallels; Gal. 3 : 15; 2 Cor. 3 : 6; Heb.
7 : 22; 9 : 15–20; 13 : 20. From all this it is clear that
originally it was not the writings themselves, whether the
"old" or the "new," that were thought of as a testament;
the writings were thought of simply as the scriptures *of*
or *concerning* a testament (covenant). The secondary
usage, applying the term directly to the writings, came
about most naturally; yet it should not be allowed to
obscure the original sense of the term.

The *names of the several books* of the Bible are for
the most part self-explanatory. The ancient Jewish
rabbis referred to the books of the Law by taking
their opening words as appellations, e.g., Genesis was
"B'reshith," "In the beginning." Our names of the Old
Testament books are, however, derived from the Greek
version through the Latin Vulgate. For example, Genesis
is the Greek for "Beginning"; Exodus means "the Departure" (from Egypt); Leviticus is the book concerning
the duties of the sons of Levi; Numbers (Latin *Numeri,*
Greek *Arithmoi*) is the book concerning the numbering

of the people; Deuteronomy is "the second giving of the Law."

The naming of the New Testament books presents no problem, except in the case of the word "Gospel" used as a title. It is well known that the primary sense of the word (Greek *euaggelion,* Latin *evangelium*) is simply "good tidings." When Jesus bids his disciples to "preach the gospel to every creature," or is himself referred to as "preaching the gospel of the kingdom," or Paul writes, "I am not ashamed of the gospel," there is, of course, no thought of a book entitled "Gospel." Moreover, even when the word became the accepted title of the memoirs of the life of Christ, nobody had the thought of claiming that these alone were "gospel," while an apostolic epistle or oral discourse was something else than gospel. Probably the key to the problem of the use of the word as the title of Christian writings of a particular class is to be found in the opening words of the oldest of our "Gospels," namely, Mark: "The beginning of the gospel of Jesus Christ, the Son of God." The words stand as the title of the book, and they probably mean: "This book is an account of the beginning or foundation of the good tidings." At all events the key word in the title is "gospel"; and from this circumstance, combined, of course, with a certain inherent fitness in the usage, the term passed into universal use as a title of the memoirs of Jesus.

Chapter IV

THE DIVERSITY AND UNITY OF THE BIBLE

The Bible, though we commonly speak of it as one book, is not, we know, really a single book but a collection of books. But we know also that the Christian church has always seemed to recognize a certain unity in this library. The books were assembled and kept together because the church was persuaded that they belonged together. So much, then, is an obvious fact; in the usage of the Church the books constitute at least an external unity. But do they possess also an essential inner unity? Is it not possible that we owe our idea of the unity of the Bible to the bookbinder? Have we not, perhaps, forced upon these writings a false appearance of unity?

If upon examination we find any essential unity in this diversified collection, then we shall have discovered something unparalleled in literary history. For this collection of books comprises all that remains of perhaps the first 1,000 years of Hebrew literary production, and to that body of Hebrew literature is added the most of what remains of the literature of primitive Christianity, and the whole has been accepted and treated by the church as representing some essential unity. Now no one ever thought of ascribing unity to the bulk of any other national literature, as the Greek or Roman. Who would undertake even to select sixty-six Greek books, bind them in one volume, and send them forth as a unity? What

would hold them together? Then what is it that holds
the books of the Bible together?

As to the Bible, some have asserted the unity without
recognizing the diversity. Others have asserted the
diversity in such a way as to deny the unity. But the
unity of the Bible, which the church asserts, is a higher
unity, which somehow includes an immense diversity.

For the diversity of the Bible is patent to all real observers. The authors represented are many—we cannot
determine the exact number. They are, moreover, real
authors, not mere penmen. Their individuality asserts
itself everywhere. In respect of time the Biblical literature shows—if we go back to the most ancient elements
incorporated in our Old Testament books as we have
them—a range of at least 1,300 years. Its different parts
represent many stages of social and intellectual advance-
ment, from the cruder beginnings of civilization to the
culture of the Græco-Roman world. The various social,
political and religious conditions under which the several
authors lived have left their mark in their writings. The
authors, too, were men of different temperaments and of
many grades of intellectuality. Again, within the limits
of the Bible we find examples of every species of literature
known among the ancient Hebrews. We have examples
of early folklore in poetry and proverb; legal and ritual
writings of various ages; narratives; annals, and other
historical writings; poetry of several types; prophetic and
apocalyptic writings; and several sorts of wisdom literature. The New Testament brings two essentially new
forms of literature (as compared with the Old Testament
forms) in the Gospels and the Epistles. But it is no mere
formal diversification that we find in the Bible. There
are some very material differences in religious thought

and practical tendency represented in the Biblical literature. Do we find the priestly doctrines of Leviticus in perfect accord with the denunciations of ceremonialism in Amos and Micah? Do the books of Jonah and Esther breathe just the same spirit? Is there no discordant note in the pessimism of Ecclesiastes? Are there not some conceptions of morality reflected in some of the Old Testament books which all who have learned in the school of Christ utterly repudiate? How, then, can we speak of a unity of the Bible?

A formal or mechanical unity is not to be claimed for the Bible. Its ideas and expressions, viewed in detail, cannot be brought into perfect harmony. In the Bible we have not a precise text-book or catechism of divine knowledge. The Bible is historically given; it is the product, in its parts and as a whole, of a great historical movement. The Scriptures are the literary remains and monument of that movement; they are the organic outgrowth of it. As the movement itself was genuinely historical, it necessarily showed at every point the limitations and incompleteness that are inherent in all human history. The movement itself involved elements of conflict, divergent currents, sometimes temporary retrogressions. Should we then be offended at finding that all these things have, in some measure, left their imprint upon the literary documents of the movement? Nevertheless, viewed in a large way, the historical movement manifestly has a certain grand unity; the spiritual history of Israel until the coming of the Messiah and the record of the life of Christ and the first era of the church—all this constitutes a great spiritual drama. If we recognize a unity in the history, we shall not fail to discern a corresponding unity in the assembled documents of that history.

The field of general history and also the realm of nature afford instructive analogies of this view of the unity of the Bible. The constitution of a state, for instance, is clearly a unity. It has had an organic development, and at any given stage, but especially in its relative maturity, it manifests a certain practical unity, inasmuch as it is the body of fundamental law, etc., according to which the organic life of the state actually expresses itself. Yet the course of constitutional history in any state often shows conflicting elements, which are gradually resolved in the constant effort of the people to realize the fullest national well-being. A larger unity in the constitutional history is evident, and the equally evident minor incongruities do not contradict that unity, for the whole tendency is to overcome them.

We all recognize the higher unity of nature; yet nature teems with conflicts. Geology, for example, in relating for us the wonderful story of how the earth came to be what it is—the fit habitation of man and beast—makes clear a grand unity in that world-process; yet how strange, how meaningless, how retrogressive some phases of the process seem to have been!

The Bible is sometimes likened to a great cathedral that was many generations in building. The style of the structure is not wholly congruous—it was the product of different periods and of many minds. The plan is not just symmetrical or strictly consistent. Here and there are to be seen relatively superfluous chambers or oratories jutting out from the main walls. Yet it is a finished cathedral that we are viewing; and clearly it possesses a very real unity. In spite of a diversification of style and the presence of some relatively non-essential elements, the process of building was guided by one great effectual purpose. Moreover, now that the work is done, the cathedral possesses a unity almost like that of a living organism; for its use is controlled by a single motive and it is hallowed by the presence and the glory of the Lord.

We may also, as some have suggested, think of the Bible as one vast drama. According to the Biblical conception the divine drama enacts itself upon the whole broad theater of human history from the beginning to the final consummation. Our Bible sketches the first and second acts, and, in terms of bold imagery and symbolism, gives us an insight into the divine purpose of a final consummation. The first part might be called "The Preparation for the Messianic Kingdom"; the second, "The Messiah and His World-Mission"; the third, "The Messianic Consummation." The first act is finished; the Old Testament sets it forth. The third is yet to come, only its general import having been revealed by the spirit of New Testament prophecy. The second part is still enacting—we are, according to the Biblical conception, living in the New Testament. The fundamental stage of it, the life of Christ and the first expansion of the Church, is already set forth in the writings recognized by the Church as narratives of the first age of Christianity. Professor R. G. Moulton, in "The Bible at a Single View," conceives the unity of the Bible in nearly the same way; a drama in two great acts, the Old Testament and the New Testament. Between the two falls the "Interlude" of the Wisdom Literature, which he holds is not an organic part of the action. Following the second act stands the "Epilogue" of the Book of Revelation.

This view of the Bible as the literature of a great

spiritual history or drama enables us to understand why the full appreciation of the first act is impossible without the second, and why the writers of the primitive books relating to the second act manifestly conceive themselves to be merely witnesses of the founding of the universal kingdom of heaven—its consummation is reserved for the future.

This point of view further enables us to understand that all parts of Scripture have not the same significance for faith.   There are parts of the Old Testament whose significance for us today is very remote and indirect. The more important books have to do with the essential structure of the divine drama.   Other books, such as the Song of Solomon, Ecclesiastes and Esther, never played a constructive part in the drama.   Still others, e.g., Leviticus, represent stages in the history of Israel, which, because of their inherent limitations, were destined to be, and now long since actually have been, left behind.   Such portions have naturally and properly fallen into a relative disuse.   Yet even these parts are not to be despised; they, too, if rightly read, will help us to understand the ways of God with man.

Without doubt the unifying center of the Bible is Jesus Christ.   What is the soul of Scripture?   Is it not its testimony to Jesus as the Christ?   Luther summed up the whole matter when he said "Scripture is that which has to do with Christ."   The New Testament writings all make him their theme.   Of the Old Testament Scriptures Jesus himself said: "They testify of me."   Not that the Old Testament prophets had the full image of Jesus of Nazareth in their minds, but that the whole Old Testament history actually prepared the way for the Christ. Those who were the chief exponents of the spiritual life of the Old Testament also gave wonderful expression to the hope of a larger glory that was to be.

This higher unity of the Bible is no mere dogma, but a pragmatic fact. The Christian church does actually use the whole Bible and the Bible as a whole; and her use of it is controlled by one concentrated purpose. That many portions of it have passed into a relative disuse does not in any way contradict this obvious general fact. Jesus Christ binds the Old and the New Testaments together in an indissoluble union.

The central thought of this discussion may be summed up in the fine words of Augustine: "Novum Testamentum in Vetere latet; Vetus Testamentum in Novo patet" (The New Testament lies hidden in the Old; the Old Testament lies open in the New).

CHAPTER V

THE BIBLE AND OTHER SACRED BOOKS

Every religion of civilized peoples has its literature, but not every such religion has its Bible. The term "Bible" we take in this generic sense as signifying not merely religious writings that are highly esteemed, but a specific body of literature acknowledged by all adherents of a given religion as possessing for them a certain sacred authority. Hence books of priestcraft, manuals of discipline for particular societies or orders, and the writings specially acknowledged by this or that sect cannot be called "Bibles," because the term "Bible" implies an acceptance and authority coextensive with a given religion. Only a highly developed and fairly unified religion can have acquired a "Bible" or "sacred canon"; that is, a fixed list of acknowledged books. The ancient Greeks and Romans could have no sacred canon, because their religions were not sufficiently well organized and unified for that. Something more or less comparable to a body of authoritative religious writings seems to have been had by the ancient Egyptians, but even they certainly had no settled sacred canon. There do exist, however, several religious literatures which bear a clear analogy to our Bible. The most important of these are the following:

(1) The Five Kings (or Canons), the sacred books of Confucianism.

(2) The Tao-teh-king (the "Canon of Virtue"), the sacred book of Taoism (written by Lao-Tsze).

(3) The Vedas, the sacred books of the Brahmans.

(4) The Tripitaka (the "Three Baskets"), the sacred books of Buddhism.

(5) The Avesta (or Zend-Avesta), the sacred books of Zoroastrianism, the religion of ancient Persia.

(6) The Mohammedan Koran.

Confucius (or Kung-fu-tsze), who lived about 551–478 B. C., is popularly supposed to be the founder of the religion (or rather ethical code) of China. Confucius himself, however, never pretended to be the author of the teaching, but only the collector and conserver of the wisdom of the sages who had lived before him. His system cannot rightly be called a religion; it is only a system of morals touched with the sentiment of veneration for the past. He entertained the magnificent idea of bringing the whole nation under the discipline of wise men. In order to accomplish his purpose he gathered about himself gifted disciples, whom he imbued with the same idea. His disciples were to aid him in carrying out his great program. An essential prerequisite of his program was a literature which should form the basis of instruction. Confucius' greatest service to his people was to edit and publish the two chief religious or moral classics of his country, the *Shu-king* and the *Shi-king,* and to win for them the deep and abiding reverence of his countrymen of every rank. The first of these two books embraces many historical or legendary documents, which were regarded as having a moral value; they dated from about 2000 B. C. to 625 B. C. The second is a collection of poems composed between 1200 B. C. and 600 B. C. A book called Yun-yu, containing ethical and philosophical aphorisms and conversations of Confucius, was edited and published by his disciples after his death. A book of ritual, the Li-ki, belongs to a still later date—in its present form not earlier than the second century after Christ. A portion of the literature of Confucianism and no inconsiderable share of influence in shaping the system are to be ascribed to Mencius, the most notable Chinese sage since Confucius.

The system called Taoism (based upon the *Tao-teh-king* of Lao-tsze) is often more or less closely associated with Confucianism. Lao-tsze was an elder contemporary of Confucius. As the aim of Confucius was the inculcation of a social or national morality, his chief emphasis was laid upon the external proprieties. Lao-tsze, on the other hand, laid much stress also upon the inwardness of virtue. He was something of a mystic and encouraged a life of contemplation. Nevertheless, even he was more ethical than religious; and as a religion—that is, a system inculcating the principles of dependence upon deity—his system has proved "a dismal failure."

The fundamental lesson which Confucianism has to teach is reverence. The reverence of the gods is mildly inculcated, but the practice of the usual acts of devotion to them is rather discouraged. The proper objects of reverence are age, wisdom, learning, established authority among men. The most characteristic expression of the principle of reverence is what is known as ancestor worship. It was really a grand conception of Confucius that only a system of national discipline in reverence—reverence for law, authority, age and wisdom—could be the true path to the attainment of the ideal state or social order. This could give to society a stability and security that arms could never bestow. Indisputably there is a certain grandeur in a system that has dominated the thought of a great nation for more than two millenniums.

There is no little human wisdom in it. Yet with all its merits it is clear that mere Confucianism is no religion, but only a system of morals. But since man is not satisfied without positive religion, religious sentiments and practices are commonly found associated with the ethical system. Confucianism a mere ethical system; Taoism an ethical system of a more inward tendency, contemplative and ascetic, and so more akin to the religious sentiment; and the crude positive religion of the common people—these are not altogether mutually incompatible systems. The common people are expected, along with their worship, to pay due heed to the teachings of Confucius and Lao-tsze, while the men of some learning generally respect—though unequally—all the "classics," both those of Confucianism and those of Taoism, and at the same time are indulgent toward the cruder worship of the common people. But obviously these classics, being chiefly books of moral wisdom rather than the standards of teaching and practice in religion, show no close analogy to our Bible, whose very soul is religion. The portions of our Bible which most resemble the Chinese classics, viz., the Wisdom Literature (apart from Job), are not the heart of the Bible.

From India have flowed two streams of religion and religious literature. Brahmanism (out of which has developed modern Hinduism) is essentially national in its spirit, while Buddhism appeals to humanity without respect to race. Of the holy books of Brahmanism the first place belongs to the four very ancient collections of poems called the *Vedas.* They are the *Rig-Veda,* the *Atharva-Veda,* the *Yagur-Veda,* and the *Soma-Veda.* To those must be added, as sacred though of a secondary order, the *Brahmanas* or ritualistic commentaries upon them, and the *Upanishads* or speculative treatises upon the philosophy of the universe which the Vedas were supposed to imply. According to the wider use of the term, all these form part of the *Veda*, or "Knowledge." They all are, according to Brahman belief, fully inspired, therefore complete, inerrant and eternal. There are also certain later religious books which, though held in high esteem, are accounted of secondary ranks. Books of the first rank were technically called "S'ruti," or "Hearing," because they were given by inspiration. The books of the second order were called "Smriti," or "Remembering" (tradition). Of the Vedas, the oldest is the Rig-Veda. It is interesting from many points of view. It sheds light not only on the earliest form of religion now traceable among the Aryan peoples, but also upon the manners and customs and the ways of thinking of those early invaders of India from the northwest. These Aryans were near kindred to the Greeks and Romans; their language was of the same stock, and their religion was similar at many points. The most interesting of the secondary books are the Laws of Menu and the Epics. The first is character-ized by an intermingling of salutary and injurious ideals. Among the latter is the law of caste, which has wrought such damage to the life of the people of India. The Epics were the chief books among the common people. Rich in myth and legend, they were mightily interesting and at the same time moralizing. And as they fairly reflected the prevailing religion, they constituted the peo-ple's Bible. The religion reflected in all this rich literature is a polytheism of a very interesting complexity. In its earlier form it had much of the "healthy-mindedness" of the Greek religion. The later development shows a sad deterioration; the caste system, the deplorable subjection of women, and some other vicious features of later Hinduism have no place in the Vedas. The books which have been so long and so highly reverenced gradually lost their hold upon the national mind, and there came in their place gross and degrading superstition among the common people, and, among the Brahmans (the highest caste) highly wrought systems of speculation that have proved themselves powerless to heal the people's misery.

For many reasons Buddhism is one of the most interesting of the non-Christian religions. It is—above all other non-Biblical systems—a religion of redemption. And because it is a religion of redemption, a religion that takes full-seriously the problem of evil in human life, it shows some marked resemblances to Christianity. Its early history is not free from obscurity. It is, however, generally agreed that it arose about the middle of the sixth century B. C. in Hindustan. According to the earliest tradition its founder was a young prince whose family name was Gotama; because of his great repute as a religious reformer he was later called "the Buddha" ("the Enlightened"). The story of how the young prince, always predisposed to a life of contemplation and asceticism, and moved by powerful direct impressions of the world's misery, forsook the luxury and splendor of the court for the life of poverty and self-abasement is very impressive. He became a mendicant, and by self-inflicted austerities, coupled with the earnest study of the books of the Brahmans, he sought for peace. Though for a time bitterly disappointed, he does not give up his pursuit. With intensest resolution to find the secret of peace he gives himself over to deep thought. For weeks he sits absorbed in contemplation. It is the misery of human life that is his problem. He finds existence itself to be an evil.

By successive stages of contemplation he reaches the conclusion that the cause of the continued existence with its hopeless struggle is ignorance. Enlightenment will overcome the fate to be continually reborn. Sitting under a certain bo-tree—the spot came to be held by his disciples as the most sacred in all the world—he experienced in his own person the great Illumination. As the "Enlightened" he now undertakes to guide others in the Way.

The system of the Buddha is based upon four principles, the "four noble truths": pain exists; its cause is desire; pain can be ended by eliminating desire; the way of virtue brings the mortification of all desire. This way of virtue he elaborates; it is an eightfold way: right faith, right judgment, right words, right purpose, right practice, right effort, right thinking, and right meditation. He further adds, as necessary to the practice of the Way, the ten "precepts of aversion": not to kill; not to steal; not to commit adultery; not to lie; not to be drunken—these five are for all his disciples; the remaining five are for those who enter upon the monastic life:—to abstain from food out of season (i. e., after midday); to abstain from personal ornaments and perfumes; to abstain from a luxurious couch; to abstain from taking gold or silver. Thus would the Buddha show the way back from the evil of individual existence to the wholeness of being. The goal he calls Nirvana; it is the state of the total extinction of desire and individual consciousness; the Buddhist ideal is a passionless peace.

The immense significance of Buddhism is due to the energy and deep earnestness with which it laid hold on certain great principles. It is a very human and humane religion. The limitations of race and caste are quite disregarded. The highest virtue is compassion, charity.

And the universal problem of human suffering is frankly, even if pessimistically, dealt with. A clear doctrine of deity is not found in Buddhism. After a time the Buddha himself became the object of special veneration, but not as a god. The reality of an eternal First Principle seems to be presupposed, but Buddhism has no doctrine of a conscious fellowship with God. Buddhism is indeed a religion of redemption, but is a self-redemption. Not by divine grace but by self-discipline is salvation to come. Nevertheless, Buddhists do pray in spite of their doctrine, for they recognize the futility of striving to do as they would without help.

The sacred canon of Buddhism is not everywhere the same; the southern canon, however, enjoys the highest repute, and on it the others seem to be based. It is a threefold literature, and is called "The Three Baskets." The first of the three is a full manual of instruction for the communities of monks, who, following the example of Gotama, are pursuing the straight path toward Nirvana. The second Basket contains reminiscences of Buddha's parables, dialogues with his disciples, and sermons, to which are added some devotional poems and stories. This group of writings represents Buddhism as adapted to common life. The third Basket contains a number of treatises of a philosophic nature bearing on the faith of Buddhism. The Three Baskets are in no part writings of Buddha himself. His doctrines were orally given; disciples wrote as they remembered; and then there were later additions and expositions. These writings are in many ways impressive. They are very carefully fitted to their purpose and have exerted a powerful influence in shaping the history of Buddhism. Yet they no longer hold the place in the religion of the people that they once occupied. The religion has gradually drifted away from the high ideals of its classic period. But the writings do fairly represent Buddhism in its early vigor. This system is to be named along with Christianity and Islam as one of the three great missionary and universalistic religions of the world. Though having sprung up in India, it has now, strangely enough, very few representatives in that country; but it made, especially in a remarkable missionary period beginning about 300 B. C., great conquests in other countries of Asia. It is still the prevailing religion of Ceylon, the Indo-Chinese Peninsula, Nepal, Thibet, Turkestan, Japan, Korea, and very large portions of China. In all these several countries it has taken on different forms. It was a profound, though (we believe) sadly one-sided, conception of life and duty that made possible its great triumphs. "The Buddha," says Max Müller, "addressed himself to castes and outcasts. He promised salvation to all men. A sense of duty extending from the narrow limits of the house, the village, and the country, to the widest circle of mankind, a feeling of sympathy and brotherhood toward all men, the idea, in fact, of humanity, were first pronounced by Buddha."

The sacred book of Zoroastrianism, the religion of the ancient Persians, is commonly called the Zend-Avesta. Properly, however, "Avesta" is the fundamental writing, or text, and "Zend" is the commentary upon it. "Avesta," like "Veda," means knowledge divinely given. But in the Avesta we have to distinguish between the *Gathas*, which contain the original teaching of Zoroaster as remembered and transcribed by his disciples, and the later portions of the Avesta. In the former the prophet appears as a very real and natural person, and his doctrine is simple and comparatively pure. In the latter the figure of the prophet is surrounded by many extravagant legends. In the former we have an approach to a genuine monotheism: there is one Lord of good, Ahura Mazda, who is the only God to worship; but there is also a mighty spirit of evil, who is in perpetual conflict with the good God. In the later portions the tendency to dualism (the recognition of *two* eternal principles or persons, one of them good, the other evil) has developed to an injurious degree; and the simpler conceptions of the unseen world have given place to a luxuriant mythology with a super-abundance of angels good and bad. Without question, early Zoroastrianism was a religion of a very high order. What various causes led to its corruption cannot be easily pointed out. But we meet here only what we meet every-where in non-Biblical systems—a decline, sometimes slow, sometimes swift, from the higher ideals. Incidentally it should be noted that some of the ideas of the Parsees (the adherents of the religion of Persia) very consider-ably affected the later religious development of Judaism. This holds true especially of the conceptions of angels and spirits. Indeed, the very name "Parsee" passed over into Jewish usage in the form of "Pharisee."

Mohammed was one of the greatest reformers. His earliest utterances have much of the purity and elevation of sentiment which we find in the prophets of the Old Testament. His religious ideas he learned in no small part from the Old Testament; there are traces also of the positive influence of Christianity, although he had met with Christianity only in a rather corrupt form. His religion was a genuine monotheism. His early zeal for the truth was worthy of very high praise; so also was his insistence upon compassion, prayer, self-control, and self-abnegation. But along with the good in his doctrine there were certain vicious elements, which brought about a swift deterioration in his teaching and its influence. He yielded much to the fleshly mind of his followers. The obligation of "holy war" against unbelievers, the solemn sanction of polygamy and slavery, together with various corrupting superstitions, all have the support of the dogma of the complete divine inspiration of every part of the Koran. The later degradation of Islam is a matter of common knowledge.

What now is the relation of our Bible to these other sacred books? Have all "Bibles" some elements or features in common? If this is affirmed, the question presents itself: What is the nature of the likeness, and what is its cause? And the differences—do these pertain only to minor or non-essential matters, or do they pertain also to matters of fundamental significance? Is our Bible merely the "best" among books of a class, or is it something unique?

The special discussion of the Christian claim of a unique place for our Bible is reserved for a later chapter. For the present it will be sufficient, by a brief comparison of the formal aspects and the historical relations of the various sacred literatures, to make clear the nature of the problem and to point out the way to its solution.

We shall consider first the things that are common to all "Bibles."

(1) In the first place, every "Bible" is a *growth;* it is, moreover, an outgrowth. It is never a production struck out at a single heat; it is the literary outgrowth of a religious history. First the religion, afterward its books. Before the stage of literary record has come, the religion has had a history, sometimes a rather long one. In the case of most sacred books the writers gathered up much

that had come down from more or less remote times. Even when a bold new movement, such as that under Moses or that under Mohammed, begins to take shape, we may be sure that there has been a long preparatory history before it. How far back, for example, the roots of Islam reach! Mohammed could not have been what he was if Moses and Jesus had not been. Whatever may be one's belief as to the divine source of the contents of a sacred literature, it is clear that every "Bible" has its natural history.

(2) An essential part of the natural history of a sacred literature is the process by which it comes to be accepted as such. No religious literature is "sacred" immediately at birth. Its full recognition or canonization is the result of a process. If exceptions to this rule are proposed, it can be readily shown that they are only apparent. If, for instance, the Koran of Mohammed was immediately accepted by his followers, it was because his oral teaching had already won its way; it was no further step for his disciples to acknowledge the transcriptions of that which they had already received by word of mouth. Now what are the steps leading to the canonization of a religious literature? First of all a considerable group accepts a certain faith; there is a religious movement. If the movement is strong and expansive, it will call forth a literature. Whatever is written in behalf of the movement finds eager readers. In the process of using the various writings in the organized life of the religious community some will appear more satisfying and serviceable than others. The relatively unavailable writings are gradually set aside; the rest are regarded, as time goes by, with increasing veneration—for time is a very important factor in the growth of the idea of sanctity—and these at length are "canon-

ized"; i.e., regarded as sacred and authoritative. In nearly every instance canonization implies the acknowledgment of the divine inspiration of the books. As every serious religion is exclusive in its claims, so also the canonization of its representative writings implies the repudiation of all books of a different faith. "Bibles" tolerate no rivals. While a candid inquiry shows that all books of religion contain much that is true and good, the largest concession that the adherents of one faith can make to the claims of the books of another faith is: Here are "broken lights," but the perfect truth is revealed in *their own* sacred books. A classic example of the extreme intolerance of a positive religion is the conduct of the Moslems in destroying the great library at Alexandria. "If the books are in agreement with the Koran, they are needless; if they are contrary to it, they are false, and should be destroyed."

When we pass on to a comparison of the world of ideas as exhibited in the several "Bibles," it is important that we fix our eyes upon the fundamental principles and not upon mere details. Some Christians read the books of other religions only to disparage them. This, of course, is without reason or excuse. There is much of truth and beauty in the sacred books of the non-Christian religions. However, to discover these things in them is by no means the same as to acknowledge their sufficiency as a whole. Whoever reads the Chinese classics is sure to find many admirable moral precepts. No saying of Confucius has been oftener quoted than the following. Being asked, "Is there any one word which may serve as a rule of practice for all one's life?", Confucius replied: "Is not reciprocity such a word? What you do not want done to yourself, do not do to others." The resemblance of this saying to the "Golden Rule" of Jesus has been often remarked. The fact that the Confucian form is negative, while that of Jesus is positive, need not be so strongly emphasized as is often done. The superiority of Jesus will be neither established nor overthrown by the comparison of mere details. Many another passage from Confucius is no less fine and noble than this. Many inspiring passages may be found also in the Vedas, in the Tripitaka, in the Avesta, in the Koran. Take, for example, this saying of Buddha: "If a man foolishly does me a wrong, I will return to him the protection of my ungrudging love. The more evil cometh from him, the more good shall come from me." Or this: "Let a man overcome anger by love, evil by good, the greedy by liberality, the liar by truth."

The occurrence of such sentiments in non-Christian books has led many to conclude that the difference between our Bible and other sacred books is "simply one of degree, not of kind." The thesis holds only within certain limits; it does not hold in respect to the innermost essence of the Biblical message. No sacred literature is without many expressions of moral earnestness and religious devotion. It could not be otherwise. Of all the interests of humanity the religious interest is the deepest. Normally it is the all-comprehensive interest. Religion springs from a sense of dependence upon a higher Power; its motive is the desire to attain peace and fellowship with that Power. Hence among all religions there must be a certain kinship in spiritual aspiration, some likeness in religious devotion, some community of moral earnestness coupled with a sense of the divine sanction of right conduct. From all this, however, it does not follow that religions differ only in degree, and not in kind. The universal "sympathy of religions"—a common sense of need, devotedness in religious practices—this is no proof that the *real content* of all religions is fundamentally one. The real issue lies deeper. Every religion must be judged by its fundamental principle and tendency. So also with the sacred books that represent a religion. It must be our aim, therefore, to determine and estimate the *fundamental peculiarity* of our Bible in comparison with other sacred books.

In the path of our quest for the *essential peculiarity of our Bible* we shall meet with some interesting and significant facts.

(1) One might be struck first of all with the unmatched *literary variety* of our Bible. In comparison all other "Bibles" are narrow in their range. Some of them are at best only collections of hymns, prayers and ritual. Besides these, prophetic oracles are in some others an important element. Still others include also a system of morals—in the books of Confucius there is virtually nothing else. On the other hand, our Bible freely and effectively uses every form and variety of literature known to the people from whom it sprang.

(2) The ethnic Bibles, taken as a whole, are *special books of religion* (or morals), while the scope of our Bible is so comprehensive as to deserve to be called a *book of life*. Yet our Bible is not on this account less a book of religion than the others, but rather much more! For while the other sacred books regard religion as one— perhaps indeed as the chief—concern of man, the Bible regards the kingdom of God as the whole of good and the service of God as embracing the whole of real life. In the Bible the vicious dualism which divides life into the "religious" and the "secular" is overcome.

(3) It is scarcely a step to our third observation. Our

Bible—at least in all its weightier portions—is fundamentally *historical,* while the non-Christian Bibles are
essentially *unhistorical.* The ethnic sacred books in no
case represent their doctrine as slowly and divinely
wrought out in the life of a people. The doctrine is
stated, explained, defended; to it is added a system of
ritual; but the religion is never conceived of as interwoven
with the whole life of a nation and of the race. The case
with our Bible is quite the reverse. With the exception
of much of the ceremonial system of the Old Testament,
all of which long ago was laid aside as an outworn gar-
ment, there is no religion in our Bible that is not interwoven with human life in its struggles, temptations, sins,
repentings, spiritual triumphs. No other book in all
literature is so intensely a book of human experiences as
our Bible; and yet the center of interest in it is not what
men have felt and thought, but what God has wrought.

(4) Again, but a step! The non-Christian sacred
books are *invariably unprogressive;* they are either retrogressive or decadent in tendency; our Bible alone is
progressive. "The oldest portions of the several collections of the Chinese, Indian, and Persian Scriptures are
confessedly the noblest in thought and aspiration; and,
secondly, ritual in each case has finally overpowered the
strivings after a personal and spiritual fellowship with
God" (Westcott). We do not forget that ritualism and
formalism also once threatened to overwhelm the prophetic spirit of the Old Testament; but they failed to
accomplish such a result. The prophetic spirit was too
persistent and powerful for that. We now see very
clearly—in the light of the fulfillment in Christ—that
ceremonialism never did truly represent the essence of
the religion of the Bible. Only a religion in which the

prophetic spirit—the spirit that is fully conscious of the progressive life of the divine Spirit among men from generation to generation—only such a religion can be progressive. A religion of ritual is always and necessarily retrogressive. The New Testament of Jesus Christ is the triumph of the religion of the Spirit. And because it is the religion of the Spirit, our relation to our Bible does not enchain us to a dead past, but bids us look not only to the Christ that was, but also to the Christ that is, and to the Christ that is to be. In the New Testament there is, strictly speaking, not one shred of mere ritual left, for the Christian sacraments are no mere rites. They are visible signs of the presence and work of the living Christ through his Spirit. Unless used in the Spirit they have neither place nor meaning in Christianity.

(5) With the exception of the Chinese classics, all the world's "Bibles" lay claim to divine revelation and inspiration. Is the claim equally false in all, or unequally true in all, or true in one and false in the rest? It is quite unnecessary to claim that God has not spoken at all to the peoples, past or present, who have been without our Bible. Nevertheless, however highly we may estimate the value of the various religious conceptions which we find in the non-Christian systems, it seems clear that those peoples have had (or have) no satisfying knowledge of God. But God, the living God, was known in Israel. He is revealed in the fulness of his grace in Jesus Christ. The ethnic conception of revelation is that *ideas* are revealed; the Biblical conception is that God reveals *himself*. The Bible purports to be the testimony of faithful men who have had fellowship with the God of history, the God who above all has revealed himself in the Christ of history. In other words, the Bible is not itself the

revelation, but is the word of testimony concerning the revelation.

This, then, is the fundamental difference between our Bible and the "Bibles" of the non-Christian world: our Bible has sprung from a sure and clear knowledge of the one true God, while the others fall short of that knowledge. *Our Bible alone gives us the Christ,* and the Christ alone gives us a full and satisfying fellowship with God. The claim that there are degrees of revelation and inspiration in all religions, "Christianity being the best and richest religion hitherto," fails to do full justice to the great fact of Christ. Is there not, after all, a measureless distance between the religions that *have not* and the religion that *has* the Christ? And does not the bearing of the message of the Christ lift our Bible out of the company of all books that know not the Christ?

Chapter VI

THE SCIENTIFIC STUDY OF THE BIBLE

To be understood the Bible must be studied. No doubt the church, through her teaching, is able to bring home the essential message of the Bible even to the unlearned. But the Bible as ancient literature, the source-book and sacred canon of Christianity, presents itself to us as a vast field for study and research. Because of its incomparable influence in the life of mankind it challenges the attention of all thoughtful men. And, in fact, no other book is the object of so much earnest inquiry. The Bible has always been studied; at no period have intelligent Christians utterly neglected to search the Scriptures. But not all Bible study is of a kind, and not all is alike fruitful. Each generation brings to bear upon the study of the Bible the intellectual resources, methods and standards that pertain to the time. Ours is a time in which a wealth of fresh light has been shed upon the Bible. The modern era of Bible study began more than one hundred years ago, but since some sixty years ago Biblical research has advanced with remarkable rapidity and in the last decades its results have become widely popularized. The modern scientific study of the Bible is characterized by a thoroughness joined with a breadth of view once quite unknown.

The breaking in of so much fresh light has wonderfully enlarged the appreciation of the Bible for many people and should naturally have been gratefully welcomed by all. But unhappily the modern scientific study of the Bible has given grave offense to many Christian people, and the confidence of some has been sorely shaken. The reason for this distress is not hard to discover. It lies in the traditional view of the nature and origin of the Bible. Out of the assurance that the Bible as a whole contained the sure word of God, the church, for the most part, came to hold that the Book was in every sense superhuman and miraculous. It was generally assumed that the very words of the Book had been given by direct inspiration and that error of any sort was thereby absolutely excluded. The Bible was thought of as a book recording history yet having no history, no development, of its own—"an historical book unhistorically given." For a very long time the great majority of Christian people rested calmly in the dogma of a strictly miraculous Bible. At length, however, the modern scientific spirit began to make even the Bible an object of inquiry. When facts pointing to the human limitations of the Bible and its genuinely historical growth and transmission began to impress themselves upon the minds of observant readers, then was born what is known as modern Biblical criticism.

Before inquiring into the special function of Biblical criticism it will be well to make clear to ourselves the nature and function of criticism in general. Criticism is the act of distinguishing things that differ, especially of separating the true from the false. As applied to art and literature, it aims to distinguish qualities and estimate values. As applied to history, it seeks, by means of an intelligent weighing of evidence, to separate between the true and the false in tradition and testimony, so that we may see past events as they actually were. The term criticism does not necessarily imply harsh or unfavorable judgment; this is a secondary and restricted use of the term. The primary and essential aim of criticism is *a just appreciation*.

As applied to the Bible the function of criticism is to discover what may be known concerning its historical and literary relations. The aim of Biblical criticism is (negatively) to remove false notions respecting the Bible and (positively) to obtain correct views of the Bible. It seeks to see the Bible as it is and to understand the process by which it came to be what it is. It would let the Bible speak for itself. Criticism *as such* neither denies nor affirms that the message of the Bible is from God; for religious appreciation is a matter that lies beyond the scope of mere science. It belongs to the realm of spiritual intuition. Biblical criticism has to do with the natural or human aspects of the Bible, not with the question of the eternal value of its religious testimony. It assumes that these writings, whatever may be their heavenly significance, have a genuinely human history and therefore may be studied as human documents. And they may be studied just as scientifically and freely by those who accept the religion of the Bible as by those who deny it.

"But," some earnest Christians are still objecting, "why criticize? Why not take the Bible just as it is?" The obvious answer is another question: Just what *is* the Bible? Now it is the sole function of criticism to determine just what the Bible is.

The right of criticism cannot possibly be questioned, except upon the presupposition that the Bible is not only a miraculous book, but also is somehow miraculously protected against non-understanding and misunderstanding. But an absolute denial of the right to the critical study of the Bible is almost unknown. It is, however, not uncommon for conservative Christians to acknowledge the right of what they call "constructive criticism" while they condemn what they call "destructive criticism." But in this view there is generally some confusion of thought. No genuine criticism tends to be destructive of anything but error, and all genuine criticism really prepares the way for positive construction. Criticism is not the advocate of unbelief; it does not represent the spirit of destruction; it is simply the search for reality. It is false to assume that whenever criticism alters a traditional view, then it is destructive. For age lends no sanctity to error. People have been troubled especially by the arguments against the tradition as to the authorship of certain books; but their reasoning here is wholly unsound. It is, for example, obviously unreasonable to assume that the Epistle to the Hebrews, if written by Paul, is worthy of all confidence, but if the work of an unknown hand, loses its value for faith. It is a fatal error to regard questions of authorship and other such matters as if they were essential to the faith. The revelational value of the Scriptures is evidenced solely by their power to help us to a conscious and saving fellowship with the living God. If our confidence in the Biblical testimony must wait until historical research has settled every doubtful question of authorship and dates and has proved that there are no historical errors in the Bible, then faith never can be secure. We must have a more direct certainty: the testimony of Biblical witnesses through the living voice of the church to-day challenges our faith, and our experience of the promised grace confirms it. It is necessary that our "faith should not stand in the wisdom of men, but in the power of God."

I have a life with Christ to live,
    But, ere I live it, must I wait
Till learning can clear answer give
    Of this or that book's date?
I have a life in Christ to live,
    I have a death in Christ to die;—
And must I wait till science give
    All doubts a full reply?

Nay rather, while the sea of doubt
    Is raging wildly round about,
Questioning of life and death and sin,
    Let me but creep within
Thy fold, O Christ, and at thy feet
    Take but the lowest seat,
And hear Thine awful voice repeat
In gentlest accents, heavenly sweet,
    Come unto Me, and rest;
    Believe Me, and be blest.
                  J. C. SHAIRP.

It would be futile to attempt to close the Bible to historical and philological research, and certainly to do so would be injurious to faith. Those who attempt this thing should have a care lest they "be found to be fighting even against God." The Bible is, at all events, far too important a heritage of antiquity to escape the thorough scrutiny of scholars. Some, perhaps, will study it irreverently, but this is no reason why the way should not be kept absolutely open to free research. "Nothing that keeps thought out is safe from thought." The only answer to vicious or false criticism is sound and true criticism. To prohibit criticism is morally and spiritually perilous if not even deadly.

Yet it must be clearly observed that there *is* such a thing as destructive criticism. But it is never mere criticism as such that is destructive, but only criticism when linked, as sometimes it is, with an unbelieving prejudice, or with a spirit of opposition to the truth. The injurious moments in criticism always come from the philosophical or dogmatic theory that controls it. Even honest criticism can and does make mistakes, and these mistakes may be disturbing factors for a time; but honest criticism carries its own antidote within itself.

The task of Biblical criticism is threefold: textual, historico-literary, and historical.

(1) Textual criticism is the task of ascertaining, as nearly as possible, the original text or wording of a writing. It has nothing to do with the interpretation of the text, except in so far as the apparent sense of a passage may afford reasons for judging of the wording at points where the traditional text is uncertain. No task could be more sharply limited than this. It is, however, a very laborious and intricate task. It involves the comparison and due appraisal of all the readings of all known manuscripts of the Bible; the use of all ancient versions for the light they may throw upon the readings in the original; and the comparison of all quotations from the Scriptures found in the writings of the Church Fathers. The inquiry concerning the correct text of the Scriptures was the earliest form of Biblical criticism to be developed. Its need was evident to all scholarly investigators. When ancient manuscripts were compared, variations in the text appeared, and the task inevitably suggested itself of determining by comparison of the manuscripts, and by other evidences, which of the several readings might be the original one. And yet when Bengel, the father of textual

criticism, began his labors in this field, the people and the clergy were sorely disturbed over this "tampering with God's word." God must—so they claimed—have protected the Bible from every error even in its transmission. Nevertheless, here were the various readings. They demanded examination and, wherever possible, correction. The need was so obvious that in course of time the work of textual criticism won universal recognition.

(2) The next form of criticism is the historico-literary, commonly called the "higher criticism," to distinguish it from the textual or "lower criticism." The task of the "higher criticism" is even more complex and difficult than that of textual criticism. It is to discover whatever may be known concerning the origin of the several writings. The inquiry takes up such questions as the following: Who wrote a given book? For what readers? When? Why? Under what conditions and circumstances? Is the book a unity in composition and authorship? What were the sources of the materials used in the book? Did the author make use of documents in composing his book? If so, what account may be given of these documents? These are, perhaps, the most important questions that "higher criticism" is called upon to answer. Naturally this form of criticism was more startling than the textual, yet happily even this line of inquiry is now justified, in principle at least, by most of the Christian people. It no longer seems like "infidelity" when we hear of the post-Mosaic authorship of the Pentateuch, the composite character of the book of Isaiah, and the various theories of the authorship of our Gospels.

(3) Historical criticism as applied to the Bible is the inquiry into the value of the historical records contained in the Bible itself. To many Christians the smallest

doubt as to the correctness of the Bible in every detail seems like a denial of the whole Bible. Even in our own day we can sometimes hear the statement that unless we can trust the Bible in every particular, we cannot be sure of it in any. Now, obviously, this is a most unnecessary assumption. We deal so with no other book and certainly with no living person. We have no warrant for assuming that God must have given us a book free from every natural limitation of human minds. And as a matter of fact, examination shows that Biblical writers were not free from the imperfections of knowledge and memory that are common to men. The value of the Bible for faith does not consist in its formal correctness, but in the fact that it brings us into sure and conscious fellowship with God.

In the last seventy-five years, and especially in the last thirty, the science of archæology and the researches of historians have shed many a light upon Bible history. People often speak of the spade as "confirming the Bible." Often, however, archæology and extra-Biblical history correct rather than confirm the Biblical tradition. As a book of religion, the Bible can never be confirmed by adducing proof of its formal accuracy; the only confirmation of a book of religion is to be found in the experience of its power to establish our fellowship with God. In matters of world-knowledge the writers of our Bible appear simply as children of their times; their special significance for us lies in this: they knew God.

The modern scientific study of the Bible is, broadly speaking, that study which uses the best scientific methods of the age in the attempt to understand the Bible in all its aspects and relations. The immense modern progress in two fields has almost revolutionized the scientific side of our relation to the Bible. Advances in archæology and modern psychological methods of study have combined to make the reading of the Bible incomparably more lively and intelligent than was possible in earlier times. Yet the religious truth of the Bible could never be wholly obscured; it has shone forth with greater or less clearness in every age. The modern Bible student reads the Bible in the light of its own history and of the general history of its times and with the application of a sane psychological and historical imagination; but he also reads it, if he has an earnest spirit, with the desire to know what these ancient writings have to say for all times.

PART II: THE BIBLE IN THE MAKING

PART II: THE BIBLE IN THE MAKING

CHAPTER VII

THE BIBLE A GROWTH

Time was when as yet there was no Bible. Then, after a process covering many centuries, men had at last a completed Bible. We have the task in this part of our study of sketching the growth of the Bible. It is only the broader outlines of the history of the growing Bible that can be offered here. The main lines of development will be indicated and the reader who is interested in the details of the problem can push his inquiries farther, and he will be amply rewarded for his pains. Every earnest student of the Bible needs to have a clear, even if rather general, knowledge of how the Bible came to be.

Now the Bible did really grow. God could have given the world a finished Bible all at once directly from heaven, or he could have given it—still in the same miraculous manner—piece by piece. Such a mechanical process, however, could not be called growth. The Bible grew in the sense of a growth in organic relation with the life of men. It is an outgrowth of historical movements. God's revelation of himself is interwoven in history, and so also the literary witness to the ways of God with men was an outgrowth of history.

The process of the Bible's becoming is twofold. First,

there is a growth of a literature; secondly, there is the sifting of that literature and the recognition of certain portions of it as divinely authoritative. We have first the writings and afterward the canonization of the writings.

The literature of the Bible grew just as any other literature grows. That it is believed to embody a divine revelation makes no difference in this respect. The literature was the spontaneous outgrowth of the life of the religious community. The several writings were put forth in the first instance with no thought of their forming parts of a future Bible. They were written to serve the immediate interests of the people. A psalmist wrote down his psalm, a prophet recorded his sermon, an evangelist wrote of the words and deeds of Christ, an apostle wrote his letters of instruction to the churches, each because of an immediate need and use that was to be served.

The Bible is a growth not merely in the sense that the *books* sprang up out of the life of the people at a given time, but also in the still deeper sense that the *ideas* of the books had a history and development before their embodiment in a book. This development of the ideas began, as a rule, long before the writing of a given book. Again, a number of the books of the Bible are a growth in the further sense that they are collections or compilations, or in some cases redactions, of older writings. The Psalter, for example, is the hymn-book of ancient Israel and as such it represents the growth of centuries. The most important of the historical books are compilations and redactions of older documents and sources.

Since the Bible grew out of the life of a people, and since the life of the people itself is largely conditioned by its physical situation and surroundings and by its con-

tact with other peoples, its writings must show evidences
of all these manifold relations. He who studies the
growth of the Bible should take into account the history
of the people from which it sprang. The literature is
really an organic part of the whole life of the people, and
the life of the people is in no small measure determined
by the land in which they live.

No book of the Bible, however rich in divine truth,
was called Holy Scripture when first written; its recognition as such came only after long use had established
it in the veneration of the people. The growth of the
Bible as a collection of writings of acknowledged authority is, therefore, an important part of our study. Books
are written for the community; they are welcomed by
the community; and those writings which prove most
satisfying continue in use and are at last officially accepted as Holy Scripture—the canon of Scripture is
fixed.

CHAPTER VIII

THE HEBREW LAND AND PEOPLE

The Old Testament is the chief literary expression of the life of the Hebrew people in their relation to Jehovah. It is a national literature. The New Testament, on the other hand, is the literary outgrowth of the Messianic faith in Jesus of Nazareth and the early preaching of that faith. As such, the New Testament is not national but universal. Nevertheless, even the writers of the New Testament were all—Luke alone excepted—Hebrews. Humanly speaking, our Bible is the product of the Hebrew race. The people of Israel felt themselves to be the chosen people and, indeed, doubtless they were a chosen people—chosen to accomplish a supreme service for the whole world. That God cared for them to the exclusion of other races, the New Testament forbids us to believe. Yet it is manifest that the prevailing Jewish conception of God's purpose for mankind was narrow and selfish. This view, however, is not that of their greatest prophets. These had a universal outlook and taught that God was the God of all men. But the people as a whole never rose to that height; and because of their lower and narrower thought of the purpose of God, the people of Israel, for the most part, rejected Jesus as Messiah. Yet we must not fail to perceive the significance of the fact that it was from Israel that the first disciples of Jesus were gathered and it was Israelites that preached the gospel of Jesus as the Christ of the whole

world. And so we have before us in our Bible a literature produced by Hebrews; and this collection of writings
by Hebrews has strangely enough become "the book of
mankind."

Now, in order to get the fullest understanding of this
most broadly human of all books, we need to know the
people from which it sprang; and in order to know the
people, we need to know their land. The divine message
of the Bible came to us through the medium of a certain
people. It was a people which would scarcely have made
for itself a very great name among the nations but for
its spiritual history and the spiritual influence that has
gone out from it. Israel was the only nation of antiquity
that learned the worship of the one universal God. Hence
the universal significance of its history. Out of Israel
came Jesus Christ. The essence of the Bible's message
is for all nations and individuals, but the form of that
message was shaped and conditioned by the characteristics and vicissitudes of the Hebrew people, and these in
turn were in no small measure conditioned by the land
in which they dwelt.

Israel was called by the prophets "Jehovah's peculiar
people," that is, the people of Jehovah's own possession.
Hence both prophets and priests warned the people to
keep themselves separate from other nations. Now this
emphasis upon the duty of separateness helped to make
the people of Israel peculiar in another sense of the word,
that is, to make them unlike other nations. Physical isola-
tion was, of course, impossible. In fact, the people of
northern Palestine were thrown into contact with other
nations in an unusual degree. Northern Palestine lay in
the direct line of the great caravan routes between many
of the principal trading nations of antiquity—Egypt,

Syria, Phœnicia, Assyria. It was therefore aptly styled "Galilee of the nations." The full recognition of this condition of life in this part of the country will greatly aid in the understanding of the social and the religious history of the Northern tribes. The intermingling of the people resulted in a rather mixed race and in a far more extensive following of the strange gods and customs than was the case with the Southern Kingdom of Judah.

The people of Southern Palestine were able to maintain a much greater degree of separateness from other nations than was possible in the North. Jerusalem was a city well surrounded by hills. Few great cities of the world have been so well protected by natural barriers or have lain so distinctly outside the zones of the great courses of commerce and travel. To the south of the city lies "the hill country of Judea" extending as far south as the desert. On the southeast the hills of Judea reach to the border of Arabah, a broad, shallow, sandy valley, the continuation of the great rift which affords the bed for the Jordan River and the Dead Sea. On the east lie the Dead Sea, flanked by steep hills, and the lower Jordan Valley. The fords of the lower Jordan are few and easily defended. Moreover, beyond the Jordan and the Dead Sea there is but a small habitable territory, and beyond this lies the great desert of Syria and Arabia. In Old Testament times this small habitable country lying to the east was held by such tribes as the Ammonites, Moabites and Edomites, who seldom were strong enough seriously to disturb the people of Judah. To the southwest and west of Jerusalem the hills extend far enough to have caused the caravans moving to and from Egypt to keep their main course at a distance from the city; only offshoots of the caravans would come to Jerusalem. There were, of course, a few tolerably good roads leading to and from Jerusalem, especially the Bethlehem road on the south, the Jericho road on the east, the Joppa road leading to the Sea, and on the north a road which branched in several directions. And so, in spite of her size and importance, Jerusalem was in an uncommon degree separated from intercourse from foreign peoples. But it was the religious teaching and policy that kept the people separate even more than their geographical situation. Separateness was inculcated as a religious duty.

There was therefore a decided difference between the religious development of "Israel" (the Northern Kingdom) and of "Judah" (the Southern Kingdom). It would, however, be possible to exaggerate the difference. In both branches of the nation Jehovah was regarded as the God of Israel; but also in both kingdoms the worship of strange gods was much practised. In the Northern Kingdom, however, this evil was far more prevalent than in Judah. All through their history both branches of the people of Israel were influenced in varying degrees by the nations and tribes with which they came in contact. The national development of Northern Israel came to an end with the fall of Samaria and the effectual scattering of the people in 721 B. C. The Southern Kingdom fared very differently. Although it endured as a kingdom only until the Babylonian Captivity, the people were able to maintain a strong national spirit even in the Exile (from 586 to 536 B. C.), and after their return to their land they developed a sense of unity and divine vocation as a people unparalleled in history. Even the destruction of Jerusalem in 70 A. D. and the loss of their country did not break their national spirit.

Israel's religion, then, was an historical development. Now the thought of the development or evolution of the religion of Israel does not signify a denial of the self-revelation of God as its foundation and source. All human life, religion included, is subject to the general law of development. This law, however, does not imply the inevitableness of improvement; it means only that everything is under the law of causal continuity. Thus religion develops in its forms and in its ideal content. But while recognizing the law of continuity as holding in the domain of religion, we may also be fully persuaded that religion is grounded in the living God and his positive relations with men. We shall do well to refuse to put evolution in the place of the living God. Genuine religion neither begins nor grows of itself; its root is in God. Yet all religion, even the highest, does grow, and the Biblical religion, not less than any other, has had its development. The only question of faith involved in the inquiry as to the growth of Biblical religion is this: Was there in the religion of Israel a real, though imperfect but growing knowledge of the true God, such a knowledge as could form the fitting background for the glory of the supreme revelation in Jesus Christ? Real religion is grounded in what God does, not in what man fancies. But there is a progressiveness in the human appropriation and understanding of God's ways with men. The recognition of the development of religion does not make religion the work of man.

To understand the Bible is to understand the religion of the Bible. Whatever, then, will throw light upon the religion of the Bible is to be seized upon and utilized in our study. We are to ask ourselves: What kinds of knowledge are calculated to help us to understand the

Bible? And, How shall we acquire and use these "auxiliary sciences"? There are many such—philology, history, archæology, race psychology, and many more. We are at the present moment concerned with one of the most important of them—Biblical geography. Ernest Renan called the land of Palestine "the fifth Gospel." But the land of Palestine throws light not only upon the life of Christ but upon the whole life of the people of Israel.

There is a popular interest in Biblical geography which, though sound and good as far as it goes, contributes little to our understanding of the Bible. It is not enough that our fancy should dwell fondly upon the local associations of Bible history and we be able, for example, to say, "Here is Carmel where Elijah slew the priests of Baal, or here is Dothan where Joseph found his brethren feeding their flocks, or here is the Sea of Galilee where Jesus taught." Every place connected with Bible history, especially with the life of our Lord, is naturally the object of a certain hallowed interest. All this, of course, is good, but the genuine student of the Bible must go further and deeper. He asks: How can the knowledge of Bible lands help me to understand the religious history of the Old and New Testament?

The term "Bible lands" should not be understood as including all countries mentioned in the Bible, but only such as have had some direct part in shaping Bible history. The Biblical world in that wider sense extended from Persia and the lands of the Tigris-Euphrates Valley in the East to Tartessus (Tarshish) in Spain in the West; from Ethiopia in the South to the Euxine or Black Sea in the North. Bible lands in the restricted sense of the term are Palestine as the home of the

Hebrews and also Mesopotamia, Egypt, the Peninsula of Sinai, Syria, Phœnicia, Babylonia, Persia, and, finally, the lands of Paul's missionary labors. Most of the lands of the Biblical world lay about the Mediterranean (or Great) Sea; even those that were most remote had extensive commercial relations with the Mediterranean lands. It is an interesting and significant fact that the most nearly central of all lands shown on the map of the Biblical world is Palestine. Indeed, if we look at a modern map embracing the three continents of the Old World, no other country seems quite so central as Palestine. It is in this land that Israel's spiritual development chiefly took place; and yet there was a most important history before they came into Palestine, and also there were exceedingly important influences from the later experiences of the Jews in the Babylonian Exile and in the contact of many of them with the Persians. When we take into account both the central location of the people and their studied aloofness, we shall be prepared to understand how Israel could be at once so broad and so narrow in its outlook. It was broad in its thought of the universality of God's kingdom and of the oneness of the human family, but narrow in its conception of its own divine vocation. In all antiquity the conception of the oneness of the human race was declared nowhere else but in Israel. The tragedy of Israel was her perversion of the grand prophetic vision of her vocation to save the whole world to a thought of the glory of her own dominion over all peoples.

The Old Testament world was essentially an Afro-Asiatic world. Israel's contact with Europe came late in her history, chiefly through the conquests of Alexander the Great. The Greek influence seems to have affected

the religious life of the Jews but little until after the
latest of the Old Testament books was written.   Thereafter a commingling of Jewish religious thought and
Greek philosophy was increasingly manifest.   Naturally
this Greek influence was more pronounced among the
Jews of the Dispersion than among the Palestinian Jews.

The New Testament world stretches northward and
westward from Palestine.   The East has almost vanished
from the view of the people of Israel.   Rome is now the
mistress of the world; but the ruling thought and the
dominant language of the world are Greek.   In spite of
the very considerable importance of Egypt and the at-
tractions of Alexandria both for Greeks and for Jews,
we read of no apostolic mission there.

Now the religious history of the Hebrews did not
begin with Moses nor did it end with him.   According
to Biblical tradition, the worship of Jehovah (or Jahweh)
was already practised in the time of Abraham and we
may be sure it was practised in the time of Moses.   Yet
we cannot affirm that even at the time of Moses the
religion of Israel had become a pure monotheism.   It was
first, doubtless, a monolatry; and it did not become a pure
monotheism until long after Moses' time.   There is,
perhaps, no problem in the history of religion more
interesting than the problem of the origin of Hebrew
monotheism.   Some hold that the desert life suggested
monotheistic worship.   It has even been said that all
monotheism has sprung up in the desert.   In answer to
this assertion, it should be stated that ancient history
shows but one perfectly clear monotheism, namely, that
of Israel.   Zoroastrianism, at its best, was almost a pure
monotheism, but it was characterized by an inherent dual-
istic tendency, and this hindered the development of true

monotheism. Besides, Zoroastrianism did not spring up in what one would call a desert country. And as for Mohammedanism, its monotheism was plainly borrowed from that of the Old Testament. Some scholars speak of "a Semitic genius for monotheism"; but most Semitic peoples were not monotheistic, though some of them were monolatrous. Monotheism is not to be regarded as the natural product of the geographical influences of the life of the desert. So much, however, is to be frankly recognized: a nomadic tribal life tends to the thought of a tribal deity and so to a pretty strict monolatry, that is, the worship of one god without the denial of the existence of other gods. The maintenance of monolatry seems to be the normal prerequisite for the rise of monotheism. At all events, the Israelites were believers in the duty of worshipping one God alone long before they came to see that there was but one God. From the desert the Israelites brought a monolatry. through long conflicts this finally rose to the heights of a pure monotheism. Moses in the land of Midian became tremendously convinced of the duty of Israel to worship the God of Israel, Jahweh. He goes back into Egypt, from whence he had fled, and leads forth the people under this standard and watchword: "Let us go forth that we may worship our God, the God of our fathers, even Jahweh." In Egypt it seems that as a people they had fallen into the worship of many gods, chiefly the gods of the Egyptians.

The influence of the forty years of the wilderness on Israel's life was great in two regards: the people grew physically strong and valiant; and they became fairly united in their worship of Jahweh. Although not yet brought to the conception of the oneness of Deity, they were brought to a concentrated worship of the God of Israel.

Palestine, as compared with the Wilderness of Sinai, might well be described as "a land flowing with milk and honey." Its boundaries cannot be sharply defined. Generally, however, its recognized limits were as follows: on the west the Mediterranean Sea; on the east the Arabian (or Syrian) Desert; on the south the indefinite line of hills descending to the desert; on the north the southern slope of Mt. Hermon and the point at which the course of the Litany (or Leontes) River turns abruptly to flow westward into the Mediterranean; but the line of division from that point to the sea must be so drawn as to leave Tyre within the bounds of Phœnicia. In the period of Israel's greatest power the city of Hamath was sometimes referred to as constituting the northern limit of the land of Israel just beyond the border. In general, however, Israel's occupation of the land did not extend beyond the southern slope of Mt. Hermon. In common speech the northern and southern limits were approximately indicated by the well-known phrase, "from Dan to Beer-sheba." The width of the land is about one hundred miles and its length from north to south about one hundred and fifty miles. In size and also in shape it is not unlike the State of Vermont.

The *geology* of Palestine is unusually interesting. Until the great volcanic upheaval about the close of the Pliocene period the whole land was covered by the waters of the sea. That upheaval gave to the land its chief permanent characteristics. The most striking of these characteristics is the great rift running north and south from the Lebanons to the Red Sea, forming the valley of the Jordan and the Dead Sea, and continuing, though with a less depression, south of the Dead Sea through the Arabah and the Gulf of Akabah. At the Dead Sea the depression is the deepest on the surface of the earth (1,292 feet below the level of the Mediterranean). The underlying rock is granite, but it is little in evidence, being for the most part well covered by red sandstone and the still later deposits of limestone and marl. In Moab and Edom the sandstone appears in abundance and sometimes in striking beauty. Some of the limestone of Palestine, especially that of Solomon's quarries in Jerusalem, is exceptionally fine. The Mediterranean for a long time extended to the very foot of the mountains of the central range. The present coastal plain was produced in part by a gradual emergence of the land from the sea and in part by the alluvial deposits from the mountains. Along the coast there is also a border of yellow sand brought in by the force of the western winds from the deposits of the Nile.

The *physical geography* of Palestine is very clearly marked. Four zones extend from north to south (in the southern half of the land it is usual, by means of a subdivision, to distinguish five). The four divisions are: (1) the coast plain; (2) the central plateau or mountain range; (3) the Jordan and Dead Sea valley; and (4) the plateau east of the Jordan. The fifth division which should be recognized in the southern portion of the land is the Shephelah, consisting of foot-hills lying between the Philistine coast plain and the more mountainous plateau. The coast plain is very narrow in the north, but in the central and southern parts we find the broader plains of Sharon and Philistia.

The central plateau is a continuation of the Lebanon mountains. The northern portion of the plateau includes some mountains of from 3,000 to 4,000 feet above sea-level. To the southwest of this division of Palestine the plateau stretches out into the beautiful and fertile plain of Esdraelon. In its central part, which is the region of Samaria, the hills are less lofty than in the north, and, gently rounding into the valleys, are tolerably fertile. The hills of Judea, on the other hand, though not more lofty than many in Samaria, are more rugged than those, and far less fertile. In the Negeb, or South Country, the hills are decidedly barren.

The valley of the Jordan and the Dead Sea is far less pleasing than one might expect. To the geologist, how-ever, its interest is great. The Jordan has several sources near Mt. Hermon. One of these is an abundant spring at Banias (the Cæsarea Philippi of New Testament times). From Banias, whose elevation is more than 1,000 feet, the river rapidly descends to about the level of the sea near Lake Huleh. Here for a distance of several miles the stream is sluggish—Huleh is in fact only the widening of the stream because of the natural obstruc-tions in the physical contour of the country—but from Huleh to the Sea of Galilee, a distance of eleven miles, the river plunges downward 682 feet. The Sea of Galilee, twelve and one-half miles in length and eight in width, is beautiful in itself and in its natural surround-ings. As it lies nearly 700 feet below the level of the Mediterranean and is well surrounded by hills, it usually escapes the severity of the winds that sweep across the country. Sometimes, however, it is not so; to-day, as in our Lord's time, the sea is occasionally very tempes-tuous. From the Sea of Galilee the Jordan flows south-ward until it empties in the Dead Sea. The distance by a straight line is only 65 miles, but so many are the river's turnings that its course measures nearly 200 miles. Here and there the river affords a beautiful view; but the narrow valley is for the most part so flat and so subject to inundations, that it is mostly given over to the luxuriance of vegetation and to wild beasts. Between Galilee and the Dead Sea there are very few convenient fords or ferries; the chief place for passage is that near Jericho, which was used by the Israelites in their invasion of the land.

The region "beyond Jordan" is again a plateau, here and there attractive, but for the most part rather forbidding. The mountains of Moab rise precipitously from near the eastern shore of the Dead Sea. Farther to the north the land is less elevated.

At the present time but little of Palestine seems fertile according to our standards. No one, indeed, fails to see fertility in the plain of Esdraelon, and in the coast plain near Haifa, and in the plain of Sharon. But the traveler is forced to ask: If then this the land flowing with milk and honey? But an examination of the face of the country reveals several things to us. We find on multitudes of hillsides the remains of ancient terraces. A system of terraces can make nearly any country productive, if water can be found. The rainfall in Palestine is rather scant, and it comes with suddenness and, because of the hilly nature of the country, it swiftly passes away. Terracing, of course, largely overcomes the difficulty, especially as the construction of reservoirs for irrigation naturally attends the terracing. Besides, there is evidence that many of the hills not used—perhaps not just available—for vineyards and olive groves were once covered with natural forests. The hills now are comparatively bare. It is possible, moreover, that (as some scientists

believe) the rainfall was more abundant in ancient times
than now.

The physical characteristics of the country are wonderfully varied. The snows of Mount Hermon are always
visible in the north. The elevations in upper Palestine
never suffer because of extreme heat, for the nights are
cool. The valley of the Jordan and the Dead Sea has a
tropical climate in summer. But the hill country of Judea
is always tolerable. Refreshing breezes from the Mediterranean are frequent, and they affect all the land except
the deep valley of the Jordan and the Dead Sea. On the
whole, the country, by virtue of excellent natural drain-
age, abundant sunshine and frequent breezes, has a very
salubrious climate.

The occupations of the people in Bible times were determined by the natural resources of the land. The plains
and some of the hillsides were available for agriculture.
In Bible times an intensive cultivation of the vine and
the fig and the olive tree was of striking importance. The
Sea of Galilee yielded an abundance of fish. The hills of
Judea were suited to flocks of sheep and goats and in
part to the cultivation of the vine, the fig and the olive.
In Samaria, and especially in Gilead and Bashan on the
east of the Jordan, cattle were raised. Ancient Palestine
supported a relatively large population. The want of
good harbors, as well as the Israelitish policy of national
separateness, prevented the development of an extensive
commerce, though Israel's neighbors and kinsmen, the
Phœnicians, were once the leading maritime nation of the
world.

History.—It is on the background of these physical
and geographical conditions that the Hebrew people developed. This development falls into several distinct

periods. The nation's history proper begins with Moses and the Exodus; what came before is largely prehistoric. And yet that pre-Mosaic period is of importance for our understanding of the life of Israel.

(1) The Pre-Mosaic Period. Its records as found in the book of Genesis are made up of traditions, legends and folk-poetry. But we need not infer that these records are without historical value. Their chief interest and value for us lies, however, not so much in the history which they purport to record as in the self-disclosure of the religion and civilization of the people at the time in which the records were finally written. The substance of these early narratives was for many centuries handed down orally. When at length the traditions came to be written down, they received the stamp of the religious thought of the time of the writing, though of course at many points they disclose also the ideas and practices of earlier times. Traditions which were the common property of the Semitic peoples were in Israel gradually transfused by the spirit of the worship of Jehovah and so also in a measure transformed. As to the direct historical value of the early narratives of Genesis there are differences of opinion among scholars. Egypt and Babylonia have monuments and inscriptions reaching back far beyond the time of Abraham. Israel's traditions, on the other hand, were merely oral until a much later period. We have no Hebrew monuments or inscriptions that date as early even as the time of Moses. Yet Abraham was doubtless a real personage and the period from Abraham to Moses is semi-historical.

(2) The age of Moses and Joshua or the period of the Exodus and the Conquest.

(3) The period of the Judges.

(4) The period of the United Kingdom, ending with the death of Solomon 942 or 935 B. C.

(5) The period from the Disruption of the Kingdom to the Babylonian Captivity. The Northern Kingdom is brought to an end by the fall of Samaria in 721 B. C., while the Kingdom of Judah lasted until the Babylonian Captivity 586 B. C.

(6) The Babylonian Captivity, or Exile, from 586 to about 536 B. C.

(7) The Persian period lasting from the rise of Cyrus the Great until the conquest of Palestine and Syria by Alexander in 333–332 B. C.

(8) The Greek (or Græco-Macedonian) period from 333 to 165 B. C. Some, however, would reckon the Greek or Seleucid period as beginning in 312, with Seleucus (Nicator) as King of Syria.

(9) The Maccabean period of independence beginning with the successful revolt of Judea under Judas Maccabæus 165 and ending with the Roman conquest, which took place 40–37 B. C.

(10) The Roman period beginning with the conquest under Pompey accomplished in the years 40–37 B. C. and ending with the destruction of Jerusalem under the generalship of Titus in 70 A. D. From this last date the Jews have had no country, though they have never ceased to be a distinct people.

Such are the stages of the general Biblical history of the people of Israel. If, however, we inquire specially concerning Israel's *religious history*, we shall find it naturally falling into five chief periods:

(1) The religion of the prehistoric period.

(2) The religion of the period from Moses to the rise of the great prophets

(3) The religion of the period from the rise of the great prophets to the Exile.

(4) The religion of the Exile.

(5) The religion of the post-exilic period.

From their early prehistoric period the Hebrews brought well-established national customs and tendencies which never were wholly obliterated. The sojourn in Egypt swept away some of these ancient customs, but the Exodus brought the people of Israel again into contact with Semitic tribes and the old traditions were largely reëstablished. The chief significance of the wanderings in the wilderness, however, lay not so much in the reestablishment of Semitic traditions as in the firm establishment of the worship of Jehovah (or Jahweh). Before Israel came from Egypt into Midian some of the inhabitants of that desert country were practising a monolatry that was well fitted for development into a genuine monotheism. It was in Midian that Moses, while a shepherd keeping the flocks of his father-in-law, Jethro, received his call to go back to Egypt, and in the name of Jahweh, the living God, to bring forth the people in order that they might worship the God of their fathers. It was at this same spot that the children of Israel were encamped, when Moses from the neighboring Mount Sinai delivered to the people the Ten Commandments. The central thought of the legislation of Sinai is a covenant to worship Jahweh only.

This covenant with Jahweh became the dominating thought in all Moses' work. He made it the watchword of the people, the foundation of all that the people did in peace and in war. All the commandments were linked with the first commandment: "I am Jahweh, thy God, that brought thee up out of the land of Egypt. Thou shalt have no other god before me." The whole Mosaic system centers in this thought. The duty of loyalty to Jahweh gradually transformed Israel from a group of tribes into a nation. It may be that at the first relatively few of the people had any deep insight into the significance of the covenant, for the people had brought with them the idolatries of Egypt. The transformation, so far as it was really carried through in this period, was due, humanly speaking, to the powerful leadership of Moses. Among the great individual forces in history Moses clearly holds a very high place. He was in all respects a great personality. It was, however, his simple, grand and intense religious conviction that gave him his unique significance. To the people he was both ruler and priest, but he had to carry on his work in an atmosphere of reluctance and sometimes revolt, for the people were disposed to cling to their Egyptian religion. Gradually, however, they became fully impressed with the thought that they were Jahweh's people. With their entrance into Canaan, however, there came a very severe test of the religious loyalty of the people. After a partial conquest of the land, the Israelites mingled much with the Canaanites, who worshipped other gods. No wonder, then, that the worship of Israel was long mingled with the idolatries of the Canaanites. Yet in the heart of the people of Israel there persisted the deep conviction that they were Jahweh's covenant people, and at length this conviction became completely dominant.

The *geographic influences* affecting the development of Israel reach back into prehistoric times. The Hebrews were of the very ancient Semitic stock, and like all the Semites, they held fast to many ancient customs and modes of thought throughout their national history.

Where was the cradle of the Semitic race? This cannot be answered with certainty. It may have been in northern Arabia, or it may have been yet farther to the eastward. The Hebrews, as we commonly understand the term, are identical with "the children of Israel," but we first meet with the name "Hebrew" in the Old Testament in connection with Abraham (Genesis 14:13: "And there came one . . . and told Abram the Hebrew"). From this and other indications it is clear that there were Hebrews long before there were children of Israel, for Israel was Jacob, the grandson of Abraham. The earliest Hebrews were a nomadic people. They seem to have come into Palestine in considerable numbers long before the time when they finally settled in the land under Joshua. The early history of the Hebrews is altogether obscure, but we may accept the Biblical tradition concerning Abraham and his descendants as representing in a general way historical reality. The tradition is that Abraham (or, as he was first called, Abram) came out of the land of Chaldæa (from "Ur of the Chaldees") and that he journeyed to the northwest and settled for a time in Haran near the sources of the Tigris and Euphrates Rivers and afterwards came into the land of Canaan. After a period of unsettled life in Haran and Canaan, a portion of the descendants of Abraham, namely, Jacob and his family, migrated into Egypt on account of the famine in the land of Canaan. With a store of provisions Moses led forth the people of Israel into the desert of the Peninsula of Sinai and after his death the people of Israel under Joshua gained a foothold in the land of Canaan and ultimately became its masters.

The period of Joshua and the Judges must remain less clear to us than we might desire. Some things, however,

are impressively clear. It is evident that both the Canaanites and the Philistines were superior to Israel in civilization. They dwelt in walled cities and they had fairly
developed the arts of settled peoples. It is a wonder that
Israel overcame them in the conflict at arms. It is even
more a wonder that Israel, though conquering thus, was
not herself in turn overwhelmed and taken captive by the
social and religious ideals of these peoples. The corruption of Israel's religious ideals was very considerable,
but it was never complete. At length the persistent forces
of her own religious and ethical ideals triumphed over the
lower conceptions of the surrounding peoples. The religion of the time of Joshua and the Judges was very
crude, and the worship of Jahweh was sadly intermingled
with the worship of false gods. Yet it seems clear that
the leaders of the people were fairly consistent in the
singleness of their devotion to Jahweh. The religious
development was held in check through all this period by
the nature of the political life of the people. Israel was a
group of tribes of a common race that felt themselves to
be the people of Jahweh. It was only when Samuel, the
greatest of the Judges, laid the foundation for a unified
national life, that the religious development of the nation
could be consistently progressive.

The development of Israel from the time of Samuel
to the time of Solomon was swift and altogether remarkable. In the time of Saul, the first King of Israel, the
progress was not great, because Saul himself was religiously and morally weak. At the death of Saul, the
sense of national solidarity was not much stronger than
at the beginning of his reign. There was a temporary
division of the nation on the question of the royal suc-
cession. It was only the immense personal popularity of

David that gave him eventually a united people to reign over. Under David, Israel became a real nation. His military successes gave him Jerusalem, hitherto the stronghold of the Jebusites, and brought the Philistines into subjection. He extended his rule also northward and eastward; but his reign had, perhaps, equally great significance for the development of religion. Saul had been essentially superstitious; David was genuinely religious, and given to the undivided worship of Jahweh. Though himself a man of war, David remembered in everything Jahweh, his God. And David would have built a temple unto Jahweh, but this was not granted to him.

Solomon's reign marks the highest stage of power and glory that Israel was destined ever to reach. In a remarkable way he built up the city of Jerusalem, and especially he built the great temple there, thus centralizing the ritual worship of the nation, but he made alliances with many surrounding peoples and permitted idolatrous practices even in Jerusalem. Religiously, his reign denotes a corrupting tendency.

Upon the death of Solomon, the Kingdom broke asunder. The occasion of the disruption was the folly of Rehoboam, the new king, in refusing to lessen the burdens of the people. The leader of the people of the North, Jeroboam, was a man of unusual force; and when he renounced allegiance to Rehoboam and called upon the northern tribes to follow him, they did so with a will. But Jeroboam's religious convictions were slight. He set up places of worship in his own realm so that the people need no longer go to Jerusalem. In this there would have been no harm to religion, if only he had sought to preserve the true worship of Jahweh. But Jeroboam "made Israel to sin" in providing for worship after the manner of the Canaanites.

From this time, until its fall in 721 B. C., the Northern Kingdom was never even approximately free from idolatry. Perhaps the extreme of idolatrous worship was reached in the reign of Ahab, whose wife, Jezebel, did all in her power to further the worship of the Canaanite and Phœnician deities. But a mighty reformation led by Elijah, the prophet, followed immediately. This reform, however, did not signify the conversion of the most of the people to a pure worship. It was followed by King Jehu's boasted "zeal for Jahweh," but this was a fearful exhibition of treachery and cruelty. Such is the picture of the religion of the Northern Kingdom—sometimes better, sometimes worse—until the fall of the Kingdom. In the Southern Kingdom the religious history is brighter; yet even in Judah idolatry sometimes swept over the land. There were, however, certain reform movements from time to time, especially the great reform under Josiah toward the close of the 7th century.

The religious life of the two kingdoms is vividly and faithfully portrayed in the Books of the Kings. The outwardly conditioning factors of the religious development in the centuries during which the two kingdoms existed side by side are chiefly two: (1) The varying political policy of the kings; and (2) the influence of neighboring peoples. The more inward factors are (1) the priestly and (2) the prophetic ideals and tendencies. These inward factors of religious development deserve careful consideration.

In all historical religions we find the priestly idea expressing itself. Its essence is a regard for outward forms of worship and sacrifice, and the establishment of the privilege of the priestly class to represent the people in worship. But in all higher religion, that is, wherever the personal communion with God is conceived as the essence of religion, we find the expression of the prophetic idea. No historical religion, however, has ever become purely prophetic and inward. The entrance of the prophetic idea does not eliminate the priestly idea, but it tends to subordinate it. Now, the essence of prophecy is not the foretelling of the future. It is the interpreting of the mind of God, or speaking for God. Incidentally, of course, prediction of the future is involved in the exercise of the prophetic function, but this is never its chief interest. The prophetic spirit can be traced in the history of Israel back to the time of Moses. Moses, as lawgiver and proclaimer of the will of God, was more prophet than priest; and yet until many centuries after his time, prophecy was on a comparatively low plane in Israel because the conception of personal and ethical religion was comparatively undeveloped.

The prophet has no confidence in forms and ceremonies. He may not wholly repudiate them, but he recognizes that godliness is something inward and personal. The will of God is righteousness in all social relations. The prophet speaks as God bids him speak and sometimes denounces the practices even of the kings. Ordinarily he denounces the priests because of their formalism and their indifference to plain righteousness.

The priest, on the other hand, has his eyes fixed upon the past; he is a slave to tradition. His conception of religion is that God is pleased and honored by our observance of forms and ceremonies. The prophet, believing in the living God, has a forward look; yet he looks also at the past and at the present. This he does, however, not in order to preserve forms, but in order to interpret the mind of God; and he looks into the future in order to picture the will of God for time to come. He is not interested in the approved traditions of men's religious performances, but in the signs of God's working and the meaning of it. The prophet has also a very wide view. He sees not only the whole life of his own nation but he looks also at the movements of the other peoples. Looking into the future he foretells, not so much the details, but the great essential reality of that which is to be. His function is not to disclose mysteries as to coming events, but to acquaint men with God.

Prophecy in some form, lower or higher, existed in Israel from the beginning, but in the 8th century B. C. it sprang up in special strength. Amos was the first of the prophets to produce a book. Indeed, the book of Amos is the oldest complete book in our Bible. Amos was a mighty preacher of righteousness, and his denunciation of the sins of the people was tremendous. At about the same period there sprang up a hope of a future glory for Israel and for the world—the Messianic hope. Having once sprung up, it never perished. This hope assumed various forms according to the nature of the experience and the spiritual development of a given prophet, but in one form or another it is henceforth the most significant feature of Israel's prophecy. Broadly speaking, it was the hope that God would send to Israel a heavenly king and redeemer who should bring to Israel and the world supreme and endless blessings.

Generally speaking, monarchy tended to support and make use of the priesthood. A primary interest of every monarch is the unifying of national life. Now, obviously, the priesthood is a powerful organizing and conservative force. Therefore, we naturally find king and priest working hand in hand, whether it be in the interests of the worship of Jahweh, or in the service of false gods. The prophet, on the other hand, tends to break down existing conditions if they are evil, and therefore in the eyes of the worldly-minded he looks like a disorganizer and destroyer; yet he himself knows that his function is to tear down only that he may build up. The priestly tendency at its worst is mere formalism; at its best, it includes a legalism that is the observance of all required forms of righteousness in social life. At its best, the priestly function is quite compatible with a genuine spirit of prophecy.

The period of the kings of Israel and Judah witnessed a great struggle between these two tendencies in religion, the priestly and the prophetic. In this period appeared some of the greatest prophets and all of them showed a frank abhorrence of mere ritual. The struggle, however, did not end with the period. It never ended absolutely.

The outward conditions of the religious development of the people of Israel in the period of the Kings were highly significant. Until the time of Solomon it was chiefly the Philistines and the Canaanite tribes with whom Israel was in contact. Solomon brought the people of Israel into contact with remoter nations. After the time of Solomon, the Northern Kingdom came into rather direct relations with Syria. The Syrian influence, along with that of the Philistines, continued to be quite pronounced until the power of Assyria not only quenched the aspirations of Syria, but also ultimately destroyed Israel. At the same time Assyria was also menacing Judah, and this menace was the background of much of the prophecy of Isaiah of Jerusalem. The destruction of the Northern Kingdom came in the midst of Isaiah's labors as prophet in Jerusalem. By paying tribute Judah averted destruction by the hand of the Assyrian, but on one memorable occasion it was a swift pestilence that drove back the invading army from the very walls of Jerusalem. At length Judah was overwhelmed and led into captivity—not, however, by that Assyria, which had so long threatened, but by Babylon, which in the meantime had gained the ascendency over Assyria herself. Nineveh, the Assyrian capital, has been destroyed and Babylon has become capital of the empire.

The Babylonian Captivity of Judah had an immense religious significance. In the last few decades before the Captivity (which began 586 B. C.) we find a movement of great importance for the religion of the Jews. It was the movement that brought forth and established Deuteronomy as the standard of religious and social practice. This book was in a large measure the work of the priests, but it is far more than a priestly document. It represents the tendency of the time to combine the priestly and the prophetic elements. Jeremiah, the great prophet of the time, recognized in the work of the priests a needful factor for the life of the people. The book of Deuteronomy is made the basis of extensive reforms during the reign of Josiah. Now, the deep ethical and spiritual influence of Jeremiah and the wholesome religious education of the people on the basis of Deuteronomy remained with the people as they were carried into captivity, and the treasure involved in this combined influence was never lost. The captivity threatened the annihilation of Israel's great hope as a nation, but in the midst of the deep depression and suffering of the time, a marvel of religious development takes place. The apparent destruction of the nation's hopes led prophetic souls to turn to God for light.

Religion became at once more individual and more universal, more inward and at the same time wider in its outlook. The promise of Jahweh cannot fail even though Israel should never realize her national hopes. It is from this period that we have the great prophecy concerning the Suffering Servant in the writings of the unknown prophet called Deutero-Isaiah (Isaiah 40–55). In all this suffering of Israel, God has a purpose—the salvation of the Gentiles.

In the Captivity another tendency manifests itself side by side with the prophetic spirit. Priestly tradition is further developed and reduced to literary form. The Priestly Code, which later formed a part of the Pentateuch, assumed shape chiefly in the Exile; and a great prophet of the time, Ezekiel, who began to prophesy before the Captivity and continued for some decades during it, is the characteristic example of the union of the prophetic and the priestly tendencies. Also many of the Psalms date from this time, and the book known as the Lamentations of Jeremiah. All these productions show the immense religious significance of the period of the Exile.

At length the Jews are permitted by the decree of Cyrus, the new master of the world, to return to Jerusalem (538–536 B. C.). With the return there develops the phase of the religion of the Jews that had its germ in the reign of Josiah. This new phase is known as Judaism. Its fundamental characteristic is, on the one hand, the amalgamating of the ceremonial with the moral law, and, on the other, the recognition of the authority of the great prophets of the past. Deuteronomy and Ezekiel are the characteristic examples of the union of legal and ceremonial principles in the era before Judaism proper became established. But the era of Judaism produced its special literature and recognized the approved writings of former times and brought them into shape and gave to them the sanction of universal recognition.

In some respects Judaism represents a great advance over the pre-exilic religion. Idolatry has now been effectually overcome. The individual responsibility to God has gained a much larger recognition. The social character of religion is emphasized and the whole nation is organized upon the basis of a moral law. Jeremiah had introduced the element of individualism into his warnings. Ezekiel, writing from the Exile, had carried the principle much further, insomuch that he has been called the prophet of individualism. Yet in the system of Judaism, the individual is never thought of in separation from the nation. It is a system of the union of the national and individual points of view. Another point of advance is the thorough organization of the people for instruction in matters of religion and social righteousness. The leader in this work was Ezra, the scribe. In order to make effective the plan of religious instruction, Ezra and others gathered up the books held in highest esteem, edited them and began to establish a canon of Sacred Scriptures. To the writings thus recognized, additions were made from time to time until about 150 B. C., when the canon was closed.

The large measure of wholesomeness in the system of Judaism cannot be questioned, but along with the elements of good and of progress, some factors of a contrary nature were at work. It was good to establish systematic religious instruction, but it was not good that a religious formalism gradually gained ascendency. It was good that there was a zeal for keeping the commandments, but it was evil that the spirit of the law was sometimes forgotten in its formal observance. Thus there grew up many traditions that obscured the real meaning of the law. Little by little needless details of outward righteousness were added until religious observance was lost in a mere formalism. It was evil, too, that the fixing of a list of authoritative scriptures led the people to despise every new voice of prophecy, and even to deny that there could be any further inspiration. Instead of the ethical and spiritual prophecy of former days, there grows up a tendency to apocalyptic prediction. The essence of apocalyptic prediction is the forecasting of future events rather than the interpreting of the mind of God. Knowing that he cannot hope to be recognized as a genuine prophet, the man with a message ascribes his revelation or apocalypse to some earlier prophet of recognized authority. The Messianic hope, of course, was continually stirring, but it tended to grow more and more narrow and selfish in its outlook.

Such, in brief, was the development of Israel until the appearance of Jesus. Every period in this development has left its mark upon the literature of the Old Testament, and that literature can only be understood as an outgrowth of these historical movements. In the pre-Mosaic period there were no writings, and yet the people of Israel brought from that dim past an immense body of ideas and customs which helped to shape their whole subsequent history. Laws, which were only written down centuries later, were largely shaped in the customs of the people long before Moses' time. Even the period of Moses and Joshua could have produced but little in the way of actual writing, yet doubtless Moses was the great lawgiver of Israel, and the heart of what is known as Mosaic legislation came from his hand. Such laws, however, as Moses may have given forth must afterwards have been transcribed and rewritten from time to time, so that we can hardly assume that we have writings directly from his hand. In the time of the Kings we have, however, a rich literary productivity. Books of history and of prophecy and of legislation belong to this time. Yet some of these writings were recast, edited and put into final form in the period after the Exile. The historical books produced in the time of the Kings represent traditions which have been handed down orally from very ancient times, but it is doubtful whether the actual literary production of the nation began to assume any considerable proportions until the time of Solomon. The earlier writings were either lost or absorbed into later writings. The period of bookmaking in the modern sense was the period after the return from the Exile. Strangely enough, virtually nothing of the literature of Israel produced before the time of the fixing of the Canon has been preserved except the books that form the Canon. The writings known as Apocrypha were produced almost entirely after the closing of the Canon.

When Jesus appeared and taught publicly he won followers, who eventually recognized in him the promised Messiah. The leaders of the people, however, were so filled with other conceptions of the kingdom of God that they could not receive him. The preaching of Jesus as Messiah by his followers brought about a tremendous change in the religious history of the nation. While a few Jews confidently proclaimed him as the Messiah, the most of the people rejected him. The Jews could have received Jesus only by radically renouncing their peculiar conception of the nature of the Messianic kingdom. In the vivid narratives of the New Testament there is enacted before our eyes the profoundest spiritual tragedy of all history: the people of the Messianic hope reject the prophet who comes bringing even more than they had hoped for.

It is not to be supposed that in the period between the closing of the Old Testament Canon and the appearance of Jesus, the religious history of Israel was at a standstill. It was rather a very stirring period, but the period between the Testaments sheds light, not so much upon the Old Testament as upon the New. The significance of this interval for the understanding of the New Testament has, in the last two or three decades, begun to receive immensely greater recognition than before.

The New Testament is, perhaps, even more clearly the outgrowth of a special religious history than is the case with the Old. The New Testament writings are in the most direct way the literary expression of the religious thought and activity of the early believers in the Messiahship of Jesus.

Chapter IX

THE ORIGIN OF THE BOOKS OF THE OLD TESTAMENT: EARLIER PERIOD

We have compared the Bible to a vast cathedral. Many centuries was this cathedral in building, and now for many centuries the Christian Church has had the finished temple, including both the Old and the New Testament, in which it finds and worships God. Our present task is to sketch the history of the building. What means have we for accomplishing this task? Where are we to find the records of this history? The answer is: We must read the history of the building in its stones. In other words, the history of the origin of the Bible must disclose itself through an examination of the books themselves. All that is built and all that grows bears in itself some record of the process of building or growth. As an architect can read the history of the building of a cathedral—and that, too, without disturbing a single stone—so the competent critic can, without desecration, without tearing anything to pieces, read the history of the construction of the Bible. Not perfectly, to be sure, for there are not a few problems which he is unable to solve; yet with much sure insight and a goodly measure of trustworthy results. He can distinguish the orders and styles of literary architecture, and with the help of manifold sidelights from history and archæology, he can tell us much concerning the dates of the several writings and the influences that shaped them and finally put them together.

109

Or—to change the simile—the critic is like the geologist who reads the physical history of the earth in the strata of the rocks and all the many marks of past changes.

As we proceed to examine the literature of the Old Testament, in order to learn what we may concerning its construction, we are quickly made aware of several obvious facts.

(1) The arrangement of the books, as we find them in the ancient or the modern Bible, affords no true key to the relative age of the writings. In the Hebrew Bibles, the books of the "Torah" and the "Former Prophets" (historical books) are placed in the supposed order of the events narrated. The books of the Latter Prophets are arranged according to their supposed order of time, though we now know that there were mistakes in this arrangement. On the other hand, the arrangement of the "Writings" (Kethubim) scarcely purports to be chronological. Generally speaking, those placed near the end of the list were the last to be acknowledged as canonical. The Torah, as a whole, is placed first because it was first to be acknowledged as Holy Scripture. The Prophets stand next because they were the next to be so acknowledged. The Writings are placed last because they were the last to be canonized.

(2) Many of the books of the Old Testament are anonymous. Not one of the books which we now class as "historical" names its own author. The same is the case with Job, Lamentations, Ecclesiastes, Song of Solomon and Jonah. But also the books traditionally ascribed to Moses are in reality anonymous, for they nowhere purport to come from the hand of Moses. The most that they have to say on this line is that "Moses wrote" the various bodies of laws as indicated in the

books.   Likewise large portions of the Psalter and of
the book of Proverbs are anonymous.

(3) Various books of the Old Testament are collections and compilations.   This is obviously the case with
the Psalter and the Proverbs.   Further examination will
reveal it to be the case also with several other books.
The work of historico-literary criticism must be both
analytic and synthetic.   That is to say, critics must first
take the books as they stand and must learn to distinguish
their separable elements.   This task of analysis is both
necessary and interesting, yet is incomparably less important than the task of synthetic reproduction.   When the
parts have been distinguished, we are ready for the far
more delightful and sympathetic task of historical reconstruction, the task of following by imagination the process of the building of the literature.   In order fairly to accomplish this task we need not only a knowledge of the
main results of the critical analysis, but even more we
need historical imagination and an insight into the
motives and influences that controlled the production of
the literature.   In the following historical sketch of the
growth of the Old Testament we shall content ourselves
with the indispensable minimum of analysis and chiefly
devote our thought to the historical reconstruction.

1. *Lost Books of the Hebrews.*   When we consider
the fact that our Old Testament includes all the extant
literature of the Hebrews down to the time of Alexander
the Great and a large part of that produced between the
time of Alexander and the middle of the second century,
B. C., we are prepared to believe that very much of their
literature perished.   Indeed, what has been lost must have
immensely exceeded in bulk what has been preserved.   In
the Old Testament specific mention is made of a number

of books no longer extant. "The Book of the Wars of Jehovah" is referred to as the source of the Song of Arnon (Num. 21: 14, 15). " Book of Jashar" (or "of the Upright") is assigned as a source of the Song of the Sun Standing Still at the Battle of Beth-horon (Josh. 10:13). Also the Song of the Bow, the lament of David over Saul and Jonathan, was found "written in the book Jashar" (2 Sam. 1: 18–27). In 1 Sam. 10: 25 there is an interesting reference to Samuel's writing in a book "the manner of the kingdom" that had just been established with Saul as King. In the Books of the Kings we generally find at the conclusion of the account of a particular reign such a reference as this : "Now the rest of the acts of (this or that king) . . . are they not written in the Book of the Chronicles of the Kings of Judah" (or "of Israel") ? These are not our "Chronicles," but older narratives now lost. In our Chronicles we find mention of no fewer than ten different books now lost. Still others are mentioned in the Kings. All this excites our curiosity. We wish to know all that may be known of the possible extent of this lost literature, of its character and contents. Above all, we should like to know to what extent our Old Testament books may have gathered up, and thus preserved, elements of real importance in these otherwise lost books. Concerning some of these questions our Biblical scholars can do no more than make their more or less well founded guesses. It is certain that in several instances older books have been largely incorporated in our canonical books, and the form of the original writings can, in some cases, be largely reconstructed.

2. *Jewish Tradition as to the Age and Authorship of the Old Testament Books.*—The assembling, editing and canonizing of the Scriptures came relatively late. This

work was systematically undertaken only from the time of Ezra (after 458 B. C.) and was not concluded until about three centuries after that date.   In the process of canonizing the Scriptures, there was a natural inclination to assign all the books to some worthy and revered author; yet in fact most of the ancient writings, except the Prophets, were anonymous.   The Jewish rabbis, therefore, in their great veneration for the great names of the nation's history, and with a like reverence for the writings, were disposed, as far as possible, to find among those worthies an author for every book.   Knowing Moses as the great lawgiver, they assigned the first five books, "the Law," to him.   The books from Joshua to Kings, inclusive, they called the Former Prophets, assuming that Samuel and other prophets had written them.   They ascribed the largest number of the Psalms to David and the bulk of the Book of Proverbs to Solomon.   To the latter they ascribed also Ecclesiastes and the Song of Songs.   Job was most strangely ascribed to Moses.   It should be made clear once for all that the tradition as to the authorship of the Old Testament books in most instances does not reach back to the time when the writings first appeared.   For the most part it dates from the time after the Exile.   The titles of the Psalms and the headings of the different collections of Proverbs and of the books of the Pentateuch are no part of the original Scriptures.   The surmises of the Jewish rabbis in the last centuries before the Christian era have for us no final authority.

3. *The Origin of the Books of the Law.*—We naturally begin our inquiry with the group of writings that stands first in our Bibles.   These were the first to be recognized as Holy Scripture; and although, in their final form, they

may not prove to be nearly as old as we supposed, they do record the earliest traditions of Israel and do contain some of the oldest materials of Hebrew literature.

The Hebrew tradition as to the authorship of these books is as follows: The late books of the Old Testament constantly refer to the Law (that is, the Law as contained in the Pentateuch) as the work of Moses (Ezra 3:2; 7:6; 2 Chron. 34:14), but even here there is nothing said concerning the authorship of the books as a whole. On the other hand, Philo, Josephus and the New Testament writers everywhere assume that the whole Pentateuch is to be ascribed to Moses. The Talmud expressly states that Moses wrote the Pentateuch, only the last eight verses of Deuteronomy, which tell of the death of Moses, being added by Joshua. Thus we see that the tradition ascribing all these writings to Moses took shape in the interval between the date of the Chronicles and the New Testament time. This tradition was generally adhered to, both in Church and in Synagogue, until the seventeenth century.

But the tradition is not supported by the testimony of the books themselves. In no way whatsoever do they bear the signature of their authorship. Certain important passages are expressly stated as having been written down by Moses (see Ex. 17:14; 24:4, "the book of the covenant" Ex. 20–23; 34:27; Num. 33:2; Deut. 1:5; 4:45; 31:9, 22, 24). Yet every other reference in the five books naturally suggests that Moses is thought of not only as other than the writer but as a figure of an age long past. The ascription of particular passages to Moses is even an indirect testimony to the non-Mosaic authorship of the rest of the work.

The facts that first provoked doubts as to the Mosaic

authorship of the Pentateuch are a number of expressions found scattered through the books which manifestly presuppose that Israel was already settled in Canaan and which look back upon Moses and his time as comparatively remote. Yet it is clear that such passages could be accounted for as having been later insertions in the text; but the observation of these incongruities led to further inquiry, with the result that many highly interesting and important discoveries were made.

It is the cumulative evidence of various passages which cannot be ascribed to Moses that has forced critical scholars to give up the thought of the Mosaic authorship of the Pentateuch. Moreover, there are passages which show the clearest evidence of having proceeded from different sources. Hence strict unity cannot be ascribed to these books.

As to the expressions in the Pentateuch, which could not have originated with Moses, perhaps the following are the most striking examples. Gen. 12:6 and 13:7, "the Canaanite dwelt then in the land," an expression which implies that at the time of the writing of this narrative the Canaanites no longer occupied the land. Gen. 14:14, "pursued as far as Dan"; but the name of this city was Laish until it was renamed in the time of the Judges (Judges 18:29). Gen. 36:31, "And these are the kings that reigned in the land of Edom, before there reigned any king over the children of Israel"; the expression is impossible before the time of Saul, the first king of Israel. Gen. 40:15, Joseph is represented as speaking of Canaan as "the land of the Hebrews," an expression possible only after Joshua. Deut. 1:1, "beyond the Jordan" (RV), in reference to the land of Moab, can only spring from the pen of one who writes from the west of the Jordan. In Deut. 4:14 the "unto this day" puts the then present time in express antithesis to the age of Moses. Now it is perfectly clear that these and similar expressions could not spring from Moses, but since they might represent later additions to the text, Moses might still be the author of the books as a whole. The really conclusive objection to their Mosaic authorship is based upon the clear evidence that the Pentateuch, and especially Genesis, is a composite work based upon documents of various ages and very diverse characteristics, so that it could not originate with any single author, whether Moses or another.

The proof of the *documentary theory* of the origin of the Pentateuch is threefold. (1) In the different sections we note a marked change of language. One section, for example, says "cut a covenant," another "raise a covenant"; one uses saphah for "language," another lashon. Such differences are rather numerous and are clearly marked. Along with the differences of idiom, we find also differences of names for the same place or person. One section, for example, calls the inhabitants of Palestine "Amorites," another, "Canaanites"; the mountain on which the law was given is now "Sinai," now "Horeb"; the third patriarch is now "Jacob," now "Israel"; Moses' father-in-law is in one section "Jethro," in another "Reuel" (or "Raguel"). But by far the most striking variation is found in the designation of God as "Jahweh" and "Elohim."—These differences strongly suggest the use of different written sources in the composition or compilation of the books.

(2) Another reason for denying the literary unity of the Pentateuch is the presence of marked discrepancies in the narratives and the legislative portions. Very obvious ex-

amples are the following: (a) Two accounts of creation (Gen. 1:1–2:3 and 2:4–25). According to the former the creation takes place in six days; according to the latter—possibly aside from the creation of Eve—in one; in the former the order is plants, animals, man; in the latter, man, plants, animals; in the former man and woman are created at one time; in the latter, the woman after the man. (b) Two accounts of the flood, which, although interlaced, are mutually inconsistent. According to the one account two of every beast are taken into the ark (Gen. 6:19), while according to the other it is seven pairs of the clean and one of the unclean (7:2); also the duration of the flood is 40 days in 7:4 and 150 days in 7:24; and there are several other differences. (c) Two irreconcilable accounts of Joseph's coming into Egypt (on the one hand Gen. 37:22–24, 28a, 29 ff.; on the other vv. 25–27, 28b). (d) Two very different accounts of the call of Moses (Ex. 3 and 6). (e) Two different statements respecting the location of the Tabernacle (Ex. 33:7 outside the camp, Num. 2:2 ff. in the midst of the camp). Of the discrepancies in the details of legislation we may mention only one, namely, that there are two statements concerning who may offer the sacrifices: according to Deut. 18:7 ff. it is all the Levites, according to Ex. 28:1 ff. only the sons of Aaron.

(3) The third reason for denying the literary unity of the Pentateuch is the presence of a number of parallel accounts of the same event. These are generally easily recognizable as doublets. In every instance these parallels show such variations in languages or circumstance, or in both, as to exclude the assumption of their springing from a single source.

If it should be objected that Moses himself might have

been the one to use the older documents in writing the Pentateuch, the obvious answer is, that, while he might have made use of documents for the narratives of Genesis, he could have had no possible use for documents concerning his own work. But the differences noted pertain just as surely to the other books of the Pentateuch as to Genesis. Now the age of these documents is only a matter of more or less probable conjecture. Yet one thing is a well-established fact: the Pentateuch as we have it grew out of several documents written in Palestine after the time of Moses.

Literary criticism has shown that there are four direct sources for the Pentateuch. They are designated respectively as the Jahvistic (J), Elohistic (E), Deuteronomic (D), and Priestly (P) sources. The first is so called because of its constant use of the name of Jahweh as the designation of the God of Israel. It is sometimes called the Judean source, because it originated in Judea. The Elohistic document is so named because of its regular use of the name Elohim for God. As this writing originated in the Northern Kingdom, some prefer to call it the Ephraimitic source. The source D constitutes the larger and most important part of our Deuteronomy. The Priestly source was a writing prepared by the priests.

All of Leviticus and portions of the other four books are from P. It is doubtless the latest of the sources. Most scholars date it after the Exile (about 500—450 B. C.), although there is reason to believe that much of it was prepared in the Exile and some of it even before. D is the next above P in age. It may have been composed about 623 B. C., that is, shortly before it was brought to light in the reign of Josiah. Some hold that at that time it was newly finished; others that it was a rediscovered writing of an earlier date. The date of E is perhaps about 800 B. C., while J is to be dated somewhat earlier, perhaps about 850 B. C. The dates for J and E are confessedly uncertain, but the relative age of the documents seems clear.

4. *The Oldest Materials in the Pentateuch.* The four great "sources" are not the oldest literary productions of the Hebrews. Still older books once existed which have been lost; and besides older writings there was a large body of oral tradition that was pretty well fixed in the minds of the people. It is certain that both J and E contain materials drawn not merely from oral tradition, but also from earlier writings. These older materials are of three kinds: poetical, legislative, narrative. Their age reaches back before the time of the Kings into the time of the Judges, and in a few instances even into the time of Moses.

(1) *The poetical portions of the Pentateuch* are—perhaps in every instance—older than the prose compositions in which they have been preserved. In Israel, as with all other peoples, the age of proper authorship was preceded by an age of minstrelsy and folk-tales. Of this early minstrelsy we find fragments in the Pentateuch as follows:

(a) The Song of Lamech, or Song of the Sword (Gen. 4:23 f.), a celebration of blood revenge, is probably of Midianite or Kenite origin, taken up by the Israelites in the time of Moses. It may well be the oldest fragment in the Bible.

(b) The Sayings of Noah concerning Shem, Japheth and Canaan (Gen. 9:25-27). Shem and Japheth are blessed, while Canaan is cursed. These sayings grew up among the people under the influence and experience of

a time long after that of Noah. They may have arisen
in a pre-Mosaic period when the Canaanites were pressed
on two sides, by the Hittites (who were of Japheth) on
the north, and by the Habiri (who were of Shem) on the
east; or they may have arisen in the period when the
Canaanites were yielding to Israel (Shem) and the Philistines (Japheth), after Israel's settlement in Palestine.

(d) Jacob's Blessing (Gen. 49) contains sayings, some
of praise, others of blame, concerning the twelve tribes.
The situation or background implied in most of the sayings is that of the time of the Judges. The saying concerning Judah, however, must have originated later, perhaps in the time of David, because it refers to Judah as
holding the royal scepter.

(e) The Song of the Red Sea (Ex. 15: 1–19) and the
song of Miriam (verse 21). The latter is here only a
fragment; possibly it represents an older and briefer form
of the same folklore poem as that found in vv. 1–18.
The song may be dated from the time of the wanderings
in the wilderness.

(f) A group of songs relating to the life of Israel in
the wilderness, mostly preserved by the Elohist. These
all belong to the latest period of the wanderings, of which
period the records are relatively clear and accurate. There
is in Ex. 17: 16 a very old Oath by the Ark of the Covenant. Moses called the altar that he raised after the vic-
tory over the Amalekites Jahweh-nissi, "Jahweh is my
banner." And he said: "A hand upon the throne of Jah!
Jahweh will have war with Amalek from generation to
generation." Then there are the Sayings (Num. 10: 35 f.)
relating to the Ark, as it went forward and as it rested in
the marches of the people in the wilderness. The Aaron-
itic Blessing is found in Num. 6: 24–27. The Song of

Arnon is given in Num. 21 : 14 f. and the charming Song of the Well in verses 17 and 18.   These both doubtless sprang from the people that had actually made the journey. A Song of Contempt of Sihon (Num. 21 : 27–30) is evidently composed out of the fresh memories of the conflicts with the Amorites.

(g)   There are four Oracles of Balaam (Num. 23 : 7–10 and 18–24; 24 : 3–9 and 15–24).   The first two are given by the Elohist, the last two by the Jahvist; they are, however, all older than the documents in which they have been preserved to us.   References to certain conditions indicate that they sprang from the time of the Kings, but before the disruption of Kingdom.

(2)   *The earliest legislative portions of the Pentateuch.*—It is now an established fact that the laws of the people of Israel were not all promulgated at a single time. They were the product of successive ages.   The legal system grew.   Long before there was a written law there was a body of well-established legal customs.   At first the written laws were inscribed on stones; later the law was written out more amply and in greater detail in books. Israel's written law was not finished until some time after the Exile, and we know that even in the time of Christ the Pharisees were observing many "traditions of the elders" which never had been written in the Law at all.   Undoubtedly Moses was Israel's great lawgiver.   The main stock or trunk of the law was given through Moses.   Later accretions or outgrowths came so gradually that the people in all good faith ascribed all their law, even its latest developments, to Moses.   But Moses himself inherited from a remoter antiquity a body of Semitic customs, which he and the people held to be binding.   There are many striking similarities between the legal system

of Israel and the Code of Laws of Hammurabi, a Babylonian king who reigned some 2000 years B. C. The points of resemblance, however, have nothing to do with the central principle of the Mosaic legislation, namely, the covenant between Jahweh and Israel, but only with a mass of individual and civil rights.

The oldest written legislation of the Pentateuch must reach back, at least in its substance, to the time of Moses himself; though it is almost certan that in form the earliest legislation had been recast before it reached the form in which we know it. The oldest legislative portions are the following: (a) the *Decalogue* as given in Ex. 20: 1–17 (and, in essential agreement, Deut. 5: 6–21); (b) the *Book of the Covenant* (Ex. 20:23–23:19); (c) the so-called *Jahvistic Decalogue* (Ex. 34:10–27; (d) the *Twelvefold Curse* in Deut. 27: 15–26; (e) the *Law of Holiness* (Lev. 17–26). The whole question of the age and source of these legislative portions of the Pentateuch is much disputed.

(a) The *Decalogue* of Ex. 20 and Deut. 5 may be regarded as substantially Mosaic, only with the rewriting assumed above. The language of both passages is unquestionably that of the age of the Kings and the Prophets and not that of an earlier period. There is a dispute among scholars as to whether the form of the Decalogue with which we are familiar represents the original Commandments as promulgated by Moses at Sinai. Some scholars hold that the so-called "J Decalogue" of Ex. 34 more nearly represents the original form of the legislation. It should be observed that the "J Decalogue" is largely ceremonial, while the other (the "E Decalogue") is more ethical. Some claim that the ceremonial must have been the earlier. To this it is replied that the legislation, which critics generally ascribe to Moses, is not less ethical than our "E Decalogue." Furthermore, it is objected that in Ex. 34 it is scarcely possible to reconstruct any decalogue at all.

(b) The *Book of the Covenant* is placed in Exodus in close connection with the giving of the Ten Commandments on Mt. Sinai. But in Deuteronomy there is an explicit account (from E) of Moses' giving the people the Law of the Covenant shortly before the close of his life and directing that, as soon as they should have crossed over into the land of Canaan, they should write it upon tables of stone and promulgate it on Mt. Ebal (or Gerizim?) near Shechem (Deut. 27:1–8). As this account of the giving of the Law of the Covenant and the portion of Exodus known as the Book of the Covenant are both from the Elohist, and as the two fit together perfectly, it seems clear that the two passages originally belonged together. Thus the Book of the Covenant is to be connected, not with the legislation of Mt. Sinai, but with the closing period of Moses' life.

This Book of the Covenant shows some direct resemblances to the code of Hammurabi. These resemblances do not at all imply that Moses, or the people of Israel at any later time, had any immediate knowledge of the Babylonian code. The similarity is to be ascribed simply to the common tradition of Semitic peoples. In respect of social relations the Code of Hammurabi is better developed than that of Moses. In matters of religion and ideals of righteousness, the Mosaic Code is incomparably the higher of the two.

(c) The so-called "*J. Decalogue*" (Ex. 34:10–27). The question as to whether this passage constitutes a decalogue was suggested by the occurrence in Ex. 34:28

of the expression: "the ten words." But it is possible that this expression is an editorial addition. Some scholars hold that we have here fragments of the original Decalogue, intermingled with some of the ceremonial ordinances of the Covenant. At all events the passage contains some very old materials.

A comparison of the two "Decalogues" will prove instructive. When we examine the "E Decalogue," we note that the essence of each Commandment can be expressed in a single sentence. It is this briefer form of the "Ten Words" that has ever been impressed in the memory of the people.

> Thou shalt have no other gods before me.
> Thou shalt not make unto thyself any graven image.
> Thou shalt not take the name of Jahweh thy God in vain.
> Remember the sabbath day to keep it holy.
> Honor thy father and thy mother.
> Thou shalt not kill.
> Thou shalt not commit adultery.
> Thou shalt not steal.
> Thou shalt not bear false witness.
> Thou shalt not covet.

The "J Decalogue," according to the reconstruction of some scholars, appears—likewise in its briefer form—as follows:

> Thou shalt worship no other god.
> Thou shalt make thee no molten gods.
> The feast of unleavened bread thou shalt keep.
> Six days thou shalt work, but on the seventh day thou shalt rest.
> Thou shalt observe the feast of the weeks;
> And the feast of ingathering at the year's end.

Thou shalt not offer the blood of any sacrifice with leavened bread.

The sacrifice of the Passover shall not be left till morning.

The first of the firstfruits of thy ground shalt thou bring into the house of Jahweh thy God.

Thou shalt not seethe a kid in its mother's milk.

(d) *The Twelvefold Curse* (or Twelvefold Commandment) of Shechem (Deut. 27: 15–26).—There are indications that for a period there was in Shechem a celebration of the Covenant. The people, it seems, repeated from time to time the form of the first promulgation of the Covenant as described in Deut. 27: 1–8. The public reading of the Covenant was followed by the liturgy of the Twelvefold Curse. This liturgy probably had its origin in the time of the Judges.

(e) *The Law of Holiness* (Lev. 17–26).—The Priestly Code incorporated within itself a much older document, known as the Law of Holiness (H). Although this document was more or less rewritten by the author or editor of P, its original character is still fairly distinguishable. Its date is uncertain; probably it belongs to the last period before the Captivity.

(3) *Earliest Narrative Portions of the Pentateuch.*—Doubtless all the narratives of Genesis were derived from sources antedating the composition of the book. These sources were chiefly oral tradition, yet it is quite possible that both the Jahvist and Elohist had access to some written narratives. In one instance we have an interesting narrative that is almost surely based upon an ancient written document, perhaps a monumental inscription. It is the story of Abraham's victorious battle against the armies of the East, and his meeting Melchizedek, King of Salem

('Gen. 14). It is probable that this passage represents a rather free working over of an ancient Canaanitish memorial writing.

Such appear to be the oldest materials in the Pentateuch, materials antedating the outstanding main written sources, yet incorporated in them. To these main written sources we now turn our attention (in sections 5–8).

5. *The Jahvistic Source.*—The most striking mark of this source is its habitual use of the name Jahweh, while E more often uses Elohim. But this peculiarity in the use of the name Jahweh is only the most striking mark of the J source, it is not its most important characteristic. There are several peculiarities of language that deserve notice. A few may be mentioned here. J has "Sinai," not "Horeb"; "Israel" (after the birth of Benjamin) instead of "Jacob"; "Canaanites," not "Amorites" for the inhabitants of Palestine. There are also many favorite words and expressions aside from the names of persons and places.

The Jahvist begins with the creation of man in the garden of Eden, continues with the entrance and growth of sin and proceeds to touch in order upon most of the important incidents in the traditional history of the Hebrews. From the very beginning Jahweh appears in very personal relations with men, especially with those who enjoy his special favor. A separation of chosen ones begins among the sons of Adam and Eve and reaches a climax in the election of Abraham, to whom the most gracious promises are given. Abraham's seed shall be a great multitude. Canaan shall be his possession, and in him all peoples shall be blessed. There is an election also among the decendants of Abraham. Jacob and his family are chosen. The coming of this family into Egypt is impressively told. Then follows the miraculous saving of the chosen people out of Egypt by the hand of Moses (it is worth noting that there is no mention of Aaron in J). Then comes the giving of the Commandments on Mount Sinai, followed by the many wonderful events of the forty years in the wilderness until the death of Moses on the eve of the entrance of Israel into Canaan. The narrative of J, it should be remarked, is continued also in the books of Joshua and Judges.

Everywhere the Jahvistic source is characterized by a very lively but simple imagination, an intense human sympathy, and a really wonderful narrative art. Its manner of expression is very picturesque; even Jahweh's actions are portrayed with a simple dramatic art. Jahweh plants a garden; he walks in the garden in the cool of the day; he calls Adam to meet him. But this simplicity is to be ascribed to the poetical gift of the writer more than to a crudity of religious conceptions. The Jahvist's religious conceptions are very simple, but they are intensely personal and ethical. They bear the prophetic rather than the priestly stamp.

The appreciation of the J source is possible only as one reads it in some continuity and in comparison with the other component parts of the Pentateuch. For the purpose of introduction into this aspect of our study, the following specimens of J (all taken from Genesis) will be found interesting.

2:4b—4:26—The creation, the garden, the entrance of sin, the penalties of disobedience, Cain and his descendants.
9:18 (or 20)–27—The fate of Canaan.
11:1–9—The dispersal of mankind.
12 (in the main)—Abram's migration from the East.
13 (in the main)—Abram's separation from Lot.

15 (portions—the rest being from E)—The covenant of
    Jahweh.

18:1–19:38 (except 19:29 from P)—The angelic guests,
    destruction of Sodom and Gomorrah, Lot and his
    daughters.

24:1–9—Abraham's charge to the servant whom he sends to
    procure a wife for Isaac.

29:2–14—The meeting between Jacob and Rachel.

It is generally agreed that the J document arose in
Judah, for it frequently shows a partiality for what per-
tains to the tribe of Judah in respect both of persons and
of places. The time of the composition is uncertain, but
the great majority of scholars hold it to be somewhere
about the middle of the 9th century B. C. Some would
place it still earlier, even as far back as the reign of Solomon or David. The writing is a unity. The author took
up the various traditions of his people and wrote them
out in his own manner.

The Jahvistic writing is a work of real genius. Its
narrative art is perhaps nowhere surpassed. The author's
horizon, in spite of his intense partiality for the people of
Israel, and for Judah in particular, is exceedingly broad.
The unity of the human race is clearly recognized and
the blessing of Israel means the blessing and not the curs-
ing of the several families of the earth. In religious depth
and earnestness it surpasses the other sources of the Pentateuch, though its religious spirit is not so conscious as
that of the Priestly Code. It breathes much of the spirit
of the prophets of the next succeeding era.

6. *The Elohistic Source.*—The inquiry into this source
is more difficult than with J. E has been interwoven with
the other sources, especially with J, in such a manner as
to render its clean separation difficult and in many places

impossible. Yet for the most part the source is fairly distinguishable by characteristics of language and religious ideals, and by its special historical tradition.

The linguistic peculiarities of E are numerous and well marked. The following may be specially noted: Elohim is the exclusive designation of Deity before the revelation of Jahweh at Sinai, and the preferred designation afterwards; the mount of God is always Horeb, not Sinai; the original inhabitants of Palestine are Amorites, not Canaanites; the third patriarch is generally Jacob rather than Israel.

Among the general religious conceptions of the Elohist, we may note the following. God is not represented, as is the case with the Jahvist, as a familiar figure in intimate relations with men, but as one who communicates with men only at important crises. He reveals himself most often by dreams in the night. Thus, for example, he reveals himself on several occasions to Abraham (see Gen. 15:1 ff.; 21:12 f.; 22:1, 3), and at least three times to Jacob (Gen. 28:12; 31:11; 46:2). Also the dreams of Joseph (Gen. 37:5 ff.) and even those of the kings of Gerar and Egypt and of the servants of the latter play an important part in the narrative. When there is occasion to communicate with men by day, God is represented as speaking through his angel "out of heaven," as in the case of Hagar and Ishmael in their distress (Gen. 21:17), and of Abraham on the point of slaying Isaac (Gen. 22:11).

There are also peculiar characteristics in the historical tradition of the Elohist. The most important of these is that the narrative begins with the call of Abraham and offers nothing of the earlier traditions. The ancestors of the Hebrews, when they "dwelt of old time on the other side of the River," are represented (Josh. 24:2) as serving other gods. In the exodus and in the wanderings in the wilderness Aaron and Miriam play an important rôle along with Moses.

The Elohist, too, like the Jahvist, has his special sectional or tribal interest. He shows his preference for the northern tribes and localities. In E, for example, it is Reuben, not Judah, that befriends Joseph and rescues him from death. But the Elohist's horizon is less wide than that of the Jahvist. While he is not more intensely Israelitish than the Jahvist, he has not the latter's lively interest in other peoples. Ishmael and Esau appear as individuals in the Elohistic narrative, but their descendants do not appear. The Elohist is more sensitive than the Jahvist respecting the good name of the patriarchs: the faults of Abraham and the trickeries of Jacob are most frankly related in J, while in E they are glossed over or excused.

In its literary aspect, the Elohistic writing is strong and fine, yet not equal to that of the Jahvist. Here and there one may note—in contrast with J—a striving for effect, or an appeal for sympathy with the subject of a narrative. An examination of the two modes of treatment is found in the two accounts of Hagar. According to J (Gen. 16:4–14), Hagar is harshly dealt with, and is angry and rebellious and flees of her own choice, but she is not in grave trouble. According to E (Gen. 21:9–21) she is an outcast in the bitterest distress, which can be relieved only by a miracle.

The characteristics of E may be studied in the following specimen passages.

Gen. 15:1–6—God's promise to Abram.

Gen. 20:1–17—The seizure of Sarah by Abimelech (Compare with the J narrative, 12:10–20).

Gen. 40–42; 45 (in the main)—Joseph in Egypt.

Gen. 48 (in the main)—The sons of Joseph.

Ex. 1:15–22—The decree of the king of Egypt to destroy the male children of the Hebrews.

Ex. 2:1–10—The birth and adoption of Moses.

Ex. 20:1–23:19—The Decalogue and the Book of the Covenant.

Deut. 31:1–8, 14–23; also chapters 32 and 33; also 34:3–6, 10—The closing scenes in the life of Moses.

While it is beyond dispute that the Elohistic writing springs from the Northern Kingdom, its date is very uncertain. There are indications that it is later than J, especially in the fact that its references to events connected with the conquest suggest a relatively remoter past than is the case with J. Some contend that the writing could not have originated later than the time of Solomon. Three reasons are offered in support of this view: There is no allusion to the division of the Kingdom; Judah heads the list of the tribes in the account of the division of the territory (Josh. 15:1 ff.); and finally Jerusalem is recognized as a sanctuary, along with Bethel and Shechem—a thing which, it is claimed, would hardly occur in the case of a book written after Jeroboam had forbidden his people to worship in Jerusalem. On the other hand, we must recognize the fact that J and E were united into one book (JE), probably not earlier than 650 B. C., and by a man of Southern Palestine. This Southern redaction might account for the naming of Jerusalem among the sanctuaries. Most modern critics place the Elohistic source much later than Solomon, namely, about 800 B. C., and some would place it even as late as the reign of Jeroboam II (785–745 B. C.).

The interlacing of J and E may be conveniently studied—with the help of any modern commentary—in connection with the story of Jacob and Esau and the story of Joseph.

7. *The Deuteronomic Source*.—In the reign of Josiah there was found in the temple at Jerusalem, about the year 622 B. C., a book then unknown to priests, king and people. Hilkiah sent it by the hand of Shaphan the scribe to the king, who, after consulting with Huldah the prophetess, made it the basis of a vigorous religious reform. It was accepted by all as the true "book of the law," or "book of the covenant," which had been allowed to lapse into oblivion. That this book is essentially our Deuteronomy, and not the whole of the Pentateuch nor some other book since lost, is now universally recognized. Among the reasons for this opinion are the following: (a) It was a writing not too long to be read by Shaphan twice through in one day—once in the temple and again before the King (2 Ki. 22:8, 10). (b) The book is called the book of the covenant, a designation that fits only Exodus 20–23 and Deuteronomy (see Deut. 5:2; 29:1 and 20; 30:10). (c) But since the nature of the reform that followed fits Deuteronomy rather than Exodus 20–23, we conclude that Deuteronomy is meant. The chief feature of the reform was the centralization of worship (2 Ki. 23:8 ff.; compare with Deut. 12:13; 16:21). But indeed all the other features of the reform—the abolition of the worship of the heavenly bodies, and putting away of all that had familiar spirits, the celebration of the Passover in the temple, and other matters—are clearly based upon the Deuteronomic code.

The book purports to be the record of the laws divinely given through Moses for the future conduct of the people when they should be established in the Promised Land. Their application in the wilderness would have been, for the most part, impossible. They are, therefore, represented as being given for promulgation only after the people should have passed over the Jordan. The laws and the needful accompanying exhortations are given in the form of a discourse from Moses to the people.

The present Deuteronomy doubtless comprises more than the original D source. Probably the basic writing included 4:45-49; 5:6-21 (the Decalogue); 6:4-15; and nearly all the matter in chapters 12-26.

The origin of the book is much in dispute. In its present form it probably represents, in the main, a combination of D with JE. Shortly before the fall of Jerusalem (586 B. C.) other additions were made, no doubt, in the process of editing the various books of the Scripture after the Exile. Our present question has to do mainly with the origin of the original D. The prevailing view of modern critics is that the book was composed by a group of priests who were in a measure under the influence of the great prophets, in the years just before the publication of the book in 622 B. C. According to this view, the book was based largely upon approved legal and priestly tradition. In this sense it was a fair representation of Israel's more ancient laws; but these critics held that the book itself was composed by priests in the reign of Josiah, and that it was, therefore, a forgery, since it was put forth as an ancient book only just discovered by accident in the course of repairing the temple. The "discovery" they suppose to have been a pious fraud, designed to further the intended reform. But there is to-day a strong tendency to believe that the book was in reality an older writing dating from the reign of Hezekiah (about 720–686 B. C.) and rediscovered in the time of Josiah. That such a book might have fallen into oblivion would not be strange in view of all the evil practices and perversions of the long reign of Manasseh (about 686–641 B. C.). At all events, however, the writing was not a very ancient one when it was brought forward in 622 B. C. The language and the religious ideas belong to the era of the great prophets. It is not necessary to assume a fraud in relation to the discovery or promulgation of the book. Whoever the writers were, they seem to have written the laws substantially as their traditions represented them. Yet they recast and elaborated them, and composed the accompanying exhortations in keeping with what they believed to have been the spirit of the Mosaic legislation. Ancient Oriental writers were in the habit of taking liberties with the names of historical personages which would not be permitted to-day.

8. *The Priestly Writing.*—The marks of this source are so plain that it can be distinguished from the others with comparative ease and certainty. The style is formal, the interest centers in ceremony and custom, and much emphasis is laid upon genealogies and the dignity of the priestly class. The idea of holiness is largely ceremonial. Then there are characteristic linguistic usages. In the historical portions there is a careful avoidance of the anthromorphisms (conceptions of Deity after the analogy of man) which are so characteristic of J. The name Jahweh is avoided until the narrative reaches the point where the name is revealed to Moses at the burning bush. But also priests and sacrifices and the distinction between

clean and unclean are unmentioned until the time of Moses is reached.

P is the only source which is found in all the books of the Hexateuch. Like J, it begins with an account of creation, and shows a dependence upon J for the outline of the history, but it differs much from that source in the details of the treatment. The entire history serves for P only as a background or introduction to the system of law and worship.

The Priestly Writing clearly bears throughout the stamp of one mind. Yet it does not form a perfect literary unity. The writer drew his materials from various sources and he was not always at pains to reduce them to harmony. Nevertheless, the general tendency of the writing is very consistent. There is a perfect unity of standpoint and purpose.

The Priestly Writing in its present form doubtless belongs to the time of Ezra and Nehemiah. It was in 458 B. C. that Ezra, a priest and "ready scribe in the law of Moses, which Jahweh, the God of Israel, had given," went up from Babylon to Jerusalem (Ezra 7:1 ff.). He had the law of his God in his hand (7:14). He purposed to inquire as to the religious state of Jerusalem and Judah, and to instruct the people according to the law as he knew it. In 444 B. C. this law was solemnly read and by oath was acknowledged and established as binding for the people (Neh. 8–10). Now the law thus introduced was surely not a substitute for D and the Book of the Covenant, but a notable addition to these. The writings J and E (as we have seen) had been combined a good while before this (the result being designated by scholars to-day as JE). Then, after the promulgation of D in 622 B. C., this also was joined with the others (JED). Between his arrival in Jerusalem in 458 B. C. and the solemn promulgation of the finished law in 444 B. C. Ezra must have combined the Priestly Writing with JED, thus forming our Pentateuch.

Among the most important characteristic sections of P are the following:

Gen. 1:1–2:4a—The account of creation.
Gen. 5—The first ten generations.
Gen. 6:9–22—The ark and its freight.
Gen. 7 and 8 (mixed with J).
Gen. 9:1–7—The introduction of animal food.
Gen. 9:8–17, 28, 29—The bow of promise.
Gen. 23—The death of Sarah.
Gen. 46:6–27—The descent into Egypt.
Ex. 8, 9, 11 (mixed with J and E).
Ex. 12:1–20—The Passover.
Ex. 25–31—The Tabernacle, etc.
Leviticus entire (chapters 17–26 being the older Law of Holiness).

The following observations will be found illuminating as to the general problem of the Pentateuch. (a) There is no ground for assuming any additions to the Pentateuch after 444 B. C. The tradition concerning the character and contents of the Torah are clear enough from that time on. (b) The prophets Deutero-Isaiah, Haggai, Zechariah and Malachi know and refer to the Deuteronomic Code, but they betray no acquaintance with the Priestly Code. Hence we infer the late introduction of P. (c) Ezekiel (whose prophetic work belongs to the early portion of the Exile, about 592–570 B. C.) knows the ordinances of the Law of Holiness (H), but he shows no knowledge of the other features of P; for example, the office of the High Priest is unknown to him. (d) Among the many reasons for recognizing D as older than P is the fact that while D *demands* the centralization of worship (which was not brought about until Josiah's reform after 622 B. C.), P views it as a *long-established fact*.

The Book of the Law which Ezra (in 458 B. C.) brought with him from Babylon could not have been composed by himself, for he ever looked upon it with reverent awe as something traditionally sacred.   But since no such book was brought back by the first returning exiles in 537 or 536 B. C., we must infer that the book which Ezra had in his possession took shape after the first return of exiles.   Perhaps about 500 B. C. may be assumed as an approximate date.   Yet since we know that this Priestly Writing incorporated the much older Law of Holiness (Lev. 17–26), we may reasonably infer that the Priestly Writing was a growth, which included other elements besides the Law of Holiness, elements which were considerably earlier in their origin than 500 B. C.   It was a comparatively new writing that Ezra brought with him from Babylon, but it was a writing that embodied many ancient materials.   Apparently Ezra and his helpers were utterly sincere in their conviction that the final introduction of this law as the standard for the people's life and worship signified a return to the ancient lawful worship of God.   In their eyes the *law* seemed ancient even though the *book* was comparatively new.

9. *The Redactions of the Pentateuch.*—Our previous scattered notices of various editings of the Pentateuch, together with some additional observations, may now be gathered up.

(1) A combination of J and E was made not earlier than the fall of Samaria in 722.   It was unquestionably made in Judah.   The evidences of such a combination are

clear to the careful student. There are seams and marks
of interlacing in a number of places.

(2) The discovery of Deuteronomy, and the reform
under Josiah based upon its code of laws, naturally suggested the combination of D with JE. Or rather, in the
first instance, of D with E, since the latter was closely
akin to D, and contained the Book of the Covenant. This
combination, DE, was probably completed before the
Captivity.

(3) The redaction which combined JE with DE probably took place in the Exile. The period of the Exile
seems to have witnessed not a little work in the way of
copying, revision and editing the older literature.

(4) The last redaction by Ezra and the scribes associated with him resulted in the Pentateuch (and even the
Hexateuch) as it now stands. It is of interest to note
that the Samaritans established their divergent form of
the Pentateuch about 430 B. C. This Samaritan Pentateuch is still preserved, probably with only slight alterations, in a very ancient manuscript which can be seen to-
day at Nablus (Shechem).

The Pentateuch (Torah) formed the basis of Judaism,
that is, of the Jewish national system developed after the
Exile. In the estimation of the people the Torah held a
higher place than the Prophets or the Psalms.

10. *The Prophets.*—We have seen that the second division of the Hebrew Scriptures bore the title of The Prophets. The Prophets were divided into two groups, the
Former and the Latter Prophets. The books of the
"Former Prophets" are the histories of the Hebrew nation
from the time of the Conquest to the Babylonian Exile
(excepting Chronicles and Ruth), and comprise, therefore, the books of Joshua, Judges, Samuel and Kings.

The "Latter Prophets" are the prophets in the stricter sense.

(a) *The Former Prophets* (the Histories).—To call these books of history prophetic writings seems strange to us. The Jewish rabbis, not knowing who wrote them, but recognizing in them great religious value, naturally enough ascribed them to the prophets. There is no ground for accepting the opinion of the rabbis on this point. Yet there is a certain fitness in classifying them with the Prophets, for the history is written from the standpoint of the prophets. It is history written to show God's dealings with men, especially with the people of Israel. The glory of these books lies not in their historical lore, nor in their literary art, but in their interpretation of the purposes of God in history; and just such interpretation is the essence of prophecy.

The writers of these books, in gathering their materials, used various sources. Here we find no such thing as "inspired history" in the sense that God informed the writers respecting the events to be recorded. The writers took the materials of history and tradition that were at hand. The element of inspiration in their writing is to be found only in the religious interpretation of the history. The writers used written as well as oral sources; indeed frequent mention is made of written sources.

In respect to the question of literary origins, it is certain that *Joshua* belongs with the Pentateuch and is made up from the same sources. All four of the documents of the Pentateuch are in evidence also in Joshua. The final redaction of Joshua must have taken place shortly after the completion of the Pentateuch. If all these books had been put forth together, it seems certain that the Samaritans, who separated from the Jews in the time of Ezra, and carried with them their Pentateuch, would have had a Hexateuch instead; for doubtless they took with them all the books that were available at the time. Hence we infer that the separation of the Samaritans from Judaism took place before the final publication of Joshua.

The *Book of the Judges* gives the history of the children of Israel from the death of Joshua to Samuel. It clearly falls into three parts: (1) A general introduction (1:1—2:5), probably from a Judean source, relates in a swift and summary fashion how the tribes west of the Jordan took possession of the districts assigned to them, yet without obtaining full mastery over the Canaanites, who still held most of the cities. (2) The main narrative of the book (2:6—16:31) begins—in immediate continuation of the narrative of Joshua—with a summary of the whole period (2:6—3:6): after the death of Joshua the people fell away from the worship of Jehovah and betook themselves to the gods of the Canaanites; to punish and bring them back Jehovah delivers them into the hand of oppressors from the surrounding nations; the people alternately repent and lapse again; but whenever the people cried unto Jehovah, he raised up for them champions and deliverers. The narrative then proceeds to give an account of these deliverers or "judges" (3:7—16:31). All told, there are twelve judges (some would reckon in three other leaders, making fifteen). The narrative deals amply with five of the judges (Ehud, Barak, Gideon, Jephthah, Samson), more briefly with the rest. (3) Chapters 17–21 are a sort of appendix, made up of narratives belonging to the time of the Judges.

The second part of the book shows kinship with the Book of Deuteronomy, but there are also materials from J and E. The book is accordingly a growth extending from a very early period until its virtual completion shortly before, or after, the fall of Jerusalem in 586 B. C.

A careful reading of the Book of Judges reveals many matters of significance for our understanding of the history of Israel. In the first place we observe (as we did in Joshua) two divergent traditions regarding the time of the completion of the conquest of Canaan. One account makes the conquest miraculously swift and conclusive. The other clearly recognizes that for a very long time it was far from complete. Another feature is the rather artificial chronology of the Deuteronomist (so many things are forty or twenty years in duration). A feature of particular importance is that in many passages the religious life and practice appear so very crude, while in others a much more advanced stage is assumed. This is one of the obvious proofs that the book is made up of several strata of widely separated ages. Whoever attentively reads Judges and compares its life with that presupposed in Leviticus will certainly perceive that the elaborate ceremonialism of the Priestly Code is unknown in the period of the Judges and even of the time of the writing of the book.

Regarded as literature the book of Judges is somewhat unequal, but it contains some admirable narratives, as the stories of Gideon and Samson, and the fine Song of Deborah.

That the Book of *Samuel*—for it is properly one book— was not written by Samuel himself is evident. His death is recounted at length in 1 Sam. 25. The chief personages are Samuel, Saul, and especially David. The book begins with a fragment of a delightful history of the childhood and youth of Samuel (1 Sam. 1–3). It then takes up the thread of the history of Israel where it was broken off at the close of Judges 16. Samuel appears as the last and greatest of the judges, and the only one of the number whose influence extended over all the tribes. He prepared the way for a united people. Before his public career begins, Israel has been subjugated by the Philistines and the ark has been captured. The liberation of Israel begins under Samuel (Ch. 7), but is fully accomplished under Saul, whom Samuel had anointed to be king, and whose reign until his rejection is described in Chapters 8–15. The remainder of his reign, together with the life of David as the object of Saul's jealous hatred, is related in Chapters 16–31. In 2 Sam. we have first the account of David's tribal kingdom with the capital at Hebron (5:6—20:26). The remaining four chapters of the book contain lists, songs and narratives pertaining to the reign of David.

The book of Samuel is based upon written sources and good oral traditions. Every attentive reader will, however, note that two lines of tradition are interlaced. Two attitudes toward the establishment of the kingdom are in evidence. According to 1 Sam. 9:1—10:16 and 11:1–15, Samuel, the *seer,* is divinely led to anoint Saul to be king, in order that he may free Israel from the yoke of the Philistines. According to 1 Sam. 8, and 10:17–24, the Philistines are already subdued, and the *judge* Samuel, against his will, yields to the entreaties of the people to have a king. But in spite of some such discrepancies the Book of Samuel as a whole must be regarded as a source of historical knowledge unsurpassed for its age. Eduard Meyer writes thus of the older source of the book of Samuel: "It is astonishing that such a piece of historical literature was possible at that time in Israel. It stands far above everything else of ancient Oriental historical writing that we know." Of the two main sources, the older is by far the clearer and surer in regard to the outward course of events, but the younger has a fine prophetic interpretation of the history. In literary style the book is peculiarly fine. As to the age of the book, the oldest source seems to belong to a period not long after the death of David. The writer was probably not a contemporary of David's, yet the freshness and vividness of the reminiscences indicate that he received them directly from those who did know David personally. The book in essentially its present form may be dated in the eighth century, with a final redaction after the Captivity.

The *Books of the Kings,* like those of Samuel, were originally one book. Indeed, Samuel and Kings stand in very close relation to each other. The one was the sequel of the other and was in no small measure derived from the same sources. The oldest source is designated as K, and is probably not only identical with the oldest source in Samuel, but possibly it is from the same hand as the J document. If this surmise is correct, it would argue that J is even older than 850 B. C.; the oldest source of Samuel and the opening section of Kings may belong to the reign of Solomon. However this may be, the Book of Kings as a whole must be dated after the end of King Jehoiachin's imprisonment in Babylon, for it brings the narrative down to this point. The book is based upon various documents. Above all, the "Chronicles of the Kings" were often referred to in the book itself; but there are also other sources. The grand narrative of Elijah, for example, is based upon some writing quite apart from the Chronicles of the Kings. It is one of the finest examples of narrative art in all literature. Like all other Hebrew literature, the Book of Kings was revised and edited after the Exile.

The Book of the Kings constitutes one of the most valuable and illuminating portions of the Old Testament. Not only is it for the most part historically trustworthy, but its spirit is intensely religious. But the religious interpretation has not distorted the narrative. The book is a condensed history from the standpoint of the national religion, and it should be read with constant reference to what is known of contemporary history.

b. The *Latter Prophets* were reckoned by the Jews as four books, viz., Isaiah, Jeremiah, Ezekiel, and the Book of the Twelve (now known, on account of their comparative brevity, as the Minor Prophets).

There were prophets in Israel long before there were prophetic writings. Throughout the history of Hebrew prophecy, the prophet was primarily a man of speech, and often of action, rather than a maker of books. There is no hint that Elijah or Elisha wrote anything; and when, a century later, the prophets Amos and Hosea began to write, the change was apparently due in part to the hindrances to the freedom of speech. In the case of Amos, it seems clear that it was only after free speech had been denied him that he wrote out the substance of his sermons in a book. Hebrew prophecy developed from crude and rather low beginnings. In the earlier stages, the prophet was essentially a soothsayer, a resolver of mysteries; but at length prophecy became an ethical and spiritual thing; not a disclosing of worldly matters concerning which men sought information, but an interpretation of the mind of God.

Amos was the earliest prophet to write a book. Indeed, the prophecy of Amos is the earliest of the books of the

Old Testament as we now have them. Other books contain far older materials than Amos, but in their present
form they are of a later date. This great prophet was a
herdsman of Tekoa in Judah, but his prophecy relates to
the Northern Kingdom, which he seems to have visited
in the conduct of his business. The date of his public
labors is about the middle of the eighth century B. C., in
the reign of Jeroboam II.; it cannot be earlier than 760
nor later than 746 B. C.

A fine passage in Amos (7: 10–17) describes the impression made by the prophet's appearance in Bethel.
The chief priest at Bethel was not minded to tolerate such
denunciations. With studied expressions of scorn he
bids Amos be gone. "O seer, be gone, go back to your
land of Judah; there make your living by your prophesy-
ings. But prophesy no more at Bethel, for here is a
royal temple and a royal residence." With splendid indig-
nation Amos replies: "I am no prophet by trade, I belong
to no prophetic order; I am a herdsman and a dresser of
sycamore figs. Jehovah took me from following the
flock, and Jehovah bade me, Go prophesy against my
people Israel. So then, hear the word of Jehovah!"

Hosea belongs to the same period. His public appearance as prophet cannot well be placed more than ten years
after that of Amos. Like the herdsman of Tekoa, he, too,
prophesied in the Northern Kingdom, but, unlike the
former, he was a subject of that kingdom. Intellectually,
morally and religiously, Amos is to be placed on a level
with Isaiah. If Hosea is intellectually less vigorous than
Amos, he is his superior in the profound appreciation of
the quality of the Divine mercy.

The mission of both was to denounce the sins of the
nation and to win the people to a repentance in the fear

of Jehovah. The specific individual appeal of prophecy came out more clearly at a later time. Amos is a prophet of national righteousness, while Hosea, though no less earnest in his warnings than Amos, wonderfully emphasizes God's yearning love and his desire to forgive. In Amos we meet with a complete monotheistic faith and a grand conception of the all-comprehending providence of God. Some scholars even hold that Amos was the first man of his people to rise to the full height of monotheism. This, however, is improbable, for Amos nowhere sets forth his conception of God as something new in Israel.

Just a little later than Amos and Hosea comes *Isaiah of Jerusalem*. He prophesied during a period of about 40 years, from 740 B. C., in the reigns of Uzziah, Jotham, Ahaz, and Hezekiah, kings of Judah. In respect of literary form Isaiah must be ranked as the greatest of the prophets. Nothing in literature surpasses some of the finest passages in his writings. In their religious aspect his prophecies are not superior to those of Amos and Hosea, and not equal to those of Jeremiah. Isaiah is the statesman prophet. He appeals not only to the people, but also directly to the kings.

The *Book of Isaiah,* unlike those of Amos and Hosea, is not a unity. Chapters 40–66 are the work of one or more later prophets. Even some of the first thirty-nine chapters are from later hands. The genuine portions of Isaiah are so charactertistic that there can be little reason for doubting that it was only by some accident or misunderstanding that the writings of the later prophets, which are so different in style, came to be joined with the prophecy of Isaiah. Isaiah deals with contemporary affairs in the most direct and concrete manner. Everything centers in Jerusalem and in the affairs of state. The background of chapters 40–55 is not that of Isaiah's time, but that of the Babylonian Captivity. The background of the remaining chapters (56–66) is the struggle to rebuild and reëstablish Jerusalem after the Exile. The writer of chapters 40–55 is now known as "Deutero-Isaiah," while chapters 56–66 are now commonly referred to as "Trito-Isaiah." The style of Isaiah of Jerusalem is wonderfully swift, vigorous and vivid, while the style of Deutero-Isaiah is smooth and flowing, showing always a quiet but lofty dignity.

Micah belongs to the same period as Isaiah. In the religious aspect he does not fall below the level of Isaiah. His style, too, is noble. Nothing of its kind in the Old Testament is finer than his condemnation of priestly ceremonialism in 6:6–8: "Wherewith shall I come before Jehovah? . . . He hath told thee; O man, what to do. And what doth Jehovah require of thee, but to do justly and to love mercy and to walk humbly before thy God?"

These four prophets of the 8th century represent the first great period of Hebrew prophecy. Another grand figure appears about a century later in the person of *Jeremiah*. If this great prophet falls below Isaiah in literary skill, he may be regarded as the greatest of all the prophets in the depth of his religious insight and conviction. He began his public work in 626 B. C., and he lived until after the beginning of the Captivity in 586 B. C. He was not carried away among the captives into Babylon, but remained in Judea, hoping to be able to help and comfort the remnant of his people. Imprisoned for a short time at Ramah, he went, upon his release, to Gedaliah the governor in Mizpah, to help him and the people as best he might. Soon, however, Gedaliah is murdered by usurpers, and a new fear falls upon the people. Many flee into Egypt against the warning of Jeremiah, and they take the aged prophet with them. Of his work in Egypt we know very little. The gloomy, or at least obscure, close of his career is of a piece with nearly all that went before. It was as a very young man —"a child" he called himself—that he began to prophesy in Anathoth, a village a little distance north of Jerusalem. Here he had meagre success, but not a little persecution. In Jerusalem he exerts considerable influence during the reign of Josiah, but with the accession of Jehoiakim began a martyrdom that lasted as long as we have an account of the course of his life. Because of his bold warning that the temple at Jerusalem would be destroyed like the ancient sanctuary at Shiloh he is accused of blasphemy. The priests were resolved on his death, but the laity saved him in his extreme need. Nevertheless, for several years the prophet was forbidden to enter the temple. It is now that he betakes himself to writing. It is prophecy full of solemn warning that he writes. His helper and scribe, Baruch, is sent to read the book before the people on a feast day. It makes a great impression upon them. Then the book is taken to King Jehoiakim and read before him. The King angrily and contemptuously burns the book (ch. 36), but Jeremiah proceeds at once to dictate it afresh to his scribe. In 597, however, Nebuchadnezzar actually comes against Jerusalem. Jeremiah renews his warnings, and for this cause is accused of treachery and cast into prison. But King Zedekiah—it is he that is now upon the throne—is a weak man, who both seeks to terrorize the imprisoned prophet and yet secretly communicates with him in order to learn what the prophet will predict. Thus is Jeremiah under persecution until the fall of Jerusalem in 586 B. C. No other prophet suffered so manifold persecutions as he. He endured his sufferings with much fortitude. Though a man of great compassion, he should not be described as a "weeping prophet." This popular designation is due to the erroneous ascription of the Book of Lamentations to Jeremiah.

The composition of the book of Jeremiah is in part described in the book itself. The chief portion is the rewritten roll of that which had been burned by Jehoiakim. Other prophecies and the historical portions were added later. Old Testament scholars attempt to distinguish three elements in the book: (1) The portions that sprang directly from Jeremiah (written by Baruch at the prophet's dictation); (2) the portions (chiefly narrative) written by Baruch; (3) a number of later additions. The materials of the book are not arranged with perfect clearness and consistency.

Two other books of prophecy, namely, Zephaniah and Nahum, belong—at least in their main substance—in this period.

With Jeremiah the first great period of Hebrew literature closes. The Captivity causes a great change in the life of the people and gives a new turn to Hebrew literature. In this period we have, as yet, no Bible in the sense of a fixed list of acknoweldged writings. Certain great writings are there, and they are reverenced and used by the people; especially the Book of the Law known as D has acquired a special authority; but the gathering together and canonizing of the Scriptures belongs to the period after the Exile.

CHAPTER X

THE ORIGIN OF THE BOOKS OF THE OLD TESTAMENT : LATER PERIOD

1. *Prophecies.*

The Book of *Ezekiel* represents the beginning of a new tendency in the religious history of Israel. Ezekiel was one of the priests of Jerusalem and was carried off to Babylon with King Jehoiachin in the "first captivity," the deportation of 597 B. C., and his book was written from the Captivity. It was the policy of Nebuchadnezzar at the first conquest of Judah, to remove a sufficient number of the upper classes of the people to insure the quiet subjection of the remainder. He made Zedekiah, an uncle of Jehoiachin, king in the latter's stead, and hoped for quiet in Judah. But after some ten years Zedekiah revolted, and the armies of Babylon a second time besieged Jerusalem. The city was completely overthrown and a great mass of the people taken into captivity in 586 B. C.

Ezekiel's prophecy falls into two parts. In the period between 597 and 586 B. C. the Jews in Babylonia and the Jews at home were so persuaded of the inviolability of the holy city that they would not believe that destruction awaited them. Many of those who had been deported even cherished the idea that Nebuchadnezzar would grow weary of the ministry of those whom he had appointed to rule in Jerusalem, and would restore the king and the princes and leaders whom he was holding in captivity. In this period Ezekiel prophesies the downfall of Jerusalem. But his word is not heeded. As soon, however, as the destruction of the city is an accomplished fact, the tone of the prophecy is altered. Up to the moment of the catastrophe he had combated the delusive hope of the people; henceforth he combats their despair. The first part of the book is all warning; the second is full of comfort and promise.

The analysis of the book is very simple. After an introduction (chapters 1–3), which recounts the call and consecration of the prophet, comes the first part of the prophecies (chapters 4–33), which may be entitled: *The Historical Israel and the Neighboring Peoples*. It is full of threats and warnings. Chapters 4–24 deal with Israel; chapters 25–32 with other peoples; chapter 33 with the watchman's call to repentance and the arrival of the news of Jerusalem's fall. The second part of the prophecy may be entitled: *The Future Israel*.

It is thought that the prophet's warnings against Jerusalem ceased for the two years of suspense in which her final doom is most imminent. In these two years we may place the warnings against other nations. But no sooner has the doom fallen upon the devoted city than the prophet begins his ministry of encouragement.

A marked feature of the Book of Ezekiel are the visions and the elaborate symbolism. These visions are bold, ample, and full of significant detail. In no other Old Testament book is the element of the ecstatic vision so prominent.

More than any other prophet Ezekiel combined the prophetic and the priestly point of view. Born and reared as a priest, yet open to the divine spirit of prophecy, he represented a conception of the priestly function that was free from mere formalism. No prophet had a truer conception of the inward nature of holiness. He was the prophet of individualism: "The soul that sinneth, it shall die."

The Book of Ezekiel shows none of the marks of compilation and amplification which are conspicuous in Isaiah and Jeremiah. We have the book substantially as it came from the author's hand. The style is unequal. At times it is vigorous and even eloquent; more generally it is rather slow. The imagination is abundant, but it is not always well restrained, nor in the best taste.

We have already mentioned five of the twelve Minor Prophets. The remaining prophets—at least for the most part—are post-exilic. Concerning the dates of some of these books there can be no certainty. Some of them, however, can be accurately or at least approximately dated. In some cases there are very clear historical allusions in the books themselves, and our knowledge of contemporary history enables us to fix the date. *Haggai* is specifically and carefully dated. The prophet received his revelations in the second year of Darius, i.e., 520 B. C. His prophecies turn about two points: it is the time to rebuild the temple, and the Messianic era is almost at hand.

The prophecy of *Zechariah* falls into two parts. Zechariah, a priest, was a contemporary of Haggai's. The first eight chapters of the book are genuine and may be dated about 520–518 B. C. The second part belongs to a much later date, perhaps about the middle of the third century B. C.

The last book of our Old Testament, *Malachi,* is certainly far from the latest in time. Allusions to the conditions of the time (e.g., Mal. 1:8, 10; 3:1, 10) point to a time shortly before the reform under Ezra and Nehemiah, or about 450 B. C.

The prophecy of *Obadiah* is very brief, but the critical questions related to it are not simple. Portions of the book clearly refer to the fall of Jerusalem, but verses 15–21 seem to be considerably later (post-exilic).

The Book of *Jonah* is one of the most interesting of the Minor Prophets. Some scholars insist that the book should not be classified with the prophets. It is said that the only ground for such classification is the fact that the book is a narrative about a prophet. At all events the justification of the traditional classification of the book does not lie in its authorship by Jonah. The book does not purport to originate with Jonah. Its form is wholly unlike that of the other prophetical books. From the first word to the last it is a story (though a psalm is incorporated in the narrative). But since it is a story designed to teach a lofty truth concerning the character of God, it is of the spirit of prophecy. For this reason and no other, it is fitting to classify it as a book of prophecy. (It may also be called a Midrashic writing.)

The hero of the story is an historical personage (see 2 Ki. 14:25). At all events, however, the book was written long after the destruction of Nineveh; and the incidents of the book are for the most part invented as the vehicle of a great religious message. From every point of view the Book of Jonah is one of the loveliest pearls of Jewish literature. Its universalistic outlook in opposition to the exclusiveness of post-exilic Judaism, and its childlike faith in the merciful Father of all men, who has compassion also upon the beasts, make the book very touching and impressive.

The date of *Habakkuk* is uncertain. Recent opinion is inclined to place it near the end of the fourth century.

Such, in brief, is the history of the Hebrew prophetical literature. There is nothing in the extra-Biblical religions to be compared with it. Only the actual self-revelation of the living God can account for Hebrew prophecy.

2. *The Holy Writings* (Kethubim).

a. The *Psalter* is Israel's Book of Praise. More specifically, it is the Song-Book of the Second Temple. But while the collection and arrangement are post-exilic, some of the individual psalms are probably very much earlier than the Exile. It is possible that in respect of the time of their origin the psalms cover a period from David to the time of the Maccabees.

The Psalter is divided, in obvious imitation of the Pentateuch, into five books, each of which closes with a doxology. The division is as follows: 1–41; 42–72; 73–89; 90–106; 107–150.

The collection of the whole Psalter was not made at one time; our Psalter represents several earlier collections. The chief proofs of this statement are the following: (a) The presence of (slightly variant) duplicates in the Psalter (compare 14 with 53; 40:13–17 with 70; 57:7–11 and 60:5–12 with 108). (b) At the close of Ps. 72 we read: "The prayers of David, the son of Jesse, are ended." This indicates that there was once a special collection of psalms ascribed to David. But since among Ps. 73–150 we find many ascribed to David, and among Ps. 1–72 there are many ascribed to other sources, it is clear that the original collection of Davidic psalms was not held to be complete nor kept intact. (c) We may infer by analogy that the psalms of the sons of Korah

(42–49; 84–89), the psalms of Asaph (50, 73–83), and other groups once formed separate collections. (d) Certain groups of psalms are decidedly "Jahvistic," others "Elohistic" (not from the same authors as the J and E of the Pentateuch, but showing the same usages in the appellations of Deity). In Psalms 3–41 the name Jahweh occurs 272 times, and Elohim only 15 times, while in Psalms 42–84 Jahweh occurs only 48 times and Elohim 208 times.

When we begin to inquire as to the origin of the several psalms, we seem at first to be particularly well informed, for about 100 of the 150 psalms bear a superscription naming the author. To David are ascribed 73, to Solomon 2, to Asaph 12, to the sons of Korah 11, to Moses, Ethan, Heman, Jeduthun 1 each. But there are clear evidences that these superscriptions are additions by late editors and therefore afford little or no sure information. This is especially obvious in the case of the 13 notations of the circumstances in which David composed given psalms. These notations are taken almost word for word from the books of Samuel; besides, David himself cannot be supposed to have given such explanations as these are.

The views as to the age of the psalms composing the Psalter are very divergent. The older view that nearly all are from the hand of David is universally given up. But even that David was the author of all the 73 ascribed to him is impossible; for some of these clearly have an historical background of a much later period. Some notable scholars not only deny that David wrote so many psalms, but even that he wrote any. Not a few critics place all the psalms in the post-exilic time. The chief questions that concern us in this connection are the following: (1) Are there pre-exilic psalms? (2) Are there even Davidic psalms? (3) Are some psalms as late as the Maccabean age?

(1) The opinion that our Psalter contains a considerable number of pre-exilic psalms has been seriously questioned by many scholars, but in recent years it has largely reëstablished itself. The arguments in favor of the presence of pre-exilic psalms are chiefly three: (1) We have a number of "psalms concerning the king," viz., 2; 18; 20; 21; 28; 33; 45; 61; 72; 110. It is unlikely that the psalms would appear in this form if kings belonged only to a remote past; and they could not well refer to the Maccabees, for these would hardly be called kings. (2) A number of the psalms express the same unfavorable view of sacrifices and ritual that we find in the great prophecies of the eighth century. (Compare Ps. 40:6; 50:9; 51:17 with Isa. 1:10 ff. and Micah 6:8.) Finally, Jeremiah, a pre-exilic prophet, uses forms of prayer which closely resemble the style and manner of many of the psalms. These forms seem to be used by him just as if they were altogether familiar in his time. Now if the "psalms concerning the king" are pre-exilic, it is more than probable that there are others also.

(2) That of the pre-exilic psalms some are Davidic seems probable. We have no reason to distrust the tradition that David, the "sweet singer of Israel," not only sang secular songs, but also composed psalms. The picture which we have of him in the Book of Samuel is that of a man of high spirit and imagination, and of a very lively religious feeling. There seems, therefore, to be no sufficient reason to deny that he wrote psalms. The question is, whether any of our present Psalter are to be referred to him. There are several that eminently fit all our ideas of the personality of David and are quite in

keeping with what we know of his times. But it is probable that any psalms that David may have composed would be more or less rewritten or reshaped in later times.

In our search for possible Davidic psalms we must pass by those which address the king or speak of him in the third person. Thus, for example, we should have to exclude such psalms as 20; 21; 72; 110. We must also pass by all the psalms that refer to the temple and its forms of worship as already existing. Finally, we must exclude such psalms as are composed in the late idioms of the Hebrew language.

On the other hand, such a psalm as 23, or 8, or 19 (verses 1–6), or 60 (verses 7–11) seem fairly to suit all that we know of David and his times. To this list we may add psalms 3, 4, 7, 16, and perhaps 18. Such psalms may fairly be regarded as Davidic, though hardly without the recognition of the probability of their having been more or less altered in the course of their being handed down from generation to generation.

(3) If we may claim that considerable portions of the psalms 3–41 and 51–72 are, at least in their original form, pre-exilic, it is even clearer that 42–50 and 73–150 are exilic and post-exilic. The psalms of these latter groups contain so many and so clear references to historical events and conditions, such as the Captivity and the sufferings in Babylon, the return from the Exile, the rebuilding of Jerusalem and the temple, and the new order of life and worship, that it is possible to fix the general period of their origin with certainty. Some of these post-exilic psalms seem to be as late as the Maccabees, i. e., after 167 B. C.

It is probable that there were as many as six stages in the compilation of the Psalter. (1) The earliest Psalter was a collection bearing the superscription of David. Some hold that there were two Davidic collections, the first comprising psalms 3–41 (except 33) and the second, psalms 51–72. (2) There was doubtless a book entitled "Of Asaph," comprising psalms 50 and 73–83. The title "Of Asaph" doubtless signified coming from a guild of singers of that name. (3) The analogous compilation "Of the Sons of Korah," another guild of singers. (4) The so-called Elohist Psalter is apparently a compilation from early collections by an editor who used the name Elohim in preference to the name Jahweh. (5) The enlargement of this group by the addition of psalms 84–89. (6) The compilation of the books entitled "Songs of Ascents," psalms 120–134.—As for the dates of the various collections, there can be no certainty. They seem to have appeared in the order of time essentially as indicated above. Probably there was a collection of so-called Davidic psalms before the Exile, but certainly the chief collecting and editing of the Psalter was post-exilic. Possibly the Psalter was not complete until about 100 B. C.

There is every reason to believe that the earlier psalms, generally speaking, were considerably reshaped in the course of the development of temple worship. It was only after the Exile that the element of song in the temple service was systematically developed. This gave occasion for the adaptation of the older poetry to the uses of public worship. Doubtless those who guided those public services dealt with traditional religious poetry even more freely than our modern hymn-book makers have done with the materials at their command, altering and editing to suit their purposes. Thus we see in the Psalter the Hymn-book of the Second Temple.

In the main the Psalter breathes the prophetic rather than the priestly spirit. Yet here and there we find a psalm that reveals the priestly interest in a rather pronounced degree. The longest of the psalms, the 119th, is an eightfold alphabetic acrostic, i.e., eight verses beginning with the first letter of the alphabet, then eight verses beginning with the second, and so on; it is a psalm in praise of the law. Here and there we find evidences of alterations or additions to a psalm in order to adapt it to the teachings of the prevailing religious party. The second part of Psalm 19 is apparently a later addition designed to constitute a religious parallel to the splendid nature-poetry of the first part of the psalm. Psalm 51 is an utterance of the old prophetic abhorrence of religious formalism and of all outward show of piety where the heart is not right with God; but the last two verses are an evident attempt to balance this rather extreme view by adding something on the values of pure sacrifices.

The Psalms are undoubtedly that portion of the Old Testament which has the greatest present significance for the Christian church. They represent on the whole the highest levels of the religious experiences of the ancient Hebrews. Their beauty, depth, and earnestness are truly wonderful.

b. The *Book of Proverbs* bears at its beginning the title: "The Proverbs of Solomon, son of David, King of Israel." But there are also here and there in the book other titles, which obviously pertain to certain lesser collections incorporated in the book. This latter fact plainly indicates that the book does not purport to be the work of Solomon alone. No doubt Solomon was the author of many wise and memorable sayings. These and many others from many sources have been gathered together during a very long period. The book represents the practical wisdom of the sages and of the whole people during their entire history until perhaps two, or less than two, centuries before Christ.

c. The *Book of Job* is generally regarded as the finest piece of literature in the Old Testament. Indeed, not a few literary critics place it at the very head of the world's great literature. Its age is unknown. The rabbinical ascription of the work to Moses is without a shadow of plausibility. Most scholars believe the book should be dated after the Exile; but there is nothing in its form or contents that could not have been pre-exilic. In the opinion of some the author was not a Palestinian. The background of the book is the desert country (Arabia). But the writer has the Jewish conception of God, and is himself probably a Jew.

The Book of Job is commonly called a drama, yet it is in many respects unlike all other dramas. Except in the prologue there is no action. The dialogue, however, is tremendously energetic. There is interaction of ideas; hence the book may be called a spiritual drama. It has also been called an epic of the inner life. The subject or problem of the book is the suffering of the righteous, or the possibility of faith in God in view of such suffering. The unnamed author has taken as a starting point the traditional story of a man called Job, who, in spite of his perfect righteousness, suffered most strangely, but was at last restored to happiness and prosperity. But this ancient story is made merely the setting or background, the prologue and epilogue for the poem. These parts are prose, while the book proper is poetry. After the "prologue in heaven" the real book begins. Job first, after long silence, utters a most bitter complaint. Then one of the three "friends" of Job makes a reply. Then Job again speaks and the second friend replies; then Job and the third friend. The argument continues for three rounds (except that the third friend is silent in the last round). Then come the speeches by a character not hitherto introduced, namely, Elihu. The argument of the three friends had been that somehow all suffering must be the just punishment for sin; Job, who had seemed so righteous, must somehow be a great sinner. Job had stoutly denied that he had done anything to deserve such treatment. He scarcely stops short of blasphemy in his bitter complaints against the divine government of the world. But now Elihu argues from the standpoint that the meaning of suffering is discipline. He seems to represent a relatively new doctrine in his day. The old theology is inadequate; he will offer the new wisdom. For several reasons the great majority of scholars hold the Elihu speeches to be an interpolation. Yet they certainly might have been introduced by the original author of the book as an exhibition of the futility of the new rational theology, which was really no less inadequate than the old. After the Elihu speeches comes the grand climax of the book in the Jehovah speeches; God manifests Himself to Job and addresses him in a most grand and impressive manner. Then Job confesses his error in reproaching God. This brief confession of Job's is followed by the epilogue. Strictly speaking, the author does not propose a direct solution of the problem. Yet the fact that Jehovah does at all manifest himself as interested in Job and in all his creation brings a certain peace to Job. The real answer to the problem of the suffering of the righteous is possible only in the light of the cross of Christ. In the light of the cross Paul is able to say: "I reckon that the sufferings of this present time are not worthy to be compared with the glory that shall be revealed in us."

d. The five *Megilloth,* or *Rolls,* were the books: Song of Songs, Ruth, Lamentations, Ecclesiastes, and Esther. The special designation "Rolls" is, of course, not due to the fact that these books alone appeared in this form— all the books of the Hebrews were rolls—but because the public use of these books made this form rather conspicuous. At each of five great religious days (four feasts and one fast) a roll was read entire in the synagogues; namely, the Song of Songs at the Passover, Ruth at Pentecost, Lamentations on the day of the destruction of the Temple, Ecclesiastes at the Feast of the Booths, and Esther at the Feast of Purim.

The *Song of Songs* is the first of this group. Its ascription to Solomon is doubtless an error; it is based, no doubt, on the frequent mention of Solomon in the poems. The book is a collection of songs of love and marriage. Solomon and the Shulamite are the hero and heroine. These poems were long regarded as having an allegorical reference to the mutual relations of Christ and his bride, the church. The inclusion of the book in the canon is doubtless due to the fact that the name of Solomon got associated with it as author. As literature the poems are very fine. They may be dated in the fifth or fourth century B. C.

The book of *Ruth,* which in our Bibles appears as "a jewel set between the ermine of the judges and the purple of the kings," belongs rightfully here among the "Writings." It is a beautiful story of a Moabitess who, because of her loyalty to her mother-in-law Naomi and her piety toward the God of Israel, became an ancestress of King David. The story forms a most effective vehicle for the

expression of the broader human sympathy, which we
have seen also in Jonah, in contrast with the narrow exclusiveness of the majority of Jews. The scene is laid
about the close of the era of the Judges. The germ of
the story is in all probability historical; a pure invention
on just this point of the attitude toward foreigners would
have met with vigorous and effectual protest on the part
of the Jews. As to the age of the book we cannot be sure.
Probably it must be dated before the fall of Prince Zerub-
babel who was governor of Judah just after the return of
the exiles; for the force of the reference to David and his
house would be largely lost after the fall of the last royal
prince of David's line.

The Book of *Lamentations* comprises five poems
(dirges and prayers) referring to the fall of Jerusalem
in 586 B. C. The tradition that ascribes the books to
Jeremiah reaches as far back as the Septuagint version,
but it is shown to be untenable because of a variety of historical allusions and sentiments which cannot be ascribed
to Jeremiah. Chapters 2 and 4 are apparently the oldest
portion of the book; they are the work of a man who had
passed through the terrible siege of Jerusalem. Chapter 1
reveals the historical background of the Captivity. Chapter 5 is the work of a man living in Jerusalem before the
rebuilding of the temple (520 B. C.). Chapter 3 is later
than the rest; as an individual song of complaint it may
be dated even after the rebuilding of the temple.

The Book of *Ecclesiastes* (Heb. *Koheleth,* "Admon-
isher" or "Preacher") belongs to the category of "wisdom literature." The book seems to purport to have been
written by Solomon. This, however, can hardly have
been intended as anything more than a fanciful or poetical
investiture of the writing for an æsthetic effect; it does

not seriously claim to spring from Solomon. Linguistic peculiarities and evidences of acquaintance with Greek philosophic ideas make it clear that the book cannot have been written before 300 B. C. (nearly 700 years after Solomon's time). The more probable date is about 200 B. C.

The fundamental idea of the book is the vanity of all things under the sun. The writer was a man weighed down by many doubts, a man of a strongly pessimistic tendency. That he was not, however, a radical pessimist is clear, since he believed in a living God (see 3:17 f.; 5:19 f.; 9:1; 11:5). In this world he saw no retributive justice and he was not sure of a hereafter (3:20 f.). Yet he believed that even in this world there were some abiding values, especially wisdom (7:11 ff.). In the passage 11:9–12:7 he sets forth a body of positive moral principles. At bottom Koheleth was a believer. The book, in spite of its doubts, deserves our sincere respect. The author had evidently suffered much, and although he had not attained to a triumphant faith, he was pressing on toward the light.

The Book of *Esther* is the story of the way in which the conspiracy of Haman at the court of Ahasuerus (Xerxes) against the life of all the Jews in the kingdom was brought to naught by the Jew Mordecai and his adopted daughter, the beautiful Queen Esther. The story is told with much dramatic power. Its special object is to portray the origin of the Feast of Purim. The book, as its language and other marks show, could not have been written before 300 B. C. The events narrated probably lay some two centuries in the past. Presumably some tradition formed the basis of the story; but that germ was doubtless fantastically developed. The Feast of

Purim seems to have sprung from several sources. Apparently it was a Jewish combination and transformation of certain Babylonian festivals. It was observed by the Jews of the eastern (Babylonian and Persian) countries long before it was introduced into Judea. It was originally a purely secular feast.

The spirit of the book is that of an intense and fanatical nationalism. This spirit of exclusiveness and hatred of the Gentiles finds some excuse in the multitude of the persecutions which the Jews suffered. Nevertheless, the contrast between the exclusiveness of Esther and the beautifully generous attitude toward foreigners displayed in Ruth and Jonah is very marked.

e. *"The Remaining Books"* are *Daniel, Ezra, Nehemiah,* and *1 and 2 Chronicles.*

The *Book of Daniel* is placed in our Bibles as one of the Major Prophets. The fact that the Jews placed it among the "Writings" is doubtless due to its very late origin. When it was written (about 165 B. C.), the Jews already had a group of scriptures called "The Prophets," and this group was regarded as complete. No new book could be admitted to it. There was, however, room for the reception of books that seemed to spring from acknowledged leaders, especially from the worthies of the past. Now some centuries had elapsed since the time of Daniel, but there was, as yet, no book of Daniel. When, therefore, a book bearing the name of Daniel appeared, it won recognition as a weighty production, but it was naturally—yes, inevitably—placed among the "Writings" and not among the "Prophets."

The book consists of two parts: (a) the narrative of the experiences of Daniel and his companions under Nebuchadnezzar, Belshazzar, and Darius the Mede in

Babylon (ch. 1–6); (b) four visions of Daniel, disclosing the course of the world empires following the fall of Babylon until the establishment of the eternal Messianic kingdom.

That the book did not spring from the Babylonian Exile, but from the time of the Maccabees, is proved by the following facts: (1) Its place among the "Writings," the latest group in the Canon. (2) It is unmentioned in "The Wisdom of Jesus, the Son of Sirach," chapter 49, where the prophets and other worthies are commemorated. (3) Its language: a part is Aramaic, the rest in a very late Hebrew; words borrowed from the Persian and the Greek are found in both parts. (4) The writer is not well informed concerning the history of the Babylonian Exile. (5) The events of Jewish history in chapters 7, 9, and 11 are portrayed with a specific exactness that belongs to history, not prediction.

It is possible to fix the date almost exactly. According to 8:14 the writer had already witnessed the dedication of the temple by Judas Maccabæus, which we know took place in 165 B. C. But the death of the abhorred Antiochus Epiphanes has not yet occurred (see 11:20–25). Now, that event occurred not long after the beginning of 164 B. C. Accordingly, the date of the book must have been about the close of 165 B. C.

The main purpose of the book is evidently to inspire the Jews with a great and victorious faith in their national destiny. The grand idea took possession of the writer that the rise and fall of empires following the fall of Jerusalem was but leading up to a glorious restoration of Israel and the establishment of the imperishable Messianic Kingdom. The magnificent success of the Maccabean revolt filled the heart of the writer with this great hope. He chooses—not as an act of deceit—to clothe his messsage in the form of an apocalypse dating from the period of the Captivity.

The Book of Daniel is the most impressive example (in chapters 7–12) of Jewish apocalyptic literature. The fundamental and essential characteristic of an apocalypse is that it discloses the very form and manner of future events—a "history written before the time." With what we may call prophecy proper it is not so. In this no essential stress is laid upon the form, manner and order of coming events, but upon the working out of the moral government of God.

It is characteristic of all apocalyptic conceptions that they grow into fuller detail and clearer form through a long period—in some instances a very long time. The apocalyptic materials in Daniel were doubtless in a large measure traditional. This fact helps us to understand that the writer of Daniel intended no fraud when he ascribed these old apocalypses to a Jewish sage of the time of the Exile. And without doubt this apocalypse—in contrast to some of the apocryphal apocalypses—shows a grand and worthy conception of the divine control of the world's history.

The four books, *Ezra, Nehemiah, 1 and 2 Chronicles,* undoubtedly were originally one comprehensive historical work. Various indications make it perfectly clear that the books Ezra and Nehemiah in their present form were not written by the men whose names they bear—they do not purport to be written by them—but by someone living not earlier than 300 B. C. One of these indications is that the book of Nehemiah contains a list of the high priests which comes down to about 300 B. C. As to the question of identity of authorship, it is to be noted that the most characteristic phrases occur in all four of the books.

The theme of the whole work was the holy people of God upon earth from Adam until the restoration of the Jewish church under Ezra and Nehemiah. The work shows throughout the Levitical-priestly tendencies and interests. In keeping with this standpoint the writer passes rapidly over the earlier times until King David comes to the throne. Henceforth Jerusalem, the temple and its worship, and all matters of ceremonial and legal religion, engage the chief attention of the writer. For his materials down to the Exile he depends chiefly upon the books of Samuel and the Kings. But he also mentions some other sources, otherwise unknown to us. At all events the historical sources are not always faithfully handled, but are frequently much transformed under the influence of priestly ideas and traditions.

For the post-exilic period the author has access to valuable sources and uses them fairly. We may, indeed, assume that the transformations of the pre-exilic history were never conscious perversions. The events in the lives of Ezra and Nehemiah seem to be told in a straightforward manner. An occasional error has been discovered, but the picture is doubtless correct in the main.

We may now briefly summarize the development of the literature of the Old Testament. First we have the earliest folk-songs, folk-tales and beginnings of the laws, next the oldest direct sources of the Pentateuch. These stages lie before the production of any of the books of our Old Testament as we possess them. In the third period falls the production of the earliest of our Old Testament books. It is the age of the earliest literary prophets. Next comes the period of literary production of the Deuteronomic Code. To it belong also a few of the Minor Prophets. The fifth period of authorship is that of the Exile, including the "First Captivity" from 597. To this period belong Ezekiel, the author of Lamentations, and the great unnamed prophet commonly known as Deutero-Isaiah. To this time we may also assign much of the work of the compilation of the Book of the Kings, and perhaps the writing of much of the Priestly Code. The sixth period, the post-exilic, might be subdivided into minor periods, yet it may also be viewed as one. To this period belong not only the production of a number of new books, but also the editing of the Pentateuch (or rather Hexateuch), the collecting and editing of the Psalms and Proverbs, and the final shaping of some of the older historical books.

Thus we see that the actual composition of the books of the Old Testament, as we now have them, stretched over more than six centuries, namely, from Amos (about 750 B. C.) to the latest Psalms (written in the latter part of the second century B. C.). But the writers and compilers of some of the Old Testament books used written materials of a much earlier date than Amos—in some cases several centuries earlier; and of course oral traditions reach back to a far remoter past.

CHRONOLOGICAL TABLE OF THE LITERATURE OF THE OLD TESTAMENT

Pre-Mosaic Era

Gen. 14 (a Canaanite document); Gen. 4:23 f.; possibly Gen. 9:25–27.

Mosaic Era
(about 1300)

(a) Various Sayings, such as that concerning the crossing of the Red Sea (Ex. 15:21); that concerning Ama-

lek (Ex. 17:16); that to the Ark (Num. 10:35 f.);
the Song of the Well (Num. 21:17 f.); also Num.
6:24–26; 21:10–16; the germ of 33:1 ff.; 21:27–29.

(b) The Decalogue (Ex. 20:1–17); later rewritten and
expanded.

(c) The Book of the Covenant (Ex. 20:23–23:19).

ERA OF THE JUDGES
(about 1250–1050)

(a) Various Songs and Sayings, e.g., the Song of Deborah
(Judg. 5); Song of Moses at the Red Sea (Ex.
15:1–18); the Blessings of Jacob (Gen. 49, except
verses 8–12); and a few others.

(b) Legal Utterances, e.g., the "J Decalogue" (Ex. 34:10–
27), though this *may* be earlier; the twelvefold commandment at Schechem (Deut. 27:15–26).

(c) The shaping of Various Traditions (chiefly oral).

DAVIDIC ERA
(about 1000)

(a) Davidic Songs and Psalms (at least in germ), such as
the Song of the Bow (2 Sam. 1:19–27); Lament
over Abner (3:33 f.); Psalm 18 and perhaps the
germ of about 10 other psalms.

(b) Sayings, such as David's Last Words (2 Sam. 23:1–7);
the Saying concerning Judah in "Jacob's Blessing"
(Gen. 49:8–12); the Balaam Oracles in Numbers 23
and 24 (these may be earlier).

(c) Probably the Book of Jashar and the Book of the Wars
of Jehovah.

(d) Possibly the beginning of the J Writing.

SOLOMONIC ERA
(about 950)

(a) Annals taken up by the writer of 1 Kings (1 Ki. 4–7;
9; 10).

(b) Possibly the completion of the J Writing extending from Gen. 1 to 1 Ki. 2.

(c) Possibly the beginning of the E Writing.

(d) Solomon's Saying at the Dedication of the Temple (1 Ki. 8:12 ff.).

(e) The germ of Proverbs 10–22.

About 850–800

(a) Song of Moses (Deut. 32).

(b) Possibly J and E writings (rather than earlier dates?).

(c) The later source of Samuel and Kings (as far as 2 Ki. 13) (?)

ERA OF JEROBOAM II
(about 750)

Amos (about 760–750); Hosea (750–735); perhaps Isaiah 15 and 16 (pre-Isaianic?).

ERA OF THE DOWNFALL OF THE NORTHERN KINGDOM
(740–722)

Portions of Isaiah; Micah 1.

ERA OF HEZEKIAH
(722–699)

(a) Remainder of genuine writings of Isaiah.

(b) Micah 2–5.

(c) Combination of J and E.

(d) Biography of Solomon (1 Ki. 3–11).

(e) Basis of Proverbs 25–29 (?).

(f) Various Psalms (later revised?).

(g) Basis of Deuteronomy (?).

ERA OF MANASSEH
(698–643)

Portions of Micah; basis of the Law of Holiness, Lev. 17–26, and other portions of the Priestly Writing; some additions to Isaiah.

Era of Josiah
(640–608)

Zephaniah; Habakkuk; finding of D and expansion of same; also combination of D with E; Nahum; possibly a po.tion of Joel.

Era of the Last Jewish Kings
(608–586)

Large portions of Jeremiah; a redaction of the Book of the Kings; various Psalms; some of the Book of Proverbs.

Era of the Exile
(586–536)

Completion of the Book of Jeremiah (by Baruch) in Egypt; Ezekiel in Babylon; Lamentations 2, 4 and 1; Deutero-Isaiah; some Psalms; combination of JE and D (or DE).

Era of the Return
(537–520)

Isaiah 56–66 (Trito-Isaiah) (?); Lamentations 5; Psalm 137; additions to Jeremiah (ch. 50 and 51).

Era of the Rebuilding of the Temple
(520–516)

Haggai; Zechariah 1-8; Ruth.

About 500

The Priestly Writing in Babylon; the Book of Job.

About 470–450

Lamentations 3; Malachi; Obadiah.

Era of Ezra and Nehemiah
(458—ca. 420)

Final redaction of the Pentateuch (P combined with JED); Ezra's memoirs; Nehemiah's memoirs; the Aramaic source concerning the restoration of Jerusalem (Ezra 4–6); Jonah (?).

About 400

Collection and general redaction of the "Former" and "Latter" Prophets. Joel. (Some additions to the prophetical books are of later date.)

In the 4th Century

Some additions to Isaiah; the most of Psalms 42-49 and 73-150; Proverbs 1-9; Song of Songs.

About 330

Habakkuk (?)

About 300

The Chronicler's writing (Chronicles, Ezra-Nehemiah); Esther (?)

About 200 (?)

Zechariah 9-14; Ecclesiastes.

MACCABEAN ERA
(after 168)

Daniel 165; collection of the "Writings" and their addition to the Law and Prophets.

About 75 B. C.

Final canonization of the Old Testament in its present compass in Jerusalem.

(This syllabus is largely based on that of Sellin.)

CHAPTER XI

THE COLLECTION AND CANONIZATION OF THE BOOKS OF THE OLD TESTAMENT

We have seen that all highly organized religions tend not only to produce their special literatures, but also eventually to establish their canons of "sacred literature." The canonization of a body of literature is in every instance the result of a relatively long process. Out of the religious movement and life springs a literature. Of the books thus produced some commend themselves to the practical sense of a religious community as being both useful and necessary, and these are at length sanctioned by the community as possessing a divine authority. The religious community never fancies that it lends authority to the books; it only acknowledges the authority which it believes to be inherent in them. It is only the content of divine truth that can ground any real and ultimate authority. At the same time it is only the sanction of a religious community that makes a writing actually canonical.

The idea of a "scripture canon," as developed in Judaism and as generally accepted in the history of Christianity, has a positive and a negative aspect. Positively, the community affirms that certain books possess the attributes of divine revelation. Negatively, it denies that any other books possess these attributes.

The Jewish canon was not fully and finally established

until about 75 B. C. Until this time the separation of
the fully acknowledged from the doubtful books had not
been definitely carried through. Indeed, there was some
dispute regarding one or two of the Writings (Kethubim)
for more than a century after this. Nevertheless, there
was a canon several centuries earlier than this, namely,
in the time of Ezra; only the canon of Ezra (fixed about
444 B. C.), and even the enlarged canon of about 200
B. C., had not yet arrived at the point of strictly excluding
all other books, present or future, from the category of
divinely inspired writings.

There were three stages or epochs in the formation of
the Old Testament canon. Indeed, there was an earlier
or preliminary stage before the three. In the preliminary
stage special acknowledgment was accorded this or that
writing, and with continued use the sense of the sanctity
of the writing grew; but there was, as yet, no attempt to
fix and declare the list of writings which should be
regarded as authoritative.

(1) The "first canon" in the proper sense of the term
was that established under the leadership of Ezra about
444 B. C. This was the canon of the Law (Torah), and
consisted of the Pentateuch. Now, we know that Ezra
and the people of the time also held other books to be
inspired; but these other books, the histories and the
prophecies, were not set up as an unconditional practical
standard. They were to be read for edification, while
the books of the Law possessed fundamental authority.

(2) The "second canon" gave sanction also to a specific list of the Prophets, the "Former" and the "Latter"
Prophets. The Prophets, however, were not placed quite
on a level with the Law. This second canon is dated

about 200 B. C. The Jewish Bible by this time consists of two parts: THE LAW and THE PROPHETS.

(3) The "third canon" added the Kethubim or Writings (called in the Septuagint version Hagiographa). These again were not placed quite on a level with the earlier collections. The full settlement of this final canon must be dated in the last century of the pre-Christian era, probably about 75 B. C. The Jewish Bible now comprises three parts: THE LAW (Torah), THE PROPHETS (Nebiim), and THE WRITINGS (Kethubim). About the time of the establishment of this completed canon, the rabbis began to teach that the line of the prophets had ceased, that no books but these were inspired, and that no inspired books were to be expected in the future.

It is certain that Ezra in magnifying the Law had no thought of denying the inspiration of the prophets. The reason for specially exalting the Law was purely pragmatic. The life of the people was to be organized and the natural basis of organization is law. This observation should aid us in clearly discriminating between the collecting of the writings and their canonization. The Jews collected various writings to be read for moral and religious instruction, and they highly honored them long before they found occasion to canonize them.

The date of the collecting of the Prophets (Former and Latter) must have been before the time of the writing of Ecclesiasticus (Wisdom of Jesus, the son of Sirach), for this book, whose date is about 182 B. C., mentions the three major prophets and the twelve minor prophets just as they occur in our Hebrew Bibles. Their *canonization* seems to have been effected at about the same time (apparently not far from 200 B. C.).

It is of special interest to note that the idea of a fixed

and closed canon should emanate only from the Palestinian Jews; the Jews of the Dispersion (in particular those of Alexandria) did not recognize a closed canon. The son of Sirach, for instance, evidently regarded his book as belonging to precisely the same category as the books of prophecy and wisdom in the "canonical" list. The Alexandrian Bible (the Septuagint) included a number of books which the Jews regarded as apocryphal. And since many of the Christian church fathers knew the Old Testament only in the Greek version, it was the Alexandrian rather than the Palestinian Old Testament that was the more generally known and accepted in the Old Catholic Church. The Old Testament Apocrypha are included in the Latin Vulgate, and the Roman Church acknowledges their inspiration.

The Old Testament (according to the Palestinian canon) was the Bible of Jesus and his disciples. Its divine inspiration was never a matter of uncertainty with Jesus. Yet it is clear that he did not share the doctrine of the scribes that the Scriptures were absolutely perfect. The Scriptures required completion, fulfilment. To our Lord, who came with the consciousness of a Messianic mission, the idea of a "closed" canon, in the sense that God had ceased to speak to men, must have been abhorrent.

Chapter XII

BETWEEN THE TESTAMENTS

Until a few decades ago it was the prevailing view that the last of the Old Testament books was written about 400 B. C., and that between the Old Testament and the time of Jesus there intervened "four centuries of silence," four centuries in which there was no revelation, no prophetic voice. We now know that there are important writings in the canonical Old Testament that date from as late as the second century B. C. Hence, even if there had been a period of silence between the Old Testament and Jesus, it could not in any event have been as long as two centuries. But even this shorter period between the Testaments was not a time of silence. It was a time of great religious activity and of real religious progress. The proofs of this statement are to be found partly in the writings called Apocrypha, but more especially in those known as Pseudepigrapha.

The canonization of the books of the Old Testament unhappily involved the denial of the inspiration of any teachers that should come after the closing of the canon. For this reason any man who had a religious message to declare to the people found it expedient to ascribe his production to some Old Testament worthy who lived not later than the time of Ezra; for the accepted doctrine was that since the completion of the accepted list of books God had ceased to speak to men. The Pseudepigrapha accordingly bear the names of such men as Enoch, Moses, Isaiah, Jeremiah, Baruch, Ezra, etc.

The Pseudepigrapha are in the main *apocalyptic*. Some of the Apocrypha are more or less so. The motives leading to the development of apocalyptic are not far to seek. Legalism and literalism had put a check upon the freedom of religious expression. To be a good Jew was, first and always, to keep the Law. But those who did not wish in the least to violate the law, and yet longed for spiritual life and movement, sought and found relief and satisfaction in a mystical, visionary religious life.

In the nature of the case the tendency was for the apocalyptists, while remaining true to the Law and laying much stress upon the ethical side of life, to revel in anticipation of the coming glory of Israel.

The last two centuries before the Christian era witnessed a very ample development of the ideas of the future life and of the events that should accompany the ushering in of the Messianic kingdom.

We may summarize the development of religion "between the Testaments" under a few main heads.

(1) The more genuine type of prophecy has given way to apocalyptic. The function of the prophet had been to preach righteousness and to point to God's workings and his moral purpose. But now the exaltation of the Law has made the preacher seem almost superfluous. As an immediate force in the spiritual life of men the prophet has largely lost his occupation. Apocalyptic, on the other hand, takes its stand upon the legal system, enforcing its precepts, and encouraging the people by visions of Israel's future glory.

(2) The "kingdom of God" in apocalyptic literature tended more and more to mean a glorious kingdom which should be established "at the end of the age" (or "world"). It was to be something more than the last

of a series of earthly kingdoms, the enduring one in contrast with all others which had fallen or must yet fall. It was to be a kingdom at once earthly and heavenly— earthly in its seat, yet more than earthly in its power and glory.

(3) The Messiah is pictured in far greater detail than in the canonical Scriptures of the Old Testament.

(4) The doctrine of a future life, which in the Old Testament remains obscure, is much developed between the Testaments. Heaven, hell, angels, the resurrection of the body are all brought into the foreground.

(5) The doctrines of personal righteousness are developed. The duty, for example, of forgiveness of one's neighbor is made clearer than it had been of old.

The most important part of the extant literature of the period between the Testaments is comprised in the Apocrypha as found in the Septuagint (see the list in Chapter II). The understanding of the religious life of Israel in this period is indispensable to a fuller appreciation of the origins of Christianity. Within the last few decades the recognition of this fact has immensely influenced the lines of New Testament study. The New Testament may no longer be studied merely in the light of the canonical Old Testament and contemporary history. The historical development of the religion of Israel did not cease with the closing of the canon. The background of the life and the work of Jesus was not merely the religion of the canonical Scriptures. At the same time, it must not be overlooked that Jesus himself honored the canonical Scriptures above the traditions of the elders. For a luminous brief treatment of the period between the Testaments, see Charles' "Religious Development between the Old and the New Testaments."

CHAPTER XIII

THE ORIGIN OF THE BOOKS OF THE NEW TESTAMENT

The Old Testament Scriptures are the product of a long movement of national religious history, the national religion of the Hebrews. The New Testament is the product of a more rapid movement covering the period of the founding and first expansion of the Christian Church. The production of the Old Testament literature covers a period (if we include the most ancient sources that are wrought into the books as we have them) of at least 1,000 years. No book of our New Testament, as we now have it, appears to have been written earlier than 50 A. D., and perhaps only one of the books can be dated much after the close of the first century.

(1) The earliest group of writings in the New Testament are the *Epistles of Paul*. This statement, however, applies only to the group taken as a whole, for it is possible that some of the other writings may have appeared before the latest of Paul's Epistles. Now, we should naturally expect the Gospels to be written before any Epistles, and it is indeed possible that one or more "sources" of our present Gospels may have antedated our Epistles; but it is certain that the Gospels, as we now have them, all appeared later than the most of the Pauline Epistles. The reason for the earlier appearance of the Epistles is not hard to discover. The memorials of the life of Jesus were recited in the congregations by wit-

nesses or by others well instructed in the tradition. The need for written accounts of the life of Christ did not begin to be felt keenly until the number of eye-witnesses began to be inadequate for the demands of the churches for personal, oral narration in the public assemblies. As the church extended into new regions and the number of believers multiplied, and the eye-witnesses became relatively few, there arose a lively demand for written records of the earthly life of Jesus; but the occasions for apostolic letters arose earlier.

All writings of real historical significance are more or less occasional. That is to say, they are writings called forth by a concrete situation or occasion. This is true in an eminent degree of the New Testament writings. The occasional character of Paul's Epistles is particularly evident. Paul's letters are the immediate outgrowth of his missionary and pastoral work. Each letter deals with a concrete situation. One of them, the letter to the Ephesians, appears to have been a circular letter to a group of churches in the province of Asia. Accordingly, its character is more general than is the case with the other letters. Generally speaking, no writings can be pointed out that are more specific in their relations to concrete situations than the Epistles of Paul.

Paul wrote letters only in lieu of direct personal communication. He preferred to meet the churches face to face, but in his absence from them he had repeated occasion to write to them, encouraging, rebuking, instructing, according to their particular needs. The Pauline Epistles are documents of the apostle's pastoral care of his various flocks. They afford us a wonderful insight into the situation and character of the New Testament churches, and also into the mind and heart of the apostle himself. In order to read Paul's Epistles understandingly one must study to get a clear, general view of his character and personal history, and yet it is just these Epistles to which we must chiefly go for a knowledge of the man and his work. But we have also the wonderful and highly trustworthy narrative of the Acts of the Apostles. The means at our command for understanding the man and his work include, therefore, the Pauline Epistles, the Acts, and the known background of the Jewish religion in which he was brought up. One Epistle will throw light upon another and our knowledge of Pharisaism will shed light upon them all. This, then, is our situation: we must know the man and his work in order to understand the earliest and primitive Christian religion. The problem is, therefore, somewhat complex. From each side of the problem light must be reflected upon the other side of the problem.

Paul's conversion probably occurred within two years, possibly within one year, of the crucifixion of Jesus, or about 29 or 30 A. D. He was not from the moment of his conversion ripe for the world's apostleship. He developed into a world apostle. This development was swift enough to set him well in advance of all the other apostles. After preaching for a time in Arabia, Syria and Cilicia, he is at length brought by Barnabas from his home in Tarsus to help in the work of evangelization in Antioch. Here Gentiles are hearing and receiving the gospel along with the Jews. The conversion of the Gentiles fills the souls of Paul and Barnabas with joy, but many of the Jews look upon it with grave doubt. If Gentiles are to be brought into the church, they must (these said) be brought in *as Jews*—they must submit to all the ceremonial requirements of the Mosaic law. From the first Paul took the broadest ground. In the death of Christ a new covenant was established which annulled the whole system of legal ordinances and put in its place the principle of *faith,* that is, a relation of trust, loyalty and inward fellowship with God. This difference between Paul and the Judaizers, or "party of the circumcision," involved the most serious and momentous controversy of the apostolic age. What sort of gospel was to be preached to the Gentiles? From the Acts of the Apostles and from the whole course of the development of the apostolic church we know that Paul's "gospel of liberty" more and more triumphed over the narrow spirit of legalism that would have imposed the Jewish ceremonial law upon the whole world. The first stage of the controversy between the "liberty of the gospel" and the "bondage of the law" culminated in an appeal of Paul to the apostles and elders at Jerusalem (Acts 15). Here Paul's position was sustained: the Gentiles should not be required to submit themselves to the ordinances of the Jewish law. And yet the controversy did not cease even then. Several of Paul's letters bear witness to the sharpness of the controversy for some years afterwards.

Paul's first letters are those to the *Thessalonians.* On his second missionary journey he, in company with Silas, had preached the gospel in Macedonia with no small success, first in Philippi, then in Thessalonica and Berea. After Paul had passed on to Athens, he learned of the state of the church at Thessalonica, and he wrote them a letter of admonition and encouragement—though perhaps not until he had reached Corinth. The special subject of his letter is the question of the Christian's proper bearing in relation to the hope of the Lord's speedy return. Now Paul himself shared in this hope, and had preached it to the Thessalonians; but he never had suffered himself to be diverted thereby from the task which the Lord had given him. The Thessalonians, on the other hand, had run into a very dangerous fanaticism. Reveling in the expectation of the Lord's appearing, many of them were neglecting the simplest Christian duties. Paul's method of dealing with the Thessalonian error is a wonderful example of his great practical wisdom and of the sanity of his own faith. While we hope for the Lord's early return, we are therefore (Paul argued) to be all the more zealous to fulfill every task and so to be found ready. The time and manner of Christ's return we do not know. The Second Epistle (whose authenticity has been questioned on rather slight grounds) continues the same theme. The date of these Epistles lies somewhere between 49 and 53 A. D., probably toward the end of this period.

The next Epistle in order was probably that to the *Galatians*. It is a fiery yet profound letter in opposition to the Judaizers who had come in after Paul in order to overturn or pervert the work he had done in Galatia. His gospel of grace and freedom they were turning into a system of legalism. The Epistle to the Galatians was Luther's favorite among Paul's writings. Its date and the place of its writing cannot now be surely determined. Most scholars place it early in the Ephesian period of Paul's ministry (about 56, or perhaps 55, A. D.).

In Corinth Paul remained in fruitful labors for a year and a half. After passing on to Ephesus, the chief city of the province of Asia, he had occasion to write certain *Letters to the Corinthians*. From notices in the second Epistle, it is clear that Paul wrote at least *three* letters to that church. It is probable that our "Second Epistle" really contains the main body of the second and third of the letters mentioned. Without doubt the Corinthian

Epistles are, historically, by far the most illuminating of Paul's Epistles. Nothing could possibly surpass the concreteness of Paul's treatment of the situation in the church at Corinth. Not only do we learn much about Paul from these letters, but they afford a wonderful insight into the religious and social life of the churches in the apostolic age. In the Corinthian church were divisions, religious and practical errors and the like; but there was also much godly zeal. These Epistles are remarkable for the number and variety of topics which Paul was called upon to discuss. They may be dated between 55 and 57 A. D.

After a rather long stay at Ephesus, Paul visits the churches of Macedonia and comes a second time to Corinth. It is from here that he writes the great *Letter to the Romans*. It is not possible for us to know as much concerning the occasion of this letter as we do in the case of the letters previously mentioned. Paul had never visited Rome, but he was very desirous of going thither. The church at Rome may have been founded by Christians from the provinces settling in the capital. No doubt Paul had some special reason to believe that the church at Rome had need of instruction upon the first principles of the gospel—salvation by grace, through faith, without the works of the law. The main theme is much the same as that of Galatians; only, in this latter Epistle Paul writes with more restraint, and his attitude toward the law is more carefully explained. He shows himself not opposed to the law in an unqualified sense; the law has not been annulled, but rather spiritualized and relieved of its formalities. Intellectually, the Epistle to the Romans is Paul's greatest writing. It is unsurpassed also in its religious fervor.

Leaving Corinth, Paul returns to Jerusalem, taking with

him the collection from various churches for the poor saints in Jerusalem. Here he meets with much bitter opposition on the part of the unbelieving Jews and also no little doubt and suspicion on the part of the Christian Jews. In consequence of false suspicions and accusations, he is arrested. The Jews are resolved upon his death, but the Roman military captain sends him under guard to Cæsarea. There he is long imprisoned in hope of bribes to be paid for his release. At length, upon his appealing to Cæsar, he is sent to Rome. Whether he is later released and is finally put to death at the end of a *second* imprisonment, or whether this imprisonment closes with his martyrdom, is uncertain. At all events, it seems pretty clear that several of Paul's letters belong to the *imprisonment period*. They are therefore called the "Imprisonment Epistles." Whether written all from Cæsarea or all from Rome, or indeed, some from the one and the others from the other place, is uncertain. Formerly nearly all scholars declared in favor of Rome. More recent discussions have shown a strong inclination to assign at least some of them to Cæsarea. These Imprisonment Epistles are Ephesians, Colossians, Philippians and Philemon. Some scholars, however, are now arguing that some, or all, of the four were written from Ephesus.

The first is not strictly *"to the Ephesians;"* it was a circular letter, and one important manuscript reads "To the church that is in Laodicea." The great theme of this Epistle is the fellowship of the faith, the church, the family of God. The sweep of thought is grand. The objections to the Pauline authorship are somewhat serious, but they are not conclusive. They are based largely upon the peculiarities of style.

The *Epistle to the Colossians* closely resembles Ephesians in many points. It is probable that Colossians was written first, for the leading ideas of this Epistle appear in the other in a more finished form.

No Epistle of Paul's is more sincerely admired than that to the *Philippians*. The Apostle's relations with the Philippian church have been almost ideal. Here Paul finds little to rebuke. He writes them a genuine love letter. The Epistle contains several highly characteristic and weighty passages.

The little *Epistle to Philemon* is a private letter—the only strictly private letter among Paul's extant writings. Paul is sending back to Philemon a runaway slave, Onesimus, whom he has won to Christ. He sends back the slave with a letter begging for mercy toward him and delicately yet powerfully suggesting his liberation.

A fourth group of Pauline Epistles is composed of *1 and 2 Timothy and Titus*. They are called the *Pastoral Epistles,* because they are written to counsel pastors or bishops as to the way in which they should conduct their office. It is probable that all three are comparatively late elaborations on the basis of Pauline notes or letters. Second Timothy may be almost all Pauline, though this is doubted by many. The others show fewer elements that look Pauline; and all three show indications of a later development of church life than would have been possible in Paul's lifetime.

Thus we have thirteen Epistles that are commonly reckoned as Pauline. Also a fourteenth, namely, the Epistle to the Hebrews, has been traditionally ascribed to Paul. This ascription, however, rests upon very slight evidence and is now almost universally rejected. Of the thirteen other "Pauline" Epistles, three or four are of doubtful authenticity, while nine or ten are now almost universally ascribed to Paul.

The Epistles whose authenticity is all but universally acknowledged are the following: Romans, 1 and 2 Corinthians, Galatians, Philippians, Philemon, Colossians, and 1 Thessalonians (8 in number). To these we add as generally acknowledged to be authentic: 2 Thessalonians and Ephesians, also the basis of 2 Timothy (which may have been worked over by a later hand). To approach the matter from the other side, very many scholars reject the Pauline authorship of 1 Timothy and Titus and a large part of 2 Timothy. A smaller but still very considerable number of critics reject the Pauline authorship of Ephesians, and not a few also deny him the authorship of 2 Thessalonians.

The Pauline Epistles are best classified (in the manner already indicated) in four groups: (1) the Early Epistles (1 and 2 Thessalonians); (2) the Chief Epistles (Galatians, 1 and 2 Corinthians and Romans); (3) the Imprisonment Epistles (Ephesians, Colossians, Philippians and Philemon); (4) the Pastoral Epistles (1 and 2 Timothy, Titus).

(2) The knowledge of the origin of the *Epistle to the Hebrews* was early lost in the church. Late in the second century, some leaders of the church were disposed to ascribe the Epistle to Paul, while a larger number seem to have doubted its Pauline authorship. Eventually, however, the growing disposition to ascribe all of the most highly esteemed Christian writings directly or indirectly to some apostle prevailed, and for many centuries Paul was credited with the authorship of this Epistle. Modern criticism, however, has made it very clear that Paul was not its author. This is proved principally by many marked

peculiarities of style. There is significance also in the entire anonymity of the writing (Paul always made his authorship of a letter very conspicuous). Finally, the early testimony is fairly decisive against the assumption of the Pauline authorship. But who, then, did write the Epistle to the Hebrews? This we do not know and probably never can know. Four well-known guesses may be mentioned: Barnabas, Apollos, Silas, and Luke. Scholars are generally inclined to either the first or the second conjecture. While the Epistle cannot have been written by Paul himself, it does represent the Pauline standpoint in doctrine. In form "Hebrews" is hardly an Epistle; it may have been originally a sermon, eventually written out for circulation.

(3) Whether the author of the *Epistle of James* was the James known as the brother of our Lord, is quite uncertain. The high esteem in which this James was held is evidenced by the fact that he was long the acknowledged head of the church in Jerusalem (see Acts 15 and Gal. 1 and 2). If the letter is rightly ascribed to him, its date may be very early, perhaps before any of Paul's Epistles. But the fact that the letter contends against a rather common misinterpretation of Paul's teaching concerning salvation by faith alone argues a somewhat later date. Some scholars place it as late as in the early years of the second century. The Epistle is a preëminently practical writing. It has all the characteristics of the best type of Jewish Christianity. The law is honored, but it is spiritualized.

(4) *The Epistles of Peter and Jude.* The *First Epistle of Peter* is probable from the hand of the apostle—at least essentially so. Doubts on this point are due chiefly to its Pauline affinities; for at the first, at least, Peter and Paul were not in perfect agreement. But it need not be assumed,

as many scholars do assume, that their early differences continued to the end. The New Testament records rather indicate that after a time these two apostles came to a substantial agreement. Perhaps the finished form of the letter was not possible to the fisherman of Galilee without the help of some more practised literary hand. But we know that Peter had no lack of competent helpers. The *Second Epistle,* on the other hand, is probably erroneously ascribed to the apostle. Several features of the letter point to a date probably past the middle of the second century. Among these are the references to heresies of that period and the significant reference to the letters of Paul as in the same class with "the other scriptures" (2 Peter 3:16). Such a view of apostolic letters was hardly possible in the lifetime of Peter. Another feature of interest is the resemblance of this Epistle to the *Epistle of Jude.* It is evident that one has borrowed from the other. The prevailing opinion is that 2 Peter is dependent on Jude. The origin of the latter is uncertain. The tradition that the author was our Lord's brother is probably unfounded.

We have yet to consider the first three Gospels, the Acts of the Apostles, and the writings ascribed to John (the Gospel, the Epistles, and the Revelation). Because of its close relation to the Pauline Epistles, there is something in favor of considering the Acts of the Apostles before we take up the Gospels, but since the Acts is the continuation of the third Gospel, we shall consider it after the Gospel of Luke and before taking up the Johannine writings. Because these last are of relatively late date, we shall consider them after the Synoptic Gospels and the Acts.

(5) *The Synoptic Gospels.* The first three Gospels

have been called the *Synoptic Gospels*. They have been so called, not because each of them severally gives an outline of the life of Jesus, but because the three so strongly resemble one another in contents, language and standpoint, that they may be *viewed together* (a synopsis is a viewing together); and they may be viewed together because they themselves show a "common view" (synopsis, conspectus) of the materials of the life of Jesus. For convenience' sake the Gospels are often arranged in parallel columns. Thus the idea of the *conspectus* or *synopsis* is visualized.

The resemblances between these three Gospels are altogether remarkable, and they challenge our curiosity. They are not of a sort that can be regarded as mere coincidences. But not only are there many marked resemblances, there are also some equally marked differences. These resemblances and differences taken together present us with a problem, the so-called *Synoptic problem*. The problem is to explain the origin of these Gospels and to account for their resemblances and differences.

The intimacy of the interrelations of the first three Gospels will quickly appear upon examination. If these Gospels had represented three independent witnesses or three independent traditions, we should expect, in the first place, the greatest variety in *the selection of subject-matter*. But we find, on the contrary, a remarkably extensive agreement in this regard. The Gospel of Mark is represented almost entirely in parallels in one or both the other Synoptics. As for Luke, only 250 verses are peculiar to this Gospel (apart from the narrative concerning the birth and childhood of Jesus, ch. 1 and 2). Matthew has only about 140 verses not represented in the parallels in Mark and Luke. In the second place we find remarkable agreements in the *arrangement of the matter*. Again and again we meet with groups of passages in which the arrangement is the same in two or even three of the Gospels. The agreement often extends to the very words. Whole sentences occur in three or two Gospels in essentially identical forms. But over against these instances of the closest resemblances there are some surprising differences.

When we seek for an explanation of these remarkable phenomena, we have before us a goodly number of abstract possibilities. It might be suggested, for example, that each evangelist wrote quite independently on the basis of his own personal knowledge or of mutually independent lines of tradition. This hypothesis, however, is altogether untenable for the simple reason that extensive verbal agreements in narrating events are unknown in human experience except where there is either collusion or dependence upon some common source or sources.

The Synoptic problem has probably been the subject of a more intensive and patient study than any other literary problem whatsoever. No one, however, claims that a complete solution has been found. Yet there is a pretty extensive agreement among scholars as to certain cardinal matters. It is clear that Mark is the earliest of our present Gospels. But it is also certain that there were some attempts at a written account of the life and sayings of Jesus before the Gospel of Mark. And before those attempts at written narratives there was a period of purely oral tradition.

For a time oral tradition satisfied the needs of the comparatively small community of believers. But as the church expanded, many of the congregations were unable to hear the story of the life of Jesus from an eye-witness or even from someone who had carefully learned it from an eye-witness. Moreover, these eye-witnesses or skillful narrators began to be taken by death. Thus the demand for the written narratives arose. At first the writings were comparatively brief and fragmentary. These earliest attempts at narratives of the life of Jesus became the basis of our Gospels. The earliest records were sifted in the process of their use in the church and the best was incorporated in the later and fuller Gospels.

Three primary written sources are assumed as underlying our Synoptic Gospels: (1) A document designated as Q (Quelle), which may have been substantially identical with Matthew's "Logia" (Sayings of Jesus); (2) the Gospel of Mark substantially as we now have it; (3) other brief or fragmentary Gospels, used by Luke and perhaps also by Matthew. Of course, it is possible that behind these earliest traceable sources there were still others which were so wrought into these sources that we cannot distinguish the various threads. Both Matthew and Luke, especially the former, freely used the matter found in Mark. It is probable that even Mark used some written sources for his gospel, but this cannot be affirmed with certainty. That Matthew and Luke drew not only upon Mark, but also upon other written sources, is perfectly clear. It is very significant that much of the material in these two Gospels that is wanting in Mark is *common to the two,* and therefore must have been derived from a *common source.* This common source—which may have been used more or less also by Mark—is designated by the letter Q (Quelle). As known and used by Luke and the person who formed our "Matthew," it was probably a Greek writing. Was it then perhaps a Greek version of Matthew's "Sayings of Jesus," which, we know, was an Aramaic ("Hebrew") writing? To this

question no certain answer can be given. It seems probable, however, that the Aramaic Gospel of Matthew (the
"Sayings of Jesus") was made the basis of one or more
Greek versions—not mere translations but adaptations and
elaborations. One such version was doubtless used by
the person who prepared our "Matthew"; either the same
or more likely a variant version was used also by Luke.
It is entirely possible that the Greek version (and elabo-
ration) of Matthew's Logia is identical with Q. Indeed,
it is hardly possible that Q was not somehow based on
Matthew's original writing. Yet Q may be regarded as
in a sense the product of the mind of the primitive church.
To what Matthew had recorded, other well-attested sayings of the Lord seem to have been added.

This source (Q) included (according to Burkitt, "The
Earliest Sources of the Life of Jesus") "very many of
the most precious jewels of the Gospel. When Justin
Martyr, in the second century, wished to exhibit to the
heathen emperor the characteristic ethical teaching of
Christ, nine-tenths of his examples came out of passages
derived from Q. It is from Q that we have the blessing
on the poor, the hungry, the reviled; from Q come 'Love
your enemies,' 'Turn the other cheek,' 'Be like your
Father, who makes his sun to shine on the evil and the
good,' 'Consider the lilies,' 'Be not anxious—your Father
knoweth that ye have need,' 'They shall come from east
and west and sit down with Abraham in the kingdom of
God.' It is Q that tells us that the adversaries of Jesus
found him not ascetic enough, and mocked at him as a
friend of tax-gatherers and sinners. It is Q that tells us
that Jesus said 'I thank thee, Father, that thou hast hid
these things from the wise and revealed them to babes—
even so, Father, for so it was pleasing in thy sight.' If

the work of Mark be more important to the historian, it is Q that supplies the starting-points for the Christian moralist. Most important of all, it gives light and shade to the somewhat austere lines of the portrait of Jesus sketched in the Gospel of Mark."

Mark's Gospel is the earliest attempt to furnish a sketch of the life of Jesus, for Q dealt specially with his discourses. It is probable that Mark uses Q in a few places. The date of Mark's Gospel is probably some two years before the destruction of Jerusalem in 70 A. D. The writer was Mark, the companion of Peter and Paul. According to tradition, he wrote as he had learned from Peter. His Gospel is swift of movement, simple and vivid in expression, and emphasizes the deeds of Jesus more than his discourses.

The *"Gospel according to Matthew"* doubtless received its name because it was believed to have been based more directly than the rest upon the Apostle Matthew's work, which dates as far back as 45–50 A. D. In its present form the Gospel according to Matthew is a composite work derived from the "Sayings" (Logia) in a Greek version (Q), from Mark, and other written or oral sources. Because of the nature of its references to the destruction of Jerusalem, it must be dated after that event—perhaps about 75 A. D., or even later. It is written from the standpoint of the Christian Jew. The Old Testament Scriptures are very frequently referred to, and Jesus is represented with emphasis as the Christ who fulfills the Law and the Prophets.

Luke professedly used many sources (see the preface to the Gospel) ; he used Mark and Q, also other sources unknown to us. But he does not seem to have used our Matthew. Whether this is because Matthew was not yet written or whether, though in existence, it had not come to his knowledge, is uncertain. The author of this Gospel and of the Acts was almost certainly Luke, the companion and helper of Paul. If written (as is generally assumed) before the Acts, and then if the latter was written before the death of Paul, about 67 A. D. (as a few assume), the date of Luke would be very early indeed. But it is more probable that both must be dated in the seventies or even in the eighties.

The Gospel according to Luke has been called by Renan "the most beautiful book ever written." Its beauty, however, does not lie so much in its style, though in this respect it surpasses Matthew and Mark, nor in its excellent choice and arrangement of matter, as in a peculiarly gracious sympathy that runs through the book. It contains several passages of the greatest interest which are peculiar to itself, e.g., the Angels and the Shepherds, the Boy Jesus in the Temple, the parables of the Lost Sheep, the Lost Coin, the Lost Son, the Good Samaritan, and the Pharisee and the Publican.

(6) *The Acts of the Apostles.* The opening words of the Acts of the Apostles represent this book as a continuation of "the former treatise," which must have been the third Gospel. Both writings are dedicated to a certain Theophilus, and both exhibit essentially the same features of vocabulary and style. That Luke is the author of both is rendered almost certain by the full agreement of ample external testimony with the internal evidence of literary form and method. In the Acts, however, there are certain sections whose style varies considerably from that which prevails in the rest of the work. This is doubtless to be accounted for by the author's free use of written sources for some matters not under his personal observation. In

the beginning of his Gospel, Luke has told us that he had examined various earlier accounts of the life of Jesus, and we may reasonably suppose that he would use the same method in writing his second work. And, in fact, as we examine the Acts we find pretty clear evidences of the author's use of documents. Certain portions of the book may be designated as "the we-sections" (see 16: 10–17; 20: 5; 21: 18; 27: 1; 28: 16). These passages are evidently the work of an eye-witness—and, as we know, Luke was for a considerable time a companion of Paul. The "we-sections," since they are the purely original work of the writer of the Acts, may be taken as the basis of our study of the composition of the book. When, then, we examine the rest of the book in the light of these manifestly original sections, we find so large a measure of similarity in vocabulary and grammatical construction as to be able to conclude that the book as a whole bears the impress of a single hand. At the same time there are some passages in the earlier chapters that appear to have been drawn almost bodily from other sources. Even in our English version we can clearly recognize the marked differences of style between such passages as the account of the Day of Pentecost, the speech of Stephen, and the addresses of Peter and John on the one hand and the we-sections on the other.

The date of the book cannot be very much later than that of the Gospel of Luke; about the year 80 may be assumed as approximately correct.

The purpose of the Acts is at bottom the same as that of the Gospel. Just as "the former treatise" was written to show clearly what is the foundation of the faith, namely, the things "that Jesus began both to do and to teach until the day in which he was received up," so this is written to show the continuance of that same working of the living Christ through the Holy Spirit. The book shows how the gospel spread and the church developed in the first age of Christianity, and it exhibits the power of the gospel as over against the weakness of the idolatry and philosophy of the Græco-Roman world.

(7) *The Johannine Writings.*

a. The *Gospel of John* was written at a considerably later date than the Synoptics. Its character is in many ways peculiar. It may be briefly described as the Gospel of the developing church. It is mystical and theological. While it is based upon the personal recollections of the writer and gives some valuable historical data more clearly and consistently than the Synoptics, it is, on the whole, not an attempt to give an objective narrative, but a spiritual interpretation of the life of Christ. The discourses are developed in a style that belongs to the writer rather than to Jesus. The original recollections have been recast and transfused by the spiritual experiences of the writer.

But who is the author? On this point scholars find no agreement. The weight of numbers among scholars of high repute is perhaps against the Johannine authorship. Yet many of the greatest scholars still stoutly maintain that the author was none other than the Apostle John. A rather favorite theory is that the Gospel is an interpretation of the life of Christ from some one of the group of men associated with the Apostle John in Ephesus. The Apostle is thus supposed to be the general source of the thought of the Gospel, which was then worked out by a younger man after John's death. At all events the Gospel is a profound and spiritual writing, which truly reflects the inward life of faith and the growth of the church's conception of Christ.

b. The *First Epistle of John* is surely, the Second and Third Epistles and the Revelation probably, the work of the same writer. Whoever is the author of one is probably the author of all. And the evidence in favor of the Johannine authorship seems at least as strong as that against it. The First Epistle is a sort of companion to the Gospel, and is certainly a work of marvelous depth. The *Second Epistle* is addressed to an individual church under the symbolic title: "the elect lady and her children." The *Third Epistle* is a private letter to one Gaius, apparently a member of the same church as that addressed in the Second Epistle.

c. The *Apocalypse* presents a peculiar problem. As a whole, it probably dates from the time of Domitian, and the persecutions under his reign (about 95 A. D.). But some of the visions seem clearly to refer to the persecutions in the time of Nero before 70 A. D. If the book is not directly from the hand of John—and the Johannine authorship can neither be proved nor disproved—it is doubtless from a Johannine circle at Ephesus. The apocalypses, which form the largest part of the book, are apparently for the most part Christian transformations of Jewish apocalyptic ideas.

CHRONOLOGICAL TABLE OF THE NEW TESTAMENT WRITINGS

While Biblical scholars, in spite of their thorough researches, have not been able to determine the precise date of even a single writing of the New Testament, they can, with full certainty, give approximate dates for many of the books. In the case of most of Paul's Epistles the margin of uncertainty is rather narrow. In the case of some of the other writings it is pretty wide. Generally speaking, the order of the writings is a matter involved in less doubt than the individual dates.

1. *Paul's First Letter to the Thessalonians,* written from Corinth very shortly after the Apostle's arrival there and about a half-year after the founding of the Thessalonian church.

2. *Paul's Second Letter to the Thessalonians,* written from Corinth very soon after the First.

3. *Paul's Letter to the Galatians.* Time and place of writing uncertain. If addressed to the churches of North Galatia, it may have been written from Ephesus, shortly after Paul's arrival there. If addressed to those of South Galatia, it was probably written from Antioch at the close of Paul's second missionary journey.

4. *Paul's First Letter to the Corinthians* was clearly written from Ephesus, apparently (see 16:8) not long before the Passover when Paul left Ephesus, which may have been as early as 55 A. D.

5. *Paul's Second Letter to the Corinthians* (really two letters merged in one) was probably written from Macedonia late in the autumn of the same year in which Paul left Ephesus.

6. *Paul's Letter to the Romans* was written from Corinth, perhaps in March of the following year (56 A. D.?).

The four next following Letters are called, and they seem to be in fact, "Imprisonment Epistles." They seem to have been written in Cæsarea or Rome, yet possibly, as some now contend, in Ephesus. The probable order is as given below, yet in this matter the only certainty seems to be that Ephesians is later than Colossians, which it resembles in thought and expression.

7. *Paul's Letter to the Philippians.*

8. *Paul's Letter to the Colossians.*

9. *Paul's Letter to the Ephesians,* so-called; it seems to have been a circular letter to the churches of Asia Minor.

10. *Paul's Letter to Philemon.*

These ten seem to be all the genuine Epistles of Paul, but it is highly probable that the Pastoral Epistles (1 and 2 Timothy and Titus), especially 2 Timothy, contain considerable elements originating with Paul.

11. *The Gospel according to Mark,* written probably after the death of Peter and Paul (which occurred about 67 A. D.) but before the destruction of Jerusalem in 70 A. D.

12. *The Gospel according to Matthew,* written within a few years after the destruction of Jerusalem.

13. *The Gospel according to Luke,* written a little later than Matthew. Both Matthew and Luke show dependence on Mark, and both use the early source Q, though in different versions. Luke seems also to have used still other sources.

14. *The First Epistle of Peter.* Written, apparently, by Silvanus at the instance and in the name of Peter, perhaps about 64 A. D.

15. *The Acts of the Apostles.* Written by Luke, perhaps about 80 A. D.

16. *The Epistle to the Hebrews.* Date not far from 80 A. D.; author unknown—possibly Apollos.

17. *The Apocalypse of John.* Written in Asia Minor, the main portion about 80 A. D., chapter 7 before 70, and some portions probably about 95 (in reference to the persecution under Domitian).

18. *The First Epistle of John.* Written in Asia Minor, later than (the main body of) the Apocalypse.

19. *The Second Epistle of John.* Asia Minor.

20. *The Third Epistle of John.* Asia Minor.

21. *The Gospel according to John.* Written at Ephesus toward the close of the first century.

22. *The Epistle of James.* Probably not by "the Lord's brother." If it were by that James, the date would naturally be very early. But, assuming another author, it may be dated 75–85 A. D., or even later.

23. *The Epistle of Jude.* Author not "the Lord's brother." The date probably near the close of the first century.

24. *The First Epistle of Paul to Timothy.* Almost surely not genuinely Pauline, yet probably embodying some Pauline materials. Written at latest about 100 A. D.

25. *The Second Epistle of Paul to Timothy.* In its present form not from Paul, yet containing a much larger body of Pauline material than the First Epistle. About 100 A. D.

26. *The Epistle of Paul to Titus.* Several portions genuine. About 100 A. D.

27. *The Second Epistle of Peter.* Not genuine. Date uncertain, but, at the earliest, well on in the second century.

CHAPTER XIV

THE CANON OF THE NEW TESTAMENT

We have swiftly traced the origin of the twenty-seven writings composing our New Testament. But we know that for a long time the church possessed these several writings without as yet possessing a "New Testament." The writings were widely known, cherished and reverently used long before the need of a New Testament canon was felt.

The beginnings of the definite process of fixing a list of acknowledged Christian writings may be set about the year 150 A. D. Long before this time, however, conditions favorable to the formation of a canon were gradually developing.

That the Christian Church should have formed a canon at all might seem strange, in the light of the fact that the whole Christian movement had burst the bands of the old Jewish Canon. That the Church should use, reverence, and acknowledge as sacred the great apostolic writings was most natural and inevitable, but that the Church should at length establish a closed canon seems to find its explanation chiefly in two important facts: the universal reverence for the apostolic word and the growing tendency to fix ecclesiastical authority. Viewed in one of its aspects, the closing of a canon is a phase of the movement which resulted in the establishment of the ancient Catholic Church.

The actual formation of our Canon of the New Testa-

ment falls into several tolerably distinct stages. But before
we trace the actual development of a canon of New Testament writings, it will be well to ask first of all what standards of authority the church acknowledged before the
specific process of forming a "New Testament" began.
Of course the supreme authority of Christian believers
could be nothing else than Jesus Christ himself. But,
since Jesus was no longer with them in person, they felt
the need of some trustworthy mediate authority that
should truly represent the teaching of Jesus. Now what
did the earliest Christians possess that might satisfy this
demand?

As first in order of time, though not first in importance
for their faith, stood the Old Testament. Since Christianity, the Messianic faith, grew out of Judaism, the
Old Testament became the inheritance of the church.
Even the Gentile converts readily received the Old Testament from the Jewish apostles and evangelists. Belief in
the full divine inspiration of the Old Testament was an
important feature of early Christianity. The early Christians used it, after the manner of the Jews, as a book of
devotion and divine instruction. Yet more and more they
used it in a special relation to the new faith—they regarded
it as a book of prophecy, of specific preparation for the
Christ. The whole Old Testament was for them a Messianic book.

The faith in Jesus as the Messiah naturally gave rise to
another authority linked with the Old Testament and yet
rising above it, namely, the words of Jesus. At first, of
course, they had not these words in written "Gospels" but
in the form of oral tradition. Paul, in several instances,
decides questions of church practice and individual life by
an appeal to the words of the Master (e.g., 1 Cor. 11:23

and Acts 20:35). For a considerable time, as we know, the words of Jesus were not handed down in a firmly fixed text, yet the oral tradition tended more and more to settle down to an established form.

Again, the earliest church recognized a certain authority in the inspiration of living prophets. In certain men the church seemed to see the unmistakable signs of the working of the Holy Spirit.

These new and specifically Christian authorities—the words of Jesus and the inspired utterances of New Testament prophets—the Church believed to be bound up with and summed up in the *apostolic office*. For from the very beginning the companions of Jesus were looked upon as the most valuable witnesses to his work and words. For a time, however, the mere fact of having been a member of the company of Jesus' personal disciples was not thought of as a reason for ascribing to their word a unique authority. It was only as teachers of doubtful competency began to appear—men whose work was not in perfect accord with that of the first preachers of the Gospel— that the thought began to take shape in the minds of the Christian people that the testimony of "the Twelve" should be the court of last resort in all matters pertaining to the teaching of the Master. After a time, and not without a considerable controversy, the right of Paul to be regarded as an apostle was acknowledged.

In all these facts we see the germs that developed into a New Testament canon. As the church grows and continually meets fresh problems, the need of clearly determining what is original and genuine Christianity, comes more and more into the consciousness of the church. The center of interest, of course, concerned the central reality of the faith—the work and words of Jesus. Hence the development tends to a special valuation of the Gospels and then of the testimony of the apostles as the only competent guarantors of the truth of the record of the life of Christ. In short, the formation of a New Testament canon is nothing else than the consistent expansion and application of the idea *that apostolic teaching and practice are the court of last resort in matters of Christian faith and life.*

The *need* of a canon (rule, standard) was felt when diverse and divisive teachings had become a disturbing factor in the church's life. The *formative principle* of the Canon was the recognition of apostolic authority. Whatever is apostolic is to be admitted, and nothing is to be admitted that is not apostolic, either directly or indirectly. Doubtless the immense intrinsic merit of certain books was, in the last analysis, the effectual cause of their being admitted to the Canon; yet invariably their admission to the Canon was coupled with the assurance that these books enjoyed apostolic sanction. Mark wrote under the teaching of Peter (and also of Paul); Luke was a companion of Paul; "Hebrews" was written by some man under Paul's influence, or perhaps by Paul himself. Such were the claims in the period of the sifting of early Christian literature with a view to fixing a list of acknowledged writings.

The stages leading up to the fixing of the Canon were about as follows. The first period reaches from the production of the earliest Christian writings to about 150 A. D. It is the period, first, of apostolic activity, including the writing of letters to the churches and the production of narratives of the life of Christ. The writings were cherished in proportion as the work of apostles and evangelists was valued. It is, secondly, the period of the collecting of valued Christian writings, chiefly those of acknowledged apostolic authorship. We know relatively little about the collecting of the writings in this period before their canonization, but we know a little. Paul's letters were collected comparatively early. It is probable that, at the first, few churches possessed more than one Gospel: here one Gospel would be in vogue and there another. Gradually these different Gospels became known to other churches, and each was valued more or less distinctly alongside the others. But there was a rather widespread thought that the use of four distinct records of the life of Christ was not desirable. It was in consequence of this that Tatian in Syria undertook the preparation of a single Gospel composed of the materials of the four—the so-called Diatesseron. This work was in extensive use in the churches of Syria. That the apostolic writings were collected and reverenced, however, is not the whole of the matter. They were continually read in the public services of the churches; hence men gradually set a special value on them—a higher value than they attached to any other writings.

The second period in the origin of the Canon reached from about 150 to about 200 A. D. The compass of the acknowledged literature was nearly fixed in this period. The sense of the need of a canon became clear in this time, and there was a general agreement as to the principles that should determine what writings should be acknowledged as authoritative. In this period, however, no final agreement was reached.

We know from various testimonies that from about 150 A. D. the Gospels were read in public worship along with portions of the Old Testament; but there was not yet any claim that they were inspired scriptures. It was for their message that they were valued, not for any alleged supernatural origin. Indeed, Papias frankly tells us that he sought for the lines of the oral tradition of the teaching of Jesus in preference to that embodied in the writings. In the references of the Church Fathers of this period to the writings now embraced in our New Testament we note some striking differences in their various estimations of their value. Justin Martyr, on the one hand, puts the Epistles of Paul very much in the background, while others show a special fondness for the Pauline writings. The extreme of partiality for Paul is shown in Marcion, who broke away from the fellowship of the general church and founded one of his own. Marcion is the first Christian writer to make use of the idea of a canonical list of books. He and his followers recognized one Gospel (Luke) and ten Epistles of Paul— no other of our New Testament writings; and they refused to acknowledge the authority of the Old Testament in the Christian church. Now Marcion was accounted a heretic; yet he did not depart from the main line of the church's teaching as widely as some others. Gnosticism sought to transmute the gospel into a system of philosophic speculation (and Marcion was not untouched with the Gnostic error). It was largely because of the encroachments of Gnosticism—much of it came even before 150 A. D.—that the church felt impelled, in the period of 150–200 A. D., to seek to establish a canon of scripture as a defense against heresy.

At about 200 A. D., then, we find in the church a general recognition of a body of New Testament scriptures. The great church teachers, such as Irenæus of Lyons, Tertullian of Carthage, and Clement of Alexandria, not only themselves recognized these scriptures, but also insisted upon their necessity as a basis for the church's teaching. The compass of the New Testament at 200 A. D., however, was not everywhere the same. In Alexandria, for example, some writings not included in the final Canon were acknowledged. Of much interest to the student is a specific list of recognized New Testament writings in a brief document out of this period, known as the Muratorian Fragment. It enumerates the four Gospels, the Acts of the Apostles, then thirteen Epistles of Paul, also the Epistle of Jude, two Epistles of John, and the Apocalypse of John. The Epistle of James and the Epistle of Peter (i.e., First Peter) do not appear, nor the Third Epistle of John, nor—as is to be expected— the Second Epistle of Peter. But we are surprised to find alongside the Apocalypse of John the Apocalypse of Peter. There is also a third apocalyptic writing which is recognized in some quarters, namely, the Shepherd of Hermas. It is still further surprising to find in the midst of this enumeration the Wisdom of Solomon, which we now find among the Old Testament Apocrypha. Generally speaking, we may say that at about A. D. 200 and in the principal churches all our present New Testament writings were included in the Canon, with the exception of the Epistle to the Hebrews, the Second Epistle of Peter, the Second and Third Epistles of John, and the Epistle of James. Here and there, however, other writings stood in the canonical lists; in Cilicia, for example, the Gospel of Peter was acknowledged and in Syria the Diatessaron.

There still remains a third principal period in the history of the Canon. The period ends, of course, with the definitive closing of the Canon. This consummation, however, was reached earlier in the West than in the East.

In the Western Church the list was finally fixed before the close of the fourth century. In some of the separate churches of the East the conclusion was not reached until much later.

From the whole history of the Canon we must learn the obvious fact that it is the church's common consciousness that gradually established the Canon of Scripture, and that this was done in accordance with the deepening sense of the availability of given writings for the church's task of instruction and edification. And, without doubt, the church wisely followed the mind of the Spirit in this process. Yet we have no reason to assume that everything included in the Canon is intrinsically better than anything that was omitted.

PART III: HOW WE GOT OUR BIBLE

The part of our study now before us presupposes the finished Scriptures and asks, in respect —first of the Old Testament and then of the New—how those writings were brought down to us. The answer to this question involves an inquiry into the history of the ancient manuscripts of the Biblical writings and a survey of ancient and modern versions of the Bible down to our own day. Light will be thrown upon our problem also by the quotations from the Holy Scriptures in the writings of the Church Fathers.

PART III: HOW WE GOT OUR BIBLE

Chapter XV

THE TRANSMISSION OF THE OLD TESTAMENT TEXT

1. *Old Testament manuscripts.* For more than four centuries Bible students have been familiar with the printed text of the Hebrew Scriptures. Before the printed Hebrew Scriptures lie the long centuries in which these writings were preserved and handed down in manuscripts. How old are the extant manuscripts of the Old Testament? Have we, perchance, in some library or museum some of the original manuscripts of the Old Testament writers? It is with some surprise that we learn that the oldest known manuscripts of the Old Testament are not really ancient. In Petrograd there is a Prophet codex written in 916 A. D. and also a manuscript of the entire Old Testament written in 1009 A. D. In comparison with the antiquity of the original writings these copies seem almost modern. We have New Testament manuscripts centuries older than these. In curious wonder we ask, How were these writings preserved and handed down in the vast interval from the time of their original composition until the printing of the Hebrew text, in the fifteenth century of our era?

We must begin with a brief inquiry into the early

manner of writing Hebrew. For many centuries the
Hebrew was written with consonants only, the vowels
being supplied by the reader. It is as if we were accus-
tomed to write our English as follows: th hrs rns fst
(the horse runs fast). So long as the Hebrew was the
vernacular of a whole people, this method of writing
presented no very serious obstacles to the clear understanding of the meaning. Even in English such a mode
of writing is not altogether impracticable. It is the
method of much shorthand writing. As soon, however,
as the spoken language became unfamiliar to the Jews
themselves, the uncertainties of a merely consonantal
writing began to appear. And as different scribes inevitably differed here and there as to which of two or more
vowel sounds should be supplied, it was clear that something must be done to remedy the confusion. The situation is well described by Professor Robertson Smith
("The Old Testament in the Jewish Church," pp. 50,
51) : "Let me ask you to realize precisely how the scribes,
at and before the time of Christ, proceeded in dealing
with the Bible. They had nothing before them but the
bare text denuded of its vowels, so that the same words
might often be read and interpreted in two different ways.
A familiar example of this is given in Heb. 11:21, where
we read of Jacob leaning upon the top of his 'staff'; but
when we turn to our Hebrew Bible as it is now printed
(Gen. 47:31), we find there nothing about the 'staff';
we find the 'bed.' Well, the Hebrew for 'the bed' is
hammittah, while the Hebrew for 'the staff' is *hammatteh.*
The consonants in these two words are the same, the
vowels are different. But the consonants only were
written, and therefore it was quite possible for one person
to read the word as 'bed,' as is now the case in our Eng-

lish Bible, following the reading of the Hebrew scribes; and for the author of the Epistle to the Hebrews, on the other hand, to understand it as a 'staff,' following the interpretation of the Greek Septuagint. Beyond the bare text, which in this way was often ambiguous, the scribes had no guide but oral teaching. They had no rules of grammar to go by; the kind of Hebrew which they themselves wrote often admitted grammatical constructions which the old language forbade, and when they came to an obsolete word or idiom they had no guide to its meaning, unless their masters had told them that the pronunciation and the sense were so and so."

The need of indicating the vowel sounds was keenly felt wherever there was serious doubt as to how a given text was originally intended to be read. Now, in order to supply the deficiency of the vowels, the Jews did not invent new letters, but merely added little marks or "points" above and below the letters of the old text. When were these vowel points added? The Jews have a tradition that they were added by Ezra, in the fifth century before Christ, and that he was fully inspired by God in this work, and so was preserved from making any mistakes. It was only in the sixteenth and seventeenth centuries that certain French scholars showed this tradition to be without foundation. It was proved that the Masoretes (that is, the scribes who through many generations sought to establish the true *Masora,* or "tradition") added the vowel points more than a thousand years after Ezra. The vowel system cannot be traced farther back than the seventh century. The Masora was completed and committed to writing at Tiberias in Palestine at the latest before the close of the ninth century. The Masora consists not only of the vowel points in the text, but also of many textual notes in the margin and at the foot of the page. Now, it was this Masoretic text that became *the received text* for Jews and Christians alike; and the doctrine of its infallibility was for centuries generally accepted. When criticism began to show that there were errors in this text, a storm of protest arose. Multitudes of good men fancied that the life and health of religion were imperiled, if the infallibility of Holy Scripture was made doubtful.

The Masoretes wrought, of course, as best they could; and to them and to a multitude of Jewish scholars since their time we must accord high praise for their scrupulous care to preserve and transmit the true text of their sacred books. Yet it is certain that this period of extreme care and diligence was preceded by a long period of laxity, in the course of which various corruptions found their way into the Hebrew text. It was only after the mischief had been done that the rabbis undertook a work which, while guarding the text against further corruptions, only tended to fix such errors as had already slipped in.

Of course, the errors of judgment in fixing the vowel points are not the only errors in the Old Testament text. Far more serious are the errors of the earlier copyists. Let us strive to make clear to our minds the conditions under which the books had to be transmitted during those earlier centuries. As yet there was no "received text," and no group of scribes coöperating in an effort to keep the text pure. The individual copyist may have written from dictation, thus being liable to the reader's errors as well as his own; or, if working without the help of a reader, errors would still be sure to slip in. The mistakes of one copyist, moreover, are destined to be perpetuated by those that follow him. But some of the most serious corrruptions of the text seem to have been due to the misplacing of some of the sheets of manuscripts. The corruptions in some of the books—Micah, for example—are seriously disturbing to the sense.

On the whole, however, the ancient Hebrew literature has been wonderfully well transmitted. The fact that we have not an errorless text should show us that our faith is not dependent on such matters. Of course, God might have miraculously prevented all scribes (and printers) from making mistakes, but in his wisdom he has not done so.

Since the time of the Masoretes the copying of the books of the Old Testament was done with much skill; many of the manuscripts were beautifully and elaborately executed. And then when the art of printing threw the copying by hand into disuse, some of the printed editions were very well done. Abundant photographic reproductions of specimens of notable Hebrew manuscripts and of important printed editions may be found in the Jewish Encyclopædia and in Geden's "Introduction to the Hebrew Bible."

2. *Ancient Versions and Their Relation to the Text.* The special account of the ancient versions of the Old Testament belongs in a later chapter. For our present purpose it is necessary merely to point out how the ancient versions assist in determining the original form of the Hebrew writings. When we have fully weighed the fact of the vast interval of time between the oldest extant and the original manuscripts of the Old Testament, we shall naturally be eager to consult the ancient versions in order to ascertain how far they seem to agree with the Masoretic text. For it is manifest that the text used by the ancient translators, being so much earlier, was probably

closer to the original than the Masoretic text. In the
ancient versions we find reflected the text that was in
vogue in the times and places in which the translations
were made. By inference we can take these ancient versions and reconstruct with approximate accuracy the text
that underlay them.

The ancient *Samaritan Pentateuch,* though it may itself
be considerably altered from its original form, gives us
some fair notion of the state of the Hebrew Pentateuch
at the time when the Samaritans withdrew from fellowship with the Jews. When the first copy of the Samaritan
Pentateuch was brought to Europe, in 1616 A. D., it
attracted great attention. Scholars observed that in many
places it agreed with the ancient Greek version, the
Septuagint, where both differed from the Masoretic
Hebrew text; but it also bore marks of careless copying
and even of arbitrary alterations for the purpose of conforming the text to the alterations in religious customs
and traditions that had been introduced by the Samaritans. On the whole the official Hebrew text is doubtless
much the purer of the two; yet at a good many points the
Samaritan version affords the means of correcting the
Hebrew text.

Of far greater importance for the textual critic is the
Greek translation of the Old Testament known as the
Septuagint. There is reason to believe that the text of
the Septuagint has been preserved in a much less corrupt
form than that of the Samaritan Pentateuch. Still, even
here errors of copyists are numerous enough. The excellence of large portions of the Septuagint version—for
example, the Pentateuch and the Psalms are generally
well done—helped to give the whole version a very wide
acceptance in its day. On the other hand, the poor ren-

dering of other books and especially their divergence from the recognized Hebrew originals, and, finally, the spread of very poor copies of the Septuagint, led to other Greek translations. Of such there were three of importance, namely, those of Aquila, Theodotion, and Symmachus.

So variant and uncertain had the current text of the Old Testament Scriptures become—especially in the Greek, which was the only form in which they were known to most Christians in the early centuries—that Origen (185–254 A. D.) made a grand effort to purify it. He prepared a vast work called the Hexapla (i.e., "sixfold"), in which he set in parallel columns the following texts: (1) The Hebrew original, (2) a Greek transliteration of the same, (3) the translation of Aquila, (4) that of Symmachus, (5) that of the Septuagint, (6) that of Theodotion. To the text he added a multitude of critical marginal notes. The work, which seems never to have been copied, was preserved in Cæsarea until the beginning of the seventh century, when it was destroyed in the Arabian conquest of the country. A few extracts have been preserved and a Syriac version of the Prophets and Hagiographa (Kethubim).

These versions, together with a number of important ones based upon the Septuagint, all shed some light upon the Hebrew text. This is true especially of Jerome's version, which came to be known as the *Vulgate,* made in the years 390 to 405. On the whole this is a magnificent work. In the course of 1500 years, Jerome was the only scholar who was entirely equal to such a task. But the translation was often ill copied, and the copies, moreover, sometimes showed a careless mingling with portions of the earlier Latin versions. Since it was produced at so early a date, and since its rendering of the Old Testament was based largely upon the Hebrew text, it throws much light upon the state of that text as it existed at the time.

Thus—in manuscript copies and through versions—was the Old Testament brought down to the time of the invention of printing. Until comparatively recently all printed editions of the Hebrew Bible followed the Masoretic text. In recent years critical editions of the Old Testament have been undertaken.

CHAPTER XVI

THE TRANSMISSION OF THE NEW TESTAMENT TEXT

1. *Manuscripts.* The New Testament scriptures were doubtless originally written upon papyrus. Where a single sheet was insufficient, the writing surface was extended at pleasure by pasting sheet to sheet; the whole then was rolled upon a small rod. Only the inner surface was written upon. It was upon such papyrus sheets and rolls that the apostles and evangelists wrote, and upon such were their books copied and again copied in the first Christian centuries. Of the ancient writings on papyrus multitudes of fragmentary remains have been discovered in Egypt, where alone of all the seats of ancient civilization the dryness of the climate made such a thing possible. A very few of these fragments contain portions of the New Testament. These papyrus fragments are for the most part older than the oldest New Testament parchment codices. In general, papyrus was preferred to the skins for the reception of writing, except where these were prepared with special skill from the choicer animals. At about the beginning of the fourth century, however, the use of parchment began to come into special favor, especially for books which were designed to be long preserved. With the use of parchment there came also a change in the outward form of books. Instead of the roll came the codex; the sheets were placed one upon the other and bound in what we know as book form.

A parchment codex could be wonderfully executed and ornamented. By the use of a rule and a metal stylus the page was lined; this enabled the scribe to give the manuscript a pleasing regularity. The letters—during a long period—were of the uncial type; at a later time this was superseded by the freer but less beautiful cursive script. Sometimes the parchment was colored with purple tints of various shades, and upon this they wrote with gold or silver ink. A chief feature of the copyist's art was the drawing of elaborate head-pieces and initials, wholly or partially filled in with gold or other beautiful colors.

The manuscripts of the fourth to the eighth century, inclusive, are all in uncial writing, those after the tenth century only in the cursive style, while in those of the ninth and tenth centuries both styles are used.

It is interesting to know that the oldest extant Greek manuscripts of any considerable compass are copies of the New Testament scriptures. The science of Greek palæography is so well developed as to enable scholars to fix the age of a Greek manuscript with fairly close approximation.

The whole number of known New Testament manuscripts, entire or partial, is about 2500. Generally speaking, the oldest manuscripts are, of course, the most important, since they have naturally suffered less than the later copies from the inadvertencies and errors of the scribes. The number of the uncial manuscripts (called also majuscules, i.e., manuscripts written with capital letters) is small in comparison with that of the cursives (called also minuscules); but the few uncials outweigh the many cursives.

It is an established custom to designate the majuscules by a letter of the Latin, Greek or Hebrew alphabet, and the minuscules by Arabic numerals. Recently, however, an entirely new system has been proposed by von Soden in his elaborate critical edition of the Greek New Testament. Whether the new system (which is based upon the idea of a genetic grouping) will displace the old is doubtful.

Of the Greek manuscripts of the New Testament only a few require special mention here. Two of these belong to the *fourth century,* namely, the Codex Vaticanus (B) and the Codex Sinaiticus (designated by the Hebrew letter Aleph ℵ). Both are very clearly and beautifully written. The first is the more accurate of the two, but unfortunately considerable portions of the (originally complete) manuscript have been lost. The existence of the Sinaitic manuscript began to come to light in 1844 through the researches of Tischendorf. It was in the library of the Monastery of St. Catherine on Mt. Sinai that he first got a glimpse of some pages of the codex, but it was not until years later that he was permitted to examine it and to have it brought to Cairo (in 1859) and finally to have it presented to the Czar of Russia. Since then it has reposed in the library in Petrograd, where it is esteemed as its chief treasure. In 1862 the Czar had it photographically reproduced and published in a magnificent edition, and thus made accessible to the scholarly world. In 1889, Pope Leo XIII. permitted the same thing to be done for the Vatican Codex. The Codex Sinaiticus has the distinction of being our only complete uncial manuscript of the New Testament.

The Alexandrian manuscript (A) dates from the fifth century, and ranks in importance next to B and ℵ. It was presented to Charles I. by Cyril Lucar, Patriarch of Constantinople, in 1682, and is preserved in the British

Museum. It lacks the most of Matthew and some leaves from John and 2 Corinthians; otherwise it presents our New Testament writings complete. At the end we find the First Epistle of Clement entire and a portion of his Second Epistle; originally the manuscript included also the Psalms of Solomon.

A fourth manuscript of great interest is the Codex of Ephraem Syrus (C). It is a palimpsest, or rescript. It was no uncommon practice, on account of the costliness of parchment, to rub out an old manuscript in order to obtain the necessary skin for a new writing. In many cases the older writing was of vastly more value than the new. This is decidedly the case in the present instance. A beautiful Biblical manuscript of the sixth or possibly the fifth century was erased to make room for some theological treatises of Ephraem, a Syrian church doctor of the twelfth century. Only by the application of chemicals was it possible to restore the earlier writing to legibility. The codex of Ephraem is in the National Library at Paris.

The four manuscripts just noticed include, in addition to the New Testament, also the Old Testament in Greek.

A very curious but important uncial manuscript remains to be mentioned. It is the Codex Bezae (D), in the University Library of Cambridge. It was presented to the University in 1581 by Theodore Beza, who had obtained it from the monastery of St. Irenæus at Lyons in 1562. It was written in the sixth century and in the West. It is a Græco-Latin manuscript, the Greek on the left-hand page, the corresponding Latin version on the right—only that the Latin does not always exactly correspond to the Greek text. In many ways it is a curious document. Would-be correctors have frequently tampered with the manuscript. Above all, we are struck by a number of interpolations in the text, the most of them being entirely unsupported by other manuscripts.

These five are by far the most important of the hundred or more uncial manuscripts of the New Testament. When we turn to the cursive manuscripts we may be sure that few of them possess great value for determining the true text. It is, however, evident that a comparatively modern cursive may have been copied from a very ancient and very excellent uncial manuscript, or have an excellent pedigree. Indeed, this has been shown to be the case with several of the cursives. On the whole, the critical study of these relatively late copies of the New Testament is more and more commending itself to the scholars of our day.

Not one of the five most important uncials and not many even of the best cursives were known to the translators of the King James Version of the Bible (published in 1611). For their translation of the New Testament they chiefly used the third and fourth editions of Erasmus' Greek New Testament.

2. *The Printed Text.* Erasmus in 1516 published in Basel his *editio princeps* of the Greek New Testament. In 1522 appeared Cardinal Ximenes' Complutensian Polyglot, of which the New Testament text was printed as early as 1514. In both instances the text was based on only a few late manuscripts. The later editions of Erasmus' New Testament introduced scarcely any improvements. Robert Stephens' New Testament in Greek appeared first in 1546 (it was in the fourth edition of this work, 1551, that the indication of verses was first introduced). Theodore Beza published a Greek New Testament in 1565, of which several editions appeared,

the last in 1598. But it was the New Testament of the Elzevir brothers in Leyden (from 1642 on) that finally won the whole field and became the *textus receptus* (the "received text"). This text maintained its place, in spite of some serious attempts at textual criticism, until about 1830. Until that time the editors contented themselves with reproducing the textus receptus and merely adding at the foot of the page the variant readings. In 1831 Lachmann broke with the textus receptus and gave the world the first critical New Testament text in modern times. Since then many great scholars have wrought at the task of restoring the primitive text. Among the most important names here are Tregelles, Scrivener, Westcott and Hort in England, and Tischendorf, Gregory (an American), Nestle, and von Soden in Germany.

3. *Early Versions.* The early versions of the New Testament have a like significance for ascertaining the true text as we found to be the case with the versions and text of the Old Testament. The earliest versions of the New Testament were the Old Latin and the Old Syriac. These belong in the second century. To the third century belongs the Coptic version. Then follow, from the fourth century on, the Gothic, Ethiopic, Armenian, Arabic, Persian and other versions. Not all of them were made directly from the Greek; some are "daughter versions."

The value of a translation as an aid in getting at the true text of the original depends upon the age of the version and upon our ability to determine where the version was made, and thus ascertain what type of text the translators must have used. Much study has been bestowed upon the problem of the genealogy and geography of the texts. So far has New Testament textual criticism advanced that experts can tell us with approximate certainty not only when and where most of the translations were made, but also the type of text that prevailed in a given locality. Evidently this knowledge is of great indirect help in determining the true original reading. Direct testimony, however, still remains the weightier, and this is to be found in the manuscripts rather than the versions. Moreover, every sober critic knows that we cannot infer with absolute certainty the exact form of the text that underlies a given translation. The difficulty is made all the greater because but few ancient languages were rich enough to afford the possibility of a really adequate rendering of the Greek.

The most important ancient version of the New Testament is, of course, the Vulgate (i.e., the Vernacular or Common Version). The Vulgate rendering of the New Testament was in the main a revision of the Old Latin (called also the Itala); and since this earlier version was not very carefully done, the Vulgate has inherited from it a good many faults. It will be of interest to note that about 8000 manuscripts of the Vulgate are known.

Of great interest to the student of the New Testament text are the Syriac versions. The famous Diatesseron (a "Gospel Harmony," or "Four Gospels in One"), compiled by Tatian in the latter part of the second century, widely used in Syria in the third and fourth centuries, and known to Bible scholars until the fourteenth century, has been lost. We have, however, Latin and Arabic translations of the work, together with an Armenian version of St. Ephraem's commentary upon it. Of the Old Syriac version, on the other hand, we have two famous manuscripts (dating from the fifth century). One of these, brought from Egypt to England, was published by Cureton in 1858. The second was discovered by Mrs. Lewis and her sister, Mrs. Gibson, in the Convent of St. Catherine at Mt. Sinai in 1892. It is a palimpsest. Inasmuch as it represents a translation of the four Gospels made in the second century, its readings are of much value to the textual critic.

4. *Quotations in the Church Fathers.* Along with the manuscripts and versions the student of the New Testament text must also pay heed to the *quotations from the Church Fathers.* These have a very real value for our purpose, since they are based upon texts more ancient than any manuscript now extant. Yet these quotations must be used with caution; for it is evident that they may, in many instances, have been made from memory and therefore sometimes inaccurately.

All these witnesses to the New Testament text must be faithfully and intelligently used. And, indeed, the text of no other ancient writing has been studied with anything like the zeal and patience that have been bestowed upon the text of the New Testament. Moreover, in most instances a thorough comparison of all the documentary testimony makes very clear what the original reading must have been. By an incredible amount of labor a vast number of errors have been corrected. All recent versions of the New Testament have been based upon a critical text.

We are not, however, to conclude that we now have, or ever shall have, an essentially perfect text. There are uncertainties that can never be removed. These are, indeed, for the most part quite unimportant. Certainly not a single fundamental truth of the Christian faith is seriously involved in any of the questions of textual criticism. Nevertheless, these uncertainties as to the exact form of the original text remain. This state of affairs warns us not to be beguiled into a false dogmatism as to the formal perfections of the Bible. The Bible is clearly not in its outward state a miraculous book. In its composition and transmission it has been subject to the same general conditions as have obtained in the case of all other books. Not in its formal aspects but in its message the true eminence of the Bible is to be found.

Chapter XVII

THE BIBLE VERSIONS: BEFORE WICKLIF

We have made a rapid survey of the way in which our Bible, Hebrew and Greek, was handed down to us. It remains for us to trace in outline the history of the bringing of the Bible to other nations, ancient and modern, who spoke neither Hebrew nor Greek. It is a wonderful story, marked by great devotion and even heroism. We shall have space for only very brief notices of other than English versions, and even the story of our English Bible can here be told only in outline.

1. *Ancient Versions of the Old Testament.* That the Old Testament should have been translated at all into other languages is a fact of striking significance. It was a national literature and not designed primarily for all races. But it must be observed that the earliest versions were not designed for Gentiles, but in one instance for the Samaritans, who were closely related to the Jews and accepted only the Pentateuch, and in another for the Jews of the Dispersion, who had become more familiar with Greek than with Hebrew.

The notice of the *Samaritan Pentateuch,* contained in the last chapter, may suffice for this important ancient version of a portion of the Old Testament. Of far greater importance in other regards is the Greek version of the whole of the Old Testament, known as the *Septuagint.* This version derived its name from an ancient legend preserved for us in the so-called "Letter of

Aristeas" and in Josephus' "Antiquities of the Jews," XII, 2 : 4. According to this account, Ptolemy Philadelphus, king of Egypt, 285–246 B. C., being zealous for matters of learning and literature, and taking pride in the great library at Alexandria, was induced by his librarian Demetrius of Phaleron to make provision for the translation of the Hebrew Scriptures renowned for their wisdom. He therefore sends ambassadors, loaded with gifts, to Eleazer, the High Priest at Jerusalem, and requests him to send in return a copy of the Hebrew Scriptures with learned men able to translate them into the Greek. Eleazer selects 72 able scribes, 6 from each of the 12 tribes, and puts into their hands a copy of the Scriptures written in golden letters. Upon their arrival in Alexandria the 72 scribes are brought to a house on the island Pharos, where, in consultation together, they accomplish their task faultlessly in just 72 days. According to a later form of the legend, the 72—the number was finally rounded off to 70—were placed in as many separate cells and at length each came forth with the complete translation of the whole body of the Scriptures. Upon comparison it was found that all the translations were exactly alike, even to the letter. Thus was the divine inspiration of their work established.

That there is little truth behind this fantastic legend is almost certain. It is clear that the whole of the Old Testament was not translated in the time of Ptolemy Philadelphus, for some of its books were at that time not yet written. It is, however, almost equally clear that in the course of his reign at least the Pentateuch was translated. The translation of the remaining books soon followed; it is, at any rate, a fact that about 130 B. C. the grandson of Jesus the son of Sirach and editor of the latter's book of "Wisdom" knew not only the books of the Law but also those of the Prophets and other Old Testament writings in Greek translation.

What may we fairly conclude as to who the translators were and as to the circumstances in which their work was done? In the first place, it is clear that the translation was only gradually accomplished, and was not the work of a group of scholars in mutual consultation. The quality of the work is very unequal. In some instances it is slavishly literal and again it is wantonly free. Here and there considerable additions are made. In the second place, it is clear that the work as a whole was undertaken on behalf of Greek-speaking Jews in Alexandria and other parts of Egypt—of Jews who no longer could read their Scriptures in the original. At the same time there are in the translation signs of a desire to commend their Scriptures to the surrounding Gentiles, for here and there expressions have been chosen with manifest accommodation to the Greek sensibilities. Finally, the translators cannot have been Palestinian Jews, because they betray, in many instances, an inadequate knowledge of the Hebrew.

Reference has already been made in the chapter on the Transmission of the Old Testament Text to other Greek versions, those of Aquila, Theodotion and Symmachus. We have, however, yet to note five translations based upon the Septuagint: (1) the Coptic version (the Coptic was one of the languages of Egypt); (2) the Ethiopic version; (3) the Gothic version of Ulfilas from the fourth century (only fragments of the book of Nehemiah have been preserved; (4) the Armenian version from the fifth century, based upon the text of Origen's Hexapla; (5) the

Old Latin version (the "Itala"), probably from the second century.

It is, however, probable that, in addition to the Itala, there were several other old Latin versions, for the fragments which have been preserved show marked variations, even where they are renderings of the same passages. They adhere as closely as possible to the original. In spite of this fact, which in itself is a merit, these versions more and more showed their inadequacy, so that Pope Damasus (366–384) committed to Jerome the task of revising it. Jerome began his work of revision with the help of the current text of the Septuagint and then of the text of Origen's Hexapla. Soon, however, he was persuaded of the necessity of an entirely new work. Thus arose an essentially independent translation from the original Hebrew. It was, however, a translation in which much use was made of the Greek versions, especially that of Symmachus; also the renderings of the Itala influenced Jerome. Jerome's version, it should be remembered, and some of the others included also the New Testament with the Old.

It would be hard to overestimate the historical importance of the Vulgate. It exerted an immense influence upon the later versions of northern and western Europe. Every version of the Old Testament, as well as of the New, since its time has received a powerful impress from the Vulgate. But its significance for the textual criticism of the Old Testament is considerably qualified by the fact that Jerome made extensive use of other versions and so was not always careful to follow the original text with absolute faithfulness.

Two other versions of the Old Testament remain to be mentioned. The first of these is the Peshitto, that is, the

Old Syriac version; the Old Testament portion of it dates probably from the second century, and is the work of a number of translators. It is valuable as a clew to the original form of the Hebrew text. Since, however, it shows itself to have been influenced by the Greek translation, its value for the textual critic is not what it might have been. The other version is that known as the Targums, that is, translations by the Jewish scribes into the vernacular Aramaic. But since these were more or less free paraphrases—they were never meant to be the *official* text for the people—they throw less light upon the original text than one might have expected.

2. *Ancient Versions of the New Testament*. For a long time the gospel was spread chiefly among peoples who understood the Greek language. There is, as we have seen, a very definite early Christian tradition that the earliest Gospel was written in Aramaic or "Hebrew," but we are sure that these first records were soon circulating in Greek versions, the Aramaic originals being early lost. All the primitive Christian literature that has been preserved to us is exclusively in Greek.

The earliest versions of the New Testament were the *Old Latin* and the *Old Syriac*. These, together with the Coptic version and those made still later into the Gothic, Ethiopic, Armenian, and Persian tongues, have already been referred to in our study of the transmission of the New Testament text. We should, however, bear in mind that the historical significance of these versions is not chiefly to provide material for the textual critic. These versions have a great interest for us in showing the power of the gospel to penetrate into all nations and languages. The version of St. Jerome is by far the most important of the ancient Latin versions of the New Testament, but we know it was not the first. But even the "Old Latin" version, which formed the basis of Jerome's work, may not have been strictly the first. There is reason to believe that portions of the New Testament were turned into Latin at a very early date and that, on the basis of these there grew up—not under a single hand, but under several —the Old Latin version (the Itala). Jerome's version, as he finally sent it forth, was either his original work or at least his own revision of early renderings. This version was often rather carelessly copied with the result that the text became rather uncertain. In 1590 Pope Sixtus V. put forth a corrected edition. This edition was, however, far from perfect, and Clement VIII. the successor of Sixtus V., almost immediately undertook a revision (1593–1598). This last has been the official standard ever since. Yet even this edition has much need of correction.

3. *Mediæval Bible Versions before Wicklif.* The impression prevails rather widely that during the whole of the Middle Ages nothing was done to give the Bible to the people in the vernacular tongues. This, however, is an error. Between the fourth and the end of the fifteenth century no fewer than sixteen translations of the Bible, or portions of it, were made into the principal languages of Europe. Yet it is true that during all the Middle Ages the Bible was nowhere the people's book.

Two chief causes brought about this deplorable estrangement of the people from their Bible. One was the general want of learning. The people, for the most part, could not read any book whatsoever, even if they could have afforded to possess books—so large a book (or library) as a manuscript Bible was a very costly thing. The other reason was that the whole method and spirit of the Roman church's dealings with the laity made direct acquaintance with the Bible quite unnecessary to them. Indeed, the church denied the right of private judgment in matters of religion. Although the Bible was a book of divine inspiration, the laity could not read it aright without the direct guidance of the clergy, hence the Bible was virtually forbidden to the laity.

It was with the dawning of the Protestant Reformation that the grand thought of giving the Bible to the common people began to be realized. The Reformation itself was begotten of a new knowledge of the Bible. It was from the direct reading of the New Testament that Luther received the light that through him blazed abroad until half of Europe was flooded with the word of the gospel. Those who had thus found the light in the Bible were then zealous to give that Bible to the people.

The remains of German translations of the Bible reach back into the ninth and even the eighth century. The earliest German translator known to us by name was Notker of St. Gall, Switzerland (died 1022). His translation of the Psalms and the Song of Solomon has been preserved, while his translation of Job has been lost. After him came Williram, a Bavarian (died 1085), from whom we possess a metrical paraphrase of the Song of Solomon, accompanied by a prose exposition of the same. Somewhat later came metrical versions of Genesis and other portions of the Bible, mostly by unknown hands. In the twelfth century the metrical paraphrases give way to prose renderings. In this period it is chiefly the historical books that are translated, since these were so much more easy to understand than the prophets and some of the poetical books. Other versions followed from time to time. None of them, however, included the whole Bible, until in 1466 there appeared in Strassburg the first printed German Bible.

But these repeated efforts to give the Bible to the German people remained comparatively fruitless until the Reformation. In other countries of Europe not much was done in this direction except in England, where, after the labors of worthy predecessors, we meet the heroic figure of John Wicklif.

4. *The English Bible before Wicklif.*—It was John Wicklif, "the morning star of the Reformation," who made the first translation of the whole Bible for the English people. But there were partial English versions— especially of the Gospels and the Psalter—even before Wicklif. These versions, however, were designed to assist the many unlearned members of the clergy rather than to make the Bible directly accessible to the common people. Very few of the laity could read—they had to obtain their knowledge of the Bible from the clergy. A vernacular version would have answered no actual demand except on the part of the members of the clergy who could not readily understand the Latin.

Before there was ever any attempt at a proper translation of the Scriptures into Anglo-Saxon the Bible was the basis of much that was sung or written. The Venerable Bede in his Ecclesiastical History gives us a very interesting account of Caedmon and his sacred minstrelsy. Caedmon was a cowherd, more than 1200 years ago, attached to the famous Abbey of Whitby. One night he was present at a feast where his masters and even some of the servants were amusing themselves, after the manner of the time, in impromptu song and easy alliterative rhyming. When the harp came toward Caedmon, he arose from the board and returned homeward. But sud-

denly, as he lay asleep in the stable, he was aroused by a
heavenly glory, and there appeared unto him One who
had been cradled in a manger six hundred years before.
"Sing, Caedmon," he said, "sing some song to me."
"I cannot sing," was the sorrowful reply; "for this cause
it is that I came hither." "Yet," said he who stood before him, "yet shalt thou sing to me." "What shall I
sing?" "The beginning of created things." And withal
a divine power came upon him, and words that he had
never heard rose up before his mind. The vision departed, but the poetic gift remained. Caedmon on the
morrow went forth a mighty poet. Hilda, the abbess,
heard the story of Caedmon's gift, and she translated for
him a story of the Scriptures, which he soon brought back
in the form of minstrel song. Other portions of Scripture followed. "He sang of the creation of the world, of
the birth of man, of the history of Genesis. He sang, too,
the Exodus of Israel from Egypt and their entrance into
the land of the promise, and many other narratives of
Holy Scripture. Of the incarnation also did he sing, and
of the passion; of the resurrection and ascension into
heaven; of the coming of the Holy Spirit, and the teaching of the Apostles."

While Caedmon was not a translator of the Scriptures,
his work deserves a place in this sketch, because it shows
in what manner a large part of the people must have
obtained their knowledge of the Bible in that age.

About the time of Caedmon's death, early in the eighth
century, certain scholars were producing Anglo-Saxon
versions of the Psalter and the Gospels. Of these by far
the greatest was Bede (d. 735 or 742?). The story of
his life and work is both impressive and charming. He
was the most famous scholar of his day in Western

Europe, and he made the monastery of Jarrow-on-the-Tyne a great center of literature, science and theology. We possess a letter written by his pupil Cuthbert to a fellow-student that gives us a touching account of the death of the Venerable Bede. A portion of the letter follows. It shows the great man's closing days and hours to have been spent in the translation of the Scriptures. "Our father and master, whom God loved, had translated the Gospel of John as far as 'What are these among so many?' . . . Then came the Tuesday before the Ascension. He began then to suffer much in his breath, and a swelling came to his feet, but he went on dictating to his scribe. 'Lose no time,' he said; 'I know not how long I may hold out, or how soon my Master may take me.' He lay awake the whole night praising God. . . . (On the following day, Wednesday, Bede continues his dictation. As the sun begins to set, the young scribe speaks.) 'There remains yet one chapter, master, but it seems very hard for you to speak.' 'No, it is easy,' Bede replied: 'take your pen and write quickly.' This he did. . . . 'And now, father, there is still one sentence unwritten.' 'Then write quickly.' . . . In a few minutes the youth said, 'It is finished.' 'Thou hast spoken truly,' replied Bede." He was then taken to the window where he had often prayed, and with the words of the Gloria Patri on his lips he breathed his last.

Among the Bible translators of a somewhat later period we find the name of Alfred the Great. Whether in his own person he was a Bible translator, as tradition affirms, may be doubted. But certainly he was zealous for the spread of the knowledge of the Bible. The Ten Commandments in Anglo-Saxon were made the very foundation of the laws of his realm. Also the Lord's Prayer and some other portions of the Scripture were given forth in the same tongue.

Not the earliest, yet by far the most celebrated, of the old Anglo-Saxon Bible manuscripts is embodied in a splendid illuminated folio known as the *Lindisfarne Gospels*. In its original form it was not an Anglo-Saxon but a Latin manuscript; the Anglo-Saxon is an interlined addition to the Latin text. The Latin manuscript is the work of Eadfrith, who afterwards became bishop of Lindisfarne (698–724). It is written on vellum, in double columns, and in a singularly beautiful script. The illuminated initials are executed with great skill. Many years afterward, namely, about 950, Aldred the priest interglossed the Latin text with an Anglo-Saxon rendering. This only slightly marred the beauty of the manuscript, and it obviously enhances its interest in other respects. After escaping destruction in many a perilous case, it is now preserved in the British Museum.

Chapter XVIII

BIBLE VERSIONS: WICKLIF AND AFTER

5. *Wicklif and the First English Bible.*—New Anglo-Saxon versions had ceased to appear about the close of the tenth century. The lapse of interest in Bible translation was probably due in the first instance to the Danish invasion of England; the continuance of the inactivity is doubtless to be ascribed to the Norman conquest (1066). Saxon prelates were displaced by Norman ecclesiastics, and the Saxon speech and Saxon Bibles were despised. The period of unsettled life and thought continued long in England. Eventually, however, there emerged an England that had overcome the feeling of conflict between peoples and languages. It was a united England, speaking neither the old Saxon nor the old Norman-French language, but a language which we call English. From the beginning of the fourteenth century the changes in language were very rapid; in the same period, too, the use of English by the upper classes was rapidly gaining ground. The latter part of the fourteenth century is notable for the beginnings of English literature proper. Sir John Mandeville published his "Travels" in 1356, and Chaucer wrote toward the close of the century. The former is one of the earliest books written in English (as distinguished from Anglo-Saxon). So we see that Wicklif's Bible (1380–1382) belongs to the first period of English literature. Had a version been put forth a few decades earlier, it must have been over-

whelmed in the tide of newly-forming speech and thus have been virtually lost to the people. But Wicklif came in the very nick of time. "If Chaucer is the father of our later English poetry, Wicklif is the father of our later English prose. The rough, clear, homely English speech of the ploughman and trader of the day, colored with the picturesque phraseology of the Bible, is, in its literary use, as distinctly a creation of his own as the style in which he embodied it, the terse vehement sentences, the stinging sarcasms, the hard antitheses, which roused the dullest mind like a whip" (J. R. Green, History of the English People, Vol. 1, p. 489).

The life of John Wicklif (ca. 1320–1384) fell in a time of grave abuses in the church in England. The people numbered about two millions, and the clergy between twenty and thirty thousand. These owned a third of the soil; their revenues were about double those of the king. Church patronage was a papal prerogative, and foreign ecclesiastics were appointed to English livings. In spite of the widespread distress caused by the Black Death the immense papal tribute from England was unabated. In the midst of these conditions Wicklif, the most eminent of Oxford schoolmen in his day, fearlessly took up the work of reformation. Unlike most of the clergy of his time, he was an earnest and genuine Bible Christian. From the simple teaching of the New Testament, which he had made his own rule of life, he looked for a revival of religion purged of corruptions and abuses. To this end he earnestly desired that the Holy Scriptures should be heard and read by the people, insisting that all Christian people "ought much to travail night and day about the text of Holy Writ, and namely (chiefly) the gospel in their mother tongue." He took a lively interest also in the political problems of his day. He was a leader in the protests of the English people against the aggressions of the papal see. On this account he was sent, along with others, as envoy to Bruges in 1374 to treat with the papal legate on Rome's disregard of the enactments of the English Commons.

On his return the King made him rector of Lutterworth near Oxford. Here he founded a fellowship of Poor Preachers. Henceforth until his death he toiled more assiduously than ever for the revival of religion and the reformation of the church. Naturally his efforts met with much opposition. His Poor Preachers the Bishops regarded as pestilent hedge-creepers, "sons of perdition under the veil of great sanctity." But the common people and not a few of the people of learning and rank recognized their worth. It may well have been one of this group—some have suggested it may have been Wicklif himself—whom Chaucer portrayed in his description of the "poor parson," the "good man of religion," who in all weathers traveled staff in hand to the widely-sundered houses in his parish, and "taught Christ's love, but first he followed it himself." Wicklif's boldness and activity with tongue and pen against religious errors and abuses naturally led to his arraignment for heresy. And indeed his doctrines were in many points opposed to the prevailing views in the church. It is, however, probable that his unorthodox views could have been tolerated but for the sharpness of his polemics, which caused personal enmities. He denounced the pretensions of the popes to temporal supremacy; a reprobate pope had no rightful power over the faithful in Christ. He insisted that the pope might be rebuked by cleric or layman; that churches habitually delinquent in ministering to the people might be deprived of their revenues; that friars should work for their living. He repudiated the prevailing doctrine of the mass and of the confessional. The pope, he declared, had no power to excommunicate a man, "unless he was first excommunicated by himself." The Bible, he affirmed, was the one ground of faith. The broad recognition of this principle carried with it the gradual repudiation of the whole Romish system, that is, of all that was peculiar to Rome. He desired that after Urban there should be no other Pope, but "Christendom ought to live, after the manner of the Greeks, under its own laws."

On two notable occasions Wicklif was publicly arraigned for alleged heresies. On both occasions he escaped with his life; on the second trial, however (at Blackfriars Monastery in London, in May, 1378), his teachings were condemned, and a few days afterwards he was excommunicated. That he was not put to death is ascribed chiefly to such powerful supporters as John of Gaunt and the Queen; but it is probable that the weakening of ecclesiastical authority through the Great Schism was also to Wicklif's advantage. When the hearing had been concluded, Wicklif, though condemned and excommunicated, was allowed to return to his quiet parish in Lutterworth.

For years Wicklif had been an ardent student of the Holy Scriptures. How fully he relied upon its teachings may be seen in the fact that in a single volume from his hand there are seven hundred quotations from the Bible. But the thing that lifts him into the rank of one of the greatest individual forces in religious history is his championship of the right of the people to the open Bible. "The Sacred Scriptures," he said, "are the property of the people, and one which no one should be allowed to wrest from them." And so it came about that, as he drew near the close of his life, he perceived that he could do no other work comparable to giving the Bible to the people in their own tongue.

In spite of his greatness in many things, Wicklif was not the man to bring about a radical reformation of the church. He was essentially a brave fighter, but he was not a constructive thinker and leader. Nor had he clearly grasped the deepest principles out of which an effectual reformation must spring. Besides, the time was not yet ripe; and the preachers, who at the first were so nobly inspired by Wicklif, afterwards in many instances ran into fanaticism and excesses.

Returning to Lutterworth from his trial at Blackfriars, Wicklif gave himself with the utmost ardor to the translation of the Bible. About the year 1380—the date cannot be absolutely fixed—the New Testament was completed. About two or three years later (1382 or 1383) the whole Bible was in the hands of the English people in their own speech. Wicklif himself is believed to have translated the whole of the New Testament with but little assistance from other scholars; the translation of the Old Testament was the work of several helpers, chiefly Nicholas Hereford, one of Wicklif's Oxford disciples. A revision and correction of the translation was issued in 1388; it is ascribed to John Purvey. The anonymous reviser states that with much labor and with the aid of "manie gode felawis and kunnynge at the correccioun of his translacion" the work was duly finished.

Wicklif's Bible was not printed until 1850. As to extant manuscripts of the same, about 170 (partial or complete) are known; the most of these give not the original Wicklif but Purvey's revision.

On the last Sunday of the year 1384 Wicklif was smitten with the palsy in the midst of the celebration of the Eucharist. He remained speechless until his death on the last day of the year. The hatred of his doctrines and even of his work as Bible translator continued with little abatement for many years. Bitter persecutions followed his adherents the Lollards; and after forty-four years his remains were exhumed and burnt and his ashes thrown into the brook at Lutterworth.

Wicklif prefixed a prologue or argument to each book in his version; some of these prologues are very interesting. He also wrote a noteworthy "Apology," in which he says: "O Lord God! sithin at the beginning of faith, so many men translated into Latin to great profit of Latin men; let one simple creature of God translate into English for Englishmen. For if worldly clerks look well their chronicles and books they shoulden find that Bede translated the Bible and expounded much in Saxon, that was English either common language of this land in his time. And not only Bede, but King Alfred that founded Oxenford, translated in his last days the beginning of the Psalter in Saxon, and would more if he had lived longer. Also Frenchmen, Beemers, and Britons han the Bible and other books of devotion translated into their mother language. Why shoulden not Englishmen have the same in their mother language? I cannot wit." (The spelling is in the main modernized.)

Wicklif's translation was, of course, based upon the Vulgate. Probably no man in England in his day would have been competent to undertake a translation out of the original Hebrew and Greek. But while Wicklif's version had not the merit of the most critical scholarship, it shows the admirable qualities of terseness, vigor and imagination. Later translators owed not a little to his happy renderings.

A few brief specimens of Wicklif's work will be of interest. The first is from the fourth chapter of Mark, at the beginning.

And eft Jhesus bigan for to teche at the see; and myche cumpany of peple is gedrid to hym, so that he, stying into a boot, sat in the see, and al the cumpany of peple was about the see, on the lond. And he taughte hem in parablis many thingis. And he seide to hem in his techynge, Heere yee. Loo! a man sowyinge goth out for to sowe; and the while he sowith, an other seed felde aboute the way, and bryddis of heuene (or of the eire) camen and eeten it. Forsothe an other felde doun on stony placis, wher it had nat myche erthe; and anoon it sprung vp, it welwide for heete, and it dried vp, for it hadde not roote. And an other felde doun into thornes, and thornes stieden vp, and strangliden it, and it gaue not fruyt. And an other felde doun in to good lond, and it gaue fruyt, styinge vp, and wexinge; and oon broughte thirtty fold, and oon sixtyfold, and oon a hundridfold. And he seide, He that hath eris of heering, heere (Mk. 4:1-9).

The following is the rendering of Matt. 3:1-6: In thilke dayes came Joon Baptist prechynge in the desert of Jude, saying, Do ye penaunce: for the kyngdom of heuens shall neigh. Forsothe this is he of whom it is said by Ysaye the prophete, A voice of a cryinge in desert, Make ye redy the wayes of the Lord, make ye rightful the pathes of hym. Forsothe that ilke Joon hadde cloth of the heeris of cameylis and a girdil of skyn about his leendis; sothely his mete weren locustis and hony of the wode. Thanne Jerusalem wente out to hym, and al Jude, and al the cuntre about Jordan, and thei weren crystened of hym in Jordan, knowlechynge there synnes.

No other noteworthy attempt to translate the Bible into English was made after Wicklif's time until some decades after the introduction of printing. This, of course, was due in part to the relative adequacy of Wicklif's version, but also in part to the church's strict prohibition of all translating or expounding of the Bible in the vulgar tongue without special permission from the proper ecclesiastical authorities. Such a decree was issued in 1408 at Oxford by the Provincial Council. And so almost a century and a half passed before the appearance of the next great figure in the history of the English Bible—William Tindale. But before Tindale comes Luther in Germany, whose work as a Bible translator has been of incalculable importance.

6. *Luther and the German Bible.*—In Germany the various efforts before the time of Luther to give the Bible to the common people were vigorously opposed by the Church. In 1486 the Archbishop of Mainz issued a decree forbidding the printing of the Bible in German. He declared that the noble Greek and Latin languages could not be rendered through the rude medium of the German; and, moreover, the laity in any event could not understand the Scriptures except as duly explained by the clergy. But the tide could not be stemmed. All the conditions of the religious and intellectual life of the people were such as to make futile every effort to suppress the growing desire to hear and read the Scriptures in the common tongue.

In March, 1517 (i.e., some seven months before the posting of the Ninety-five Theses), Luther published his version and exposition of the Seven Penitential Psalms, then in 1518 the Lord's Prayer and Psalm 110. Gradually the idea of a complete translation of the Bible matured in his mind. He began with the New Testament. The work was accomplished largely in his room in the Wartburg, near Eisenach, in the Thuringian forest, where he was kept for some time under the protection of Frederick the Elector of Saxony. On the 22nd of September, 1522, he issued the New Testament; the Old Testament, including the Apocrypha, was published twelve years later.

Luther translated the New Testament without assistance, using Erasmus' edition of the Greek New Testament for a text. For the Old Testament, however, he gladly availed himself of the help of various scholars. The text used was a Hebrew Bible printed in Brescia, Italy, in 1494. The work on the Old Testament was done chiefly in Wittenberg, where (as before his conflict with Rome) Luther was professor of theology. Here from week to week he gathered his friends together in his own house for his "Collegium Biblicum"—Melanchthon and Cruciger, and Bugenhagen, and various Jewish rabbis. And how they toiled to make the Hebrew writers speak German! Luther has given us a lively though brief account of his work. It was, he says, his constant habit "to look men everywhere in the mouth" in order to learn how they expressed themselves. "Not infrequently we sought and inquired two, three, and four weeks for a single word, and even then sometimes failed to find it." When we make clear to ourselves how very inadequate was the philological apparatus of the time, we shall begin to be able to appreciate Luther's stupendous work as Bible translator. On this point the poet-scholar Klopstock wrote: "Let no one that knows what language is come into Luther's presence without reverence! In no other nation

has a man done so much in the forming of its language."
But Luther had gifts as a translator that quite transcend
mere scholarship. He was a man of large and robust
personality, a man of the broadest human sympathy and
of a fine poetic feeling. And then, above all, he had a
devout and fervent Christian spirit. All these qualities
go to make up the ideal translator of the Bible, and no
other man in modern times so united these qualifications
in his own person as Luther did.

Luther's Bible instantly found the widest acceptance
among the German people. A second edition of the New
Testament had to be issued after three months, and before the publication of the Old Testament Luther had
issued seventeen editions of the New Testament, to say
nothing of some fifty reprints by others. It has maintained its place as the Bible of German Protestants until
this day. The standard text is that prepared by Canstein
and others (1667–1719); it is merely a corrected text,
with modernized spelling.

Luther's Bible was almost the creator of the modern
German language. Up to the time of this great work
the German people had no standard of speech; every
region had its peculiar dialect. Luther chose as his
medium the Saxon dialect. Under his hand its plastic
susceptibilities were wonderfully developed. He enriched
its vocabulary by expressions borrowed from many circles
and from many quarters. Take him all in all, Luther is
the greatest of Germans. Döllinger (a Roman Catholic
and later a leader of the "Old Catholic Church") said
of Luther: "It was Luther's supreme intellectual ability
and wonderful versatility that made him the man of his
age and of his nation. . . . He gave more to his nation
than any other one man ever did—language, popular

education, the Bible, sacred song. . . . It was he who put a stamp upon the German language as well as upon the German character. And even those Germans who heartily abhor him as a great heretic and betrayer of religion cannot help speaking his words and thinking his thoughts."

As was to be expected, the authorities of the Roman Church were very hostile to Luther's Bible. They felt it to be a work animated by the spirit of heresy; one of their scholars pointed out 1,400 heresies and falsehoods in the New Testament alone. It was particularly offensive to them that Luther had translated directly from the original Hebrew and Greek instead of the standard Vulgate. They determined, therefore,—though with reluctance—to meet the arch-heretic with an orthodox version. This plan they carried out, not by making an independent version, but by "correcting Luther's Bible according to the Vulgate." But the Catholic German Bible met with very little popular favor.

Luther's version was a powerful influence in all subsequent work of Bible translation in all languages. In England, Holland, France—indeed, in all the countries of Western and Northern Europe—its influence has been immense.

7. Before turning to Tindale in England, it will be found convenient briefly to sketch the work of *Bible translation in other countries of the Continent outside of Germany.* Less brilliant, yet not less loyal, were the efforts to give the Bible to the people in the *Dutch language.* As in Germany so also in Holland there was a long period of translating portions of the Scriptures for the common people—Rhyme-Bibles and the like. After the invention of printing there were Dutch Bibles from

the years 1477–1479, translated from the Vulgate. A better version from the Vulgate was issued in 1516. In the same year Erasmus published a Dutch translation of the New Testament from the Greek. When, however, Luther's New Testament became known, it was immediately (1523) translated into the Dutch and published at Antwerp and Amsterdam. It was far more in demand than Erasmus' version. Again in 1834 Luther's Old Testament was made the basis of a Dutch version. In 1526 the first complete Dutch Bible was published at Antwerp by Jacob Liesveldt. The translators are unnamed. This version also was based upon Luther's Bible, so far as that had been issued; for the rest it was based upon an older German version. A sixth edition of this work, carefully corrected, was published at Antwerp in 1542 and became the standard version for the Netherlands. As the notes were frankly anti-Romish, the Catholic Church issued injunctions forbidding anyone to read it. A canon of Louvain warned the people against the Liesveldt Bible as being a translation "not from the Latin, but from a foreign Bible, which had been translated into German by M. Luther and some others, helpers of his, notorious and damned heretics of our times, who, as they are rejectors of the holy Church, have Germanized the Bible out of different new translations, not following the old Latin or Vulgate of the universal Roman Church, and thus have they in many places stated things differently from what is contained in the Bible, and have perverted the Holy Scripture in such a way as to support their evil notions." The first warnings not proving effectual, it was announced that all who refused to burn heretical Bibles should themselves be burned at the stake. In 1545 Liesveldt himself was seized and beheaded because he had inserted a marginal note in his edition of the Bible declaring that our salvation depends on Christ alone. But of course the martyrdom served only to intensify the popular interest in the Bible in the vernacular.

The immense demand for the "heretical" Bibles soon led Roman Catholic scholars to issue an edition corrected according to the Vulgate. Several other Protestant revisions, based upon the German versions, followed until in 1591 Philip de Marnix, Lord of St. Aldegonde (referred to either as Marnix or St. Aldegonde) began a translation from the original tongues. It was never completed. Marnix's work was scholarly, but wanting in warmth and spiritual insight. It rendered a good service, however, and was the forerunner of the excellent Dutch authorized version published in 1637. The undertaking to make a really adequate translation was set in motion by the National Synod of Dort (Dordrecht) in 1618. The company of translators was perhaps the best that the nation could afford. Their work, though opposed (as every new version has been) by the unlearned, soon won its way to universal esteem. For scholarly accuracy, no version surpassed it until the various "revised versions" of the most recent decades. It remains the standard Dutch version until this day.

The history of the *French versions* is of far less interest than the importance of the French nation would lead us to expect. Yet we must remember that France is a Catholic country, and in no Catholic country has the work of Bible translation been pursued with the vigor that is characteristic of the work in Protestant countries.

As in all countries, so also among the French there were partial translations of the Bible in the Middle Ages. The earliest known translations date from the twelfth century. Kindred undertakings followed. The first highly significant version was that of Jacques le Fèvre d'Étaples (Jacob Faber Stapulensis), a professor in the Sorbonne, Paris. His zeal for the Bible was kindled by his acquaintance with Luther's work. He published a translation almost simultaneously with Luther (New Testament 1523–25, Old Testament 1530). His New Testament translation brought about his expulsion from his professorship, and he was forced to flee from France. In 1546 an edict was issued against him and his work, in which among other things, it was declared: "It is neither expedient nor useful for the Christian public that any translation of the Bible should be permitted to be printed; rather, they should be suppressed as injurious." Those who possessed a copy of this work were ordered to deliver it up within eight days.

As le Fèvre's version was based upon the Vulgate it has no such significance as that of Luther. It did not become the popular Bible of the French people. It was a version that satisfied neither the Catholic leaders nor the Protestants. It was printed chiefly outside of France. Several revisions of le Fèvre's work were made for the purpose of conforming it more perfectly to the Vulgate and to Roman Catholic ideas.

A better version in every way was that of the brothers Antoine and Louis de Sacy (1667 and 1668). This again was based upon the Vulgate, and it enjoyed the approval of Catholic authorities. A new translation had become indispensable because the French language had undergone great changes; but apart from the necessary modernization of the language this was doubtless a more correct version than le Fèvre's. It remains the most common version among French Catholics. In 1877 a considerably improved Catholic version (by the Abbé Glaire) was published, having the sanction of the clerical authorities. Like all other official versions it embodied notes which carefully guarded against heretical interpretations of the Scriptures. Again in 1886 a translation was issued with the sanction of the Archbishop of Paris. The translator was Henri Lassere. The work was received with great popular approval, but suddenly— about a year after its first publication—the ecclesiastical sanction was withdrawn. The book was placed in the Index Expurgatorius.

French versions of the Bible are notable for the marked difference between the Catholic and Protestant renderings. Le Fèvre's work was done by a man who was half reformer. It was therefore unacceptable to the Romans, and at the same time, scarcely acceptable to the Protestants. In 1535 Olivetan endeavored to supply the demand for a version that should embody the new evangelical ideas. Taking le Fèvre's work as a basis, but with the application of much independent research—especially in the Old Testament,—he produced a very meritorious version and one destined to play a most important part in the history of French Protestantism. In Olivetan's own lifetime many revised or altered editions of his work were put forth, some of them by other hands than his own. A more general revision of the Olivetan Bible by Martin appeared in 1696–1707, and this revision was in turn itself more than once revised—the last time near the middle of the nineteenth century. Another revision of Olivetan was made by Osterwald in 1724 (an improved edition 1744). This has enjoyed even more favor among Protestants than that of Martin and was itself revised in 1868 and 1887.

The history of Bible versions in other non-English lands merits our study, but for our present purposes it may be omitted.

8. *William Tindale.* Some ten or fifteen years after the death of Wicklif there was born in the city of Mainz (Mayence) a boy destined to deathless fame as the inventor (for the Western world) of the art of printing with movable type. The boy was Johann Gensfleisch by name. The name Gensfleisch, though not a pleasing one (in English it would be "Gooseflesh"), belonged to a family of excellent repute. Our Johann, however, eventually exchanged it for Gutenberg, a name belonging to a certain piece of property that had been acquired by his grandfather. After a residence of some duration in Strassburg, John Gutenberg returned to Mainz in 1444, and before the middle of the century he set up—in partnership with John Fust—his printing-press.

It is the time of the Renaissance. Already in Italy the revival of ancient lore had gone on apace; in other countries of Europe it was spreading rapidly. The fall of Constantinople in 1453 sent many Greeks into Italy. Some of these brought with them precious manuscripts. It was an interesting coincidence that just as Constantinople was falling to the Turks, the sheets of Cardinal Mazarin's Latin Bible were issuing from Gutenberg's press. It was the first entire book to be printed in Europe. The passion for learning had by this time become as intense in the countries of Northwestern Europe as it had been in Italy. Men of a degree of learning everywhere were impoverishing themselves by the purchase of Greek manuscripts. "As soon as I get money," wrote young Erasmus, "I shall buy Greek books; and then I shall buy some clothes." The new learning was not always fostered or approved by the Church.   On the contrary, the Revival of Learning was rightly regarded by many ecclesiastics as signifying a tendency to break away from the Church's authority.   The clergy, therefore, warned the people against the new learning.   As late as 1530 a French priest said from the pulpit: "They have found out a new language, called Greek; we must carefully guard ourselves against that language.   It will be the mother of all sorts of heresies.   I see in the hands of many people a book in that tongue called the New Testament.   It is a book full of brambles, with vipers in them."   But fortunately there were many zealous Christians, even before the Lutheran Reformation, who thought otherwise.   John Colet, one of Oxford's greatest lights, returned from travels in Italy on fire with zeal for Greek learning.   But not for the sake of mere learning.   "The knowledge of Greek seems to have had one almost exclusive aim for him. . . . Greek was the key by which he could unlock the Gospels and the New Testament, and in these he thought he could find a new religious standing-ground." (Green, A Short History of the English People.)   As Dean of St. Paul's in London, Colet delivered famous lectures on some of Paul's Epistles and other portions of the New Testament.   He died in 1519.

Six years before the close of the 15th century the Hebrew Bible was printed at Brescia; one year before Luther's Ninety-five Theses Erasmus issued his Greek New Testament.   Luther's translation, as we have noted, was made from the original tongues; the same is true of the English Bible of William Tindale.

William Tindale was born in 1484, that is, a year after the birth of Luther and just one hundred years after the death of Wicklif.   He early acquired distinction as a scholar at Oxford. Later he went to Cambridge. Here Erasmus had been professor for a time; indeed, it is possible that Tindale's earliest residence in Cambridge was before the departure of Erasmus. At all events Erasmus' Greek learning had inspired Tindale; especially the Greek New Testament (1516) was a joy to him. It was about this time that the thought of a new English version of the Bible began to stir in Tindale's mind. He went to London to obtain from the Bishop of that see the authority to make the translation of the New Testament; he desired also the Bishop's patronage in the undertaking. He brought with him a translation of an oration of Isocrates as proof of his competency for the task. The Bishop put him off, but he did not forbid the undertaking. His house, he said, was full, and he had more than he could feed; he advised Tindale to seek help elsewhere in London. And there, indeed, he did find friends and helpers. For half a year he was a welcome guest at the house of Humphrey Monmouth, a rich cloth merchant. From the ecclesiastical authorities he received not the least encouragement. Rather he was made to feel that he should meet direct opposition from that source. Therefore he concluded it was expedient to go abroad in order to finish his work. His purpose to give the Bible to the people was profound and immovable. Once, in disputing with an ardent supporter of the papacy as against personal liberty in religious matters, he had declared: "If God spare my life, ere many years I will cause a boy that driveth a plough shall know more of the Scripture than thou dost." Already for some time before his departure from London he had been toiling upon his translation. In May, 1524, furnished with means by "Humphrey Monmouth and certain other good men," he "took his leave of the realm and departed into Germanie." He took up his abode in Wittenberg, the home of Luther, the seat of the first Protestant university and center of the German Reformation. Here he finished his translation of the New Testament.

In the summer of 1525 we find Tindale and his amanuensis in Cologne, supervising a quarto edition of 3,000 copies of the New Testament. In the midst of the work a spying priest, John Cochlaeus of Frankfort, discovered his secret and betrayed him. Tindale made a hasty escape, bearing with him the sheets already printed, and journeyed by boat up the Rhine to Worms. Here a fresh edition was set up and printed—this time in octavo; it is believed that the quarto edition also was completed here. The two editions together would number 6,000 copies. These were ready for shipment to England so soon as the ice upon the river should yield. The books had to be smuggled into England and Scotland, and they were eagerly bought. King and Cardinal had been forewarned, and great efforts were put forth to suppress the edition. And indeed they were able to gather up a great number of copies and destroy them. But in Holland and elsewhere pirated editions appeared. After a time, of course, the early opposition to the giving of the Bible to the people was removed, for in the years 1531–1534 Henry VIII. effected a complete breach with Rome. While on the King's part this was not at all an expression of the principles of the Protestant Reformation, it was natural that it should have involved a policy of considerable toleration for all the anti-Romish doctrines. There was a powerful movement in the English Church toward a genuinely evangelical reformation. Just as soon, then, as the allegiance to Rome had been renounced, there came a degree of favor for liberal views. In the meantime, however, Tindale suffered the bitterest persecutions. After finishing the translation of the Old Testament and making revisions in that of the New, he was arrested at Antwerp by order of the Spanish Emperor, Charles the Fifth, in spite of the fact that he was lodged in the privileged house of the English Merchant Adventurers. After an imprisonment of about a year and a half in the bastile at Vilvorde he was brought forth on October 6, 1536, and burned at the stake. His last words—spoken in a loud voice—were: "Lord, open the King of England's eyes." His chief helper, the charming, blithe and youthful Frith, had been executed in England three years before this because he denied the Romish doctrine of transubstantiation.

Tindale's sense of the need of a vernacular version of the Bible is set forth in his Preface to Genesis: "I had perceaved by experyence, how that it was impossible to stablysh the laye people in any truth, except in their mother tonge, that they might se the processe, ordre and meaninge of the texts."

His purpose in translating the Scriptures we find expressed in the Prologue to the New Testament (the Cologne—quarto—edition, of which only eight sheets, less the title-page leaf, or 62 pages have survived to us) :—"I have here translated (brethren and susters moost dere and tenderly beloued in Christ) the newe Testament for youre spirituall edyfyinge, consolacion, and solas: Exhortynge instantly and besechynge those that are better sene in the tonges than y, and that have hyer giftes of grace to interpret the sence of the scripture and meanynge of the spyrite then y, to consydre and pondre my labour, and that with the spyrite of mekenes. And yf they perceyve in eny places that y have not attayned the very sence of the tonge, or meanynge of the scripture, or haue not geven the right englysshe worde, that they put to there handes to amende it, remembrynge that so is there duetie to doo. For we have not receyved the gyftes of god for oure selues only, or for to hyde them; but for to bestowe them unto the honouringe of god and christ, and edyfyinge of the congregacion, which is the body of christ."

Tindale translated in addition to the whole of the New Testament, "the v bookes of Moses, Josua, Judicum, Ruth, the bookes of the Kynges and the books of the Paralipomenon, Nehemias or the fyrste of Esdras, the Prophet Jonas, and no more of the holy scripture." Information as to who rendered help in the translation of the Old Testament is very incomplete. It is probable that the work on the Old Testament is less independent of the Vulgate and of Luther's version than is the case with the New Testament; and yet even for the Old Testament the original language was the basis of the translation.

Tindale was not an imposing personality like Wicklif and Luther, and yet he showed a constancy and fortitude that were beyond all praise. He possessed rare gifts for the work of a translator of the Scriptures. Much of the work of translation had to be carried on in places where he had not access to the versions of his predecessors on English soil. His dependence upon Wicklif was not so great as one might have expected; such as it was, it was largely due to the faithful impressions of his memory. His skill in handling the treasures of the English language and to develop its latent powers was altogether remarkable. In view of the influence of his version upon all later attempts to render the Bible into English, Tindale has been called "the father of the English Bible as we now have it." So compelling has been this influence that even in the Revised Version of 1881 and 1885 as many as 80 per cent of the words stand as Tindale fixed them.

The octavo edition of Tindale's New Testament contained, in addition to a long prologue, ninety-one marginal notes, of which the larger half were borrowed from Luther's New Testament and the rest were Tindale's own. He affixed notes also to the version of the Old Testament. A few examples of his notes will be of interest on all accounts and in particular will largely explain the animosity that was stirred up against their author. On Genesis 24 : 60 ("They blessed Rebekah") : "To bless a man's neighbour is to pray for him and to wish him good, and not to wag two fingers over him." On Exodus 32 : 35 ("And the Lord plagued the people") : "The Pope's bull slayeth more than Aaron's calf." On Numbers 23 : 8 ("How shall I curse whom God curseth not?") : "The Pope can tell how."

It will be profitable to compare the following specimen of Tindale's version with Wicklif's on the one hand and with the King James version on the other. The passage is Mark 4 : 1–9.

"And he began agayne to teache them by the see syde; and there gadered to gedder unto hym moche people, so greatly that he entered into a shippe, and sate in the see, and all the people was by the see syde, on the shoore. And he taught them many thynges in similitudes. And sayde unto them in his doctrine, Herken to. Beholde! the sower went forth to sowe. And it fortuned as he sowed, that some fell by the waye syde, and the fowles of the ayre cam, and devoured it uppe. Some fell on a stony grounde, where it had not moche erth; and by and by sprange uppe, because it had not deepth of erth. And as sone as the sun was uppe, it caught heet, and because it had nott rotynge, it wyddred awaye. And some fell amonge the thornes, and the thornes grewe uppe, and choked it, so that it gave no frute. And some fell apon good grounde, and did yield frute, that spronge, and grewe; and brought forthe some thirty folde, some fourty folde, and some an hundred folde. And he sayde unto them, He that hath eares to heare, lett him heare."

9. *Miles Coverdale.* We have seen William Tindale seized at Antwerp in the midst of his strenuous labors to bring his version of the Old Testament to a conclusion. He was not permitted to achieve the longed-for consummation. But it is significant that in the year of his imprisonment (1535) another Englishman was publishing a complete Bible in the language of the people. This was Miles Coverdale, and his translation was the *first complete Bible in the English tongue.*

The fierce opposition of the Bishops to Tindale's version was due, as we have seen, not so much to any fundamental objection to giving the Bible to the people as to the feeling that the translator was a heretic and his version ministered to heresy. Tindale was known to be in sympathy with Luther, and King Henry hated Luther and all his works. But the King did not deny the lawfulness or even desirability of a version of the Bible for the people, if it might be a translation duly supervised and sanctioned by the ecclesiastical authorities and by his royal self. In 1530 he joined with a prohibition of Tindale's New Testament a promise of a properly accredited version. On December 18, 1534, the upper house of the Convocation of the province of Canterbury, consisting of the Bishops, Abbots and Priors, petitioned the King to sanction the preparation of such a version, setting forth that there was need of such a version and praying that "the king's majesty should think fit to decree that the holy scripture shall be translated into the vulgar English tongue by certain upright and learned men to be named by the said most illustrious king and be meted out and delivered to the people for their instruction." In all this, of course, there is no reference to Miles Coverdale, yet it is clear from other testimony that Coverdale had already for some years been at work on a translation of the Scriptures, and that he had the encouragement and informal sanction of the Bishops for his undertaking. When therefore in the course of the following year he was ready with his translation, his work received the formal sanction of King and Bishops. His Bible must have been in press—probably at Zurich—at the very moment that Convocation put forth its petition to the King. The Coverdale Bible was published in October, 1535, and dedicated to "the most victorious Prynce and oure most gracyous soueraigne Lorde, Kynge Henry the eyght." In 1537 it was reprinted in England in folio and in quarto; one of these was the first Bible ever printed on English soil.

Coverdale, unlike Tindale, was a man of quiet spirit and altogether disinclined to controversy. He had, it would seem, less scholarship than Tindale, also less originality and vigor of expression; but he had a very fine literary instinct and admirable taste. It is especially worthy of note as a proof of the latter statement, that it is Coverdale's beautiful version of the Psalter that still holds its place in the Book of Common Prayer of the Church of England.

On the title-page of the first edition of Coverdale's Bible it is stated that it was translated "out of the Douche and Latyn," that is, probably, the German of Luther, the Swiss-German of Zwingli, the Latin of the Vulgate and of Pagninus. In the dedication to the King, Coverdale says: "I have nether wrested nor altered so moch as one worde for the mayntenaunce of any manner of secte; but have with a clear conscience purely and faythfully translated this out of fyve sundry interpreters, havyng onely the manyfest truth of the scripture before myne eyes." As Coverdale here mentions no names, we cannot know with certainty who "the fyve sundry interpreters" (translators) were. It is his title-page that mentions the "Douche and Latyn." It is, however, manifest that besides German and Latin versions he made much use of Tindale's translation, in so far as that had appeared. His dependence upon Tindale is especially marked in the New Testament; so great, indeed, that some have called the Coverdale Bible a revised Tindale. Nevertheless, Coverdale's work was of really great importance. If he had less originality and vigor than Tindale, he had more grace and good taste.

As far back as 1531 Tindale made, by the hand of a friend, the following communication to the King: "I assure youe, sayde he (Tindale), if it wolde stande withe the kinges most gracious pleasure to graunte only a bare text of the scriptures to be put forthe emonge his people, like as is put forthe emonge the subgectes of the emperour in these parties, and of other cristen princes, be it of the translation of what person soever shall please his magestie, I shall ymedyatly make faithful promise, never to wryte more, ne abide ij dayes in these parties after the same, but ymedyatly to repayre into his realme, and there most humbly submytt my selfe at the fete of his royall magestie, offerynge my bodye, to suffer what payne or tor-

ture, ye what dethe his grace will, so this be obteyned."
Of course the King's general attitude precluded an acceptance of the offer of one whom he regarded as a heretic.
But it must not be inferred that Coverdale, though he
enjoyed the favor of Bishops and King, put himself forward as an opponent of Tindale. Indeed, a positive
appreciation of Tindale's work is manifest in the "Prologue Myles Coverdale Unto the Christen reader" :—

"Considerynge how excellent knowledge and lernynge
an interpreter of scripture oughte to have in the tongues,
and ponderynge also myne owne insufficiency therein,
and how weake I am to perfourme the office of transla-
toure, I was the more lothe to meddle with this worke.
Notwithstondynge when I consydered how greate pytie it
was that we shulde wante it so longe, and called to my
remembraunce the adversite of them, which were not onely
of rype knowledge, but wolde also with all theyr hertes
have perfourmed that they beganne, yf they had not had
impediment: considerynge (I saye) that by reason of
theyr adversyte it coulde not so soone have bene broughte
to an ende, as oure most prosperous nacyon wolde fayne
have had it : these and other reasonable causes consydered,
I was the more bolde to take it in hande."

10. *Matthew's Bible and Its Revision by Taverner.*
The next English Bible is known as Matthew's Bible.
It was printed we do not know where—probably at
Antwerp—in 1537 by the same man that printed Tindale's revised New Testament in 1534. Two English
printers superintended the printing. The work was not
really a new translation, nor was the editor Thomas Matthew, this name being but a pseudonym of the real editor,
John Rogers, a friend of Tindale's. As Tindale's version
had been condemned and as Coverdale's could not be re-

garded as the special translation called for by Convocation in 1534, even though it circulated with royal sanction, there seemed to be room for another aspirant for the favor of both king and people. It was, however, no really new version that was offered, but only a revision of the versions. For reasons of policy these names were suppressed; and, as we have seen, even the name of the real editor (Rogers) does not appear. Cranmer, the Archbishop, took an interest in this new venture, and wrote to the Prime Minister of King Henry, asking him to obtain from His Majesty license for the free circulation of this book "untill such tyme that we, the Bishops, shall set forth a better translation, which I think will not be till a day after domesday." The title-page of Matthew's Bible bears the words: "Set forth with the Kinge's most gracyous lycense." Rogers' work of editing was judiciously done. There are marginal notes, as in Tindale's Bible, but they are more moderate than Tindale's. The first edition of the Matthew Bible numbered 1,500 copies.

In 1539 appeared *Taverner's Bible*. It was a revision of the Matthew Bible, with a few real improvements, and a further abating of the offensiveness of the notes as found in Tindale and in the Matthew Bible.

11. *"The Great Bible."* But the year 1539 is signalized by a still more important event in the history of the English Bible. This was the publication of what is known as "The Great Bible" (sometimes also called "Cranmer's Bible" or "Cromwell's Bible"). For various reasons it was the judgment of the Bishops that a better translation and withal a better imprint of the Bible should be procured than any that had yet appeared. Coverdale was appointed to be the "Corrector" of this new Bible. He went to Paris with the King's printer, because there

the facilities for printing were better than in England. Various events, however, threatened to bring the whole project to nought. While the edition was passing through the press the Inquisitor General suddenly stopped the work and undertook to destroy the sheets already printed. But fortunately the printed sheets (at least a part of them), the type and the presses were rescued and taken to England, with the printers themselves; there the edition was completed. It made a rather superb book. The title-page is a fine and elaborate engraving ascribed to Holbein. This engraving represents the Lord in the clouds of heaven sending forth his Word; the King kneeling to receive it; then the King on his throne delivering it to the clergy and laity, Cranmer and Cromwell distributing it; the preacher expounding it in the open air; and lastly the people with their shouting of "God save the King!"

The Great Bible was, by the order of the King, distributed to all the churches of the land, where it should be for the free use of the parishioners. Severe penalties were enacted for any church neglecting to provide itself with a copy. It was the first fully "authorized" Bible in England. And undoubtedly it was the best version that had yet appeared in England. A space of one hundred and eleven years had intervened since the ashes of Wicklif had been cast into the brook at Lutterworth, and now the open Bible is set up in every church in the King's realm, the visible acknowledgment of the supremacy of the Word of God.

Edition after edition of the Great Bible was printed. Of the first edition the copy owned by Thomas Cromwell, printed on vellum, is preserved in the Cambridge University Library. A still more superb copy of the second edition is to be seen in the British Museum; it was a presentation copy for King Henry himself.

The Great Bible was no new version, only a correction or revision of the previous versions. It was, indeed, chiefly the work of the heretic and martyr Tindale. On the title-page of the fourth edition (1540) it is stated that the text has been "overseen and perused at the commandment of the King's Highness by the ryghte reverende fathers in God, Cuthbert bishop of Duresme (Durham) and Nicholas bishop of Rochester." Now the Bishop of Durham was no other than Cuthbert Tonstal, who could find no room in his palace in London for Tindale's labors, and who afterwards did all in his power to destroy his New Testament, even himself hurling into the flames from the pulpit of 'Paul's Cross the translation which (in substance) now goes forth with his own sanction on the title-page. Such are time's revenges!

The extraordinary significance of the Great Bible does not lie in the skill of the correctors. Not all the changes from the renderings of Tindale and Coverdale were happy. This Bible is so important for two causes: the lesser is the beauty of the typography; the greater is the royal decree giving it the widest circulation possible.

One must not suppose that Henry the Eighth was in any sense a Protestant. Except for his repudiation of papal claims in England he remained orthodox to the last. He was "as prompt to burn a Protestant for the denial of transubstantiation as he was to behead a Catholic for impugning his supremacy." And so it came about that the freedom in the use of the Bible that was granted at the time of the publication of the Great Bible was afterwards curtailed. In 1543 the use of the Bible was restricted to noblemen and their wives, and merchants:

"no ordinary woman, tradesman, apprentice, or husband-man" was allowed to possess it.   In addition to the proscription of Tindale's version it was ordered that the notes in all others must be expunged.   At the same time Henry caused the devastation of the monastic houses in England and the confiscation of their lands, all simply as a blow against Rome.   As far as was possible, he was contending against both the Papacy and Protestantism.

Henry died on January 27, 1547.   He was succeeded by Edward VI., the Boy-King.   Now Edward was an adherent of the Reformed doctrine.   Under his reign the breach with Rome was carried out in dogma as well as in dominion.   One of his earliest acts was the injunction requiring the Great Bible to be placed in every parish church in the land within three months and that everyone should be exhorted by the clergy to read it.   His first Parliament set in motion important reforms.   Among these was the displacement of the Latin by the English liturgy in public worship.   Liberty was granted even to reprint Tindale's New Testament—two editions of it appeared in 1548.

We may swiftly pass by the few years of the reign of Queen Mary, with its fearful persecution of the Protestants.   The Catholic reaction was as sweeping as royal authority and fanatical zeal could make it.   Of course in Mary's time the publication of the Bible ceased in England.   But the English Protestant refugees in Geneva began the version which next demands our attention. There were also in the years of Protestant domination in England, Catholic refugees in Rheims, Douay, and Rouen, and in Catholic times Protestant refugees in Antwerp, Amsterdam and Geneva.   All of these places are associated more or less intimately with the history of our English Bible.

12. *The Geneva Bible* dates from the year 1560.   But already in 1557 Whittingham has issued in Geneva his New Testament; it is noteworthy as the first English New Testament that adopted the division of the text into verses (according to the example of Stephens' Greek New Testament of 1551).   It is not a new version, only a careful revision of Tindale's with the aid of other versions and the Greek text.   The whole Bible was issued in 1560, revised in the same way, from previous versions and reference to the Hebrew text.   Whittingham and several helpers are the men responsible for this version.   Among these helpers may have been John Knox and Coverdale— it is uncertain.   The Geneva Bible was a really improved version, printed in convenient form, in Roman type.   Besides, it contained "most profitable annotations upon all the hard places, and other things of great importance." As Protestantism in 1559 was restored to the ascendancy in England upon the accession of Queen Elizabeth, there were henceforth no barriers to the free circulation of the Scriptures in England.   The Genevan Bible became immensely popular.   Between 1560 and 1644 it was reprinted in at least 140 editions, comprising either the whole Bible or the New Testament alone.   These reprints, of course, were made chiefly in England and Scotland rather than on the Continent.

13. In respect of scholarship and literary skill the Genevan Bible represents a distinct improvement upon all its predecessors in the English tongue.   But for an obvious reason it did not satisfy the Bishops or what we now should call the High Church party; for the marginal notes, though in general both clear and scholarly,

often showed a strong Calvinistic or Puritan tendency. This led to the publication, in 1568, of *the Bishops' Bible*. Archbishop Parker was the chief promoter of this revision, and it was put forth as a fulfillment of the purpose, announced more than thirty years earlier, to issue a Bible prepared under the direct supervision of the Bishops. Here and there this revision shows admirable judgment and good scholarship, but it is on the whole inferior to the Genevan Bible. It was for the most part merely a revision of the Great Bible. Its place in the history of the English Bible is relatively unimportant.

14. *Rheims-Douay Bible*. The next venture in the field of English Bible translation is the Catholic version known as the Rheims-Douay Bible (1582–1609). In 1582 at Rheims some members of the English Catholic colony at that place supervised the publication of a translation of the New Testament, made "out of the Authentical Latin, according to the best corrected copies of the same; diligently conferred with Greeke and other Editions in divers language"; . . . "In the English College of Rhemes." The leader in this enterprise was Cardinal Allen, who, in a letter of the year 1578, had bitterly complained because the Protestants had such advantage from possessing their various versions of the Bible. "Our adversaries . . . have on their fingers' ends all those passages of scripture which seem to make for them, and by a certain deceptive adaptation and alteration of the sacred words, produce the effect of appearing to say nothing but what comes from the Bible. This evil might be remedied if we too had some Catholic version of the Bible, for all the English versions are most corrupt." The Rheims New Testament was the work of Gregory Martin, an Oxford man, who in 1578 and thereafter was

a lecturer on the Holy Scripture at the Catholic College at Rheims. A preface to the reader explains the reasons for the version, especially for basing it upon the Vulgate. The Old Testament (or rather the complete Bible) was issued at Douay in 1609. The College had its seat now at one, now at another, of the two places named (Rheims and Douay); the issue of the Bible in 1609 was from Douay; hence the authorized Catholic English Bible is commonly known as the Douay version.

The work in this version is in some respects excellent, and it had more influence upon the King James version of 1611 than has generally been recognized. On the whole, however, it is not to be named in comparison with the latter. A certain peculiarity of the Catholic version is the use of many words of Latin origin from the Vulgate.

After the manner of other versions of the period, the Rheims New Testament contained a good many polemical notes. In the more modern editions of the book these notes have given place to others, which, while no less positively Roman Catholic in contents, are quite inoffensive in form. The history of the Rheims-Douay Bible and an exposition of its contribution to the evolution of the English Bible are well set forth in Dr. J. G. Carleton's book, "The Part of Rheims in the Making of the English Bible." As to the general value of the work the estimate of Dr. W. F. Moulton ("The History of the English Bible," 3 ed. 1887) may safely be accepted: "Nothing is easier than to accumulate instances of the eccentricity of this version, of its obscure and inflated renderings; but only minute study can do justice to its faithfulness, and to the care with which the translators executed their work. Every other English version is to be preferred to this, if it must be taken as a whole; no other English version will prove more instructive to the student who will take the pains to separate what is good and useful from what is ill-advised and wrong." In translating the New Testament, Martin made free use of what he held to be good in the abhorred "most corrupt" Protestant versions, especially the Genevan and the Bishops' Bible; but then in turn the King James revisers freely availed themselves of whatever they deemed excellent in his work. The Old Testament in the Catholic version appeared too late to be of use to them.

15. We come now to the most important of all English versions of the Bible—*the King James version,* A. D. 1611. This is commonly known as the Authorized Version.

When James V. of Scotland was on his way from Edinburgh to London to take the crown of a united kingdom as "James I, King of Great Britain, France and Ireland," there was presented to him what is known as the "Millenary Petition." This was an appeal of almost a thousand Puritan clergy for the removal of grievances and relief from "the burden of human rites and ceremonies" which had been imposed upon them in the Church of England. The King, who, though the son of Queen Mary, was a decided Protestant yet no Puritan, promised to look into these matters. It was 1603 that he ascended the English throne, and as early as January, 1604, there met at Hampton Court a Conference called by the King for the consideration of the matters of controversy. The hierarchy was represented by Whitgift, Archbishop of Canterbury, eight bishops, five deans and two doctors. Four divines, the chief man among them being Dr. Reynolds, President of Corpus Christi College, Oxford, represented the Puritans. To give an account of the course and result of the discussions of this Conference is hardly within the scope of our present inquiry. Let it suffice to say that the Puritan demands, which were very far-reaching, were for the most part denied; only a few minor concessions were made. Indeed, a policy of rigid enforcement of conformity was adopted, with the result that many of the Puritans were driven to Holland and to America. But there was made at this Conference one proposal that issued in immense blessing. It was the proposal to provide for a new translation of the Bible.

When the proposal was first put forward it met with no favor in the Bishops' party, perhaps because it came from the leader of the Puritan party, Dr. Reynolds. The feeling of the dominant party seems to have been expressed by Bancroft, Bishop of London, who declared that "if every man had his humor about new versions, there would be no end of translating." But here the Bishops' party "reckoned without their host." The King, who in all other matters was in hearty accord with the hierarchy, immediately showed a lively interest in the idea of a new version. What his reasons or motives may have been it is not so easy to say. Doubtless his zeal for learning and literature furnished the best part of the motive; but he was doubtless moved also by his dislike of the Genevan Bible. In sanctioning a new translation James (who held most zealously to the doctrine of the divine right of Kings) "gave this caveat . . . that no marginal notes should be added, having found in them which are annexed to the Geneva translation (which he sawe in a Bible given him by an English Lady), some notes very partiall, untrue, seditious, and savoring too much of daungerous and trayterous conceites. As for example Exod. 1:19 where the margin note alloweth *disobedience to Kings*. And 2 Chron. 15:16, the note taxeth *Asa* for deposing his mother *onely*, and *not killing her*." In the first of these passages the text says that the Hebrew midwives "did not as the king of Egypt commanded, but saved the men-children alive" and the marginal note declares "their disobedience to the king was lawful, though their dissembling was evil." "It is false," cried the King: "to disobey a king is not lawful; such traitorous conceits should not go forth among the people." The reference to Asa and his mother implied a hearty approval of the fate of Queen Mary, the mother of James.

Whatever may have been the vanities and weaknesses of James, he showed admirable discretion in the measures which he took for carrying out the work proposed. Fifty-four learned men were selected without regard to party. These were appointed to the work by the end of June, 1604; after about three years—which time was presumably spent in private preparation—the task was formally begun. A complete and accurate list of the names of the translators has not been preserved; the most trustworthy is probably that given by Bishop Burnet in his "History of the Reformation in the Church of England." Of the original fifty-four translators the names of forty-seven seem to have been handed down with sufficient correctness. Among them we note Launcelot Andrewes (afterwards Bishop of Winchester and author of the well-known Manual of Devotions); Miles Smith (afterwards Bishop of Gloucester); Dr. Reynolds, the Puritan; John Boyes (or Bois), a famous Hebrew scholar; and George Abbot, later Archbishop of Canterbury.

The translators were divided into six companies, two

sitting at Westminster (London), two at Oxford and two at Cambridge. A portion of the Bible was allotted to each group. As soon as the translation of any book was finished, it was sent to all the others for suggestions; and upon the completion of the whole Bible, the work passed under a final revision at the hands of six or twelve of the leading members of the whole company. Certain important "Rules to be observed in the translation of the Bible" were established. They were fifteen in number; the most important points are the following: The Bishops' Bible is to be as little altered as the truth of the original will permit; but other versions are named which might be followed where these agree better with the original than the Bishops' Bible, namely, Tindale's, Matthew's, Coverdale's, Whitchurch's (the Great Bible), and the Geneva Bible; old ecclesiastical terms are not to be disturbed (e.g., the word *church* must be used instead of *congregation*); no marginalia references to other passages; scholars and divines not members of the company are invited to volunteer suggestions.—It is to be observed that the list of versions which the translators might consult did not include the Rheims-Douay Bible, yet this version (as has already been pointed out) was in fact quite influential in determining the new version. But it is certain that the King James translators availed themselves freely also of several other versions not named in the Rules.

The translators' mode of working is described by John Selden (the famous contemporary lawyer) in his Table Talk as follows: "That part of the Bible was given to him who was most excellent in such a tongue. . . . And then they met together and one read the translation, the rest holding in their hands some Bible, either of the learned tongues or French, Spanish, Italian, etc. If they found any fault, they spoke; if not, he read on." The entire work occupied but two years and nine months after the regular sittings of the companies began. This time is relatively exceedingly brief: the Anglo-American revision represents ten and a half years devoted to the New Testament and fourteen years to the Old.

The preface of this version ("The Translators to the Reader") is of much interest. Miles Smith is reputed to be its author. In it the "good Christian Reader" is assured that the translators "never thought to make a new translation, not yet to make of a bad one a good one, but to make a good one better, or out of many good ones, one principall good one, not justly to be excepted against; that hath bene our indeavour, that our marke." The writer says further: "Neither did we disdain to revise that which we had done, and to bring back to the anvil that which we had hammered, fearing no reproach for slowness nor coveting praise for expedition."

The work was published in 1611. It bears on its face the marks of its varied and noble ancestry; for (as Eadie, "The English Bible," says) "while it has the fulness of the Bishops' without its frequent literalisms or its repeated supplements, it has the graceful vigour of the Genevan, the quiet grandeur of the Great Bible, the clearness of Tindale, the harmonies of Coverdale, and the stately theological vocabulary of the Rheims." Of the combined scholarship and literary skill of the King James Bible it would be difficult to speak too highly. As to style it is "the greatest English classic." No other book in any language has been so often printed, so much read, or so influential in moulding the thought of so many people as the English version of 1611. Its power and beauty have been acknowledged by all competent critics. A particularly significant tribute has been paid it by Frederick W. Faber, the English Roman Catholic hymn-writer. "Who will say," writes Father Faber, "that the uncommon beauty and marvellous English of the Protestant Bible is not one of the great strongholds of heresy in this country? It lives on the ear like a music that can never be forgotten, like the sound of church bells, which the convert scarcely knows how he can forego. Its felicities seem often to be almost things rather than words. It is part of the national mind, and the anchor of the national seriousness. Nay, it is worshipped with a positive idolatry, in extenuation of whose fanaticism its intrinsic beauty pleads availingly with the scholar. The memory of the dead passes into it. The potent traditions of childhood are stereotoyped in its verses. It is the representative of a man's best moments; all that there has been about him of soft, and gentle, and pure, and penitent, and good speaks to him forever out of his English Bible. It is his sacred thing, which doubt never dimmed and controversy never soiled; and in the length and breadth of the land there is not a Protestant with one spark of religiousness about him whose spiritual biography is not in his Saxon Bible."

The title-page of the King James Bible reads as follows:

"THE HOLY BIBLE, conteyning the Old TESTAMENT and the New; newly translated out of the Originall tongues; and with the former translations diligently compared and revised, by his Majesties speciall Commandement. Appointed to be read in churches. Imprinted at London by Robert Barker, Printer to the Kings most Excellent Majestie. Anno Dom. 1611."

Because it was "appointed to be read in churches" (the words still appear on the title-page of editions of the book printed in England) it has been called the "Authorized Version." But the authorization was in no sense exclusive; we have no record of any special act of Church, Parliament, or King that would give it any exclusive place. All that the words "Appointed to be read in Churches" seem to have signified is only that the book was printed by the King's printer with the approval of King and Bishops for use in churches.

Our present-day copies of the King James Bible are not exact reproductions of the original edition. The spelling, as one would naturally expect, has been modernized. But this is not all. In the course of time many slight changes have been silently introduced into the text. These are for the most part obvious improvements; they are to be traced generally to the two editions of certain scholars bearing the dates 1762 and 1769, respectively. An example of these slight alterations is the following from Matthew 16:16: "Thou art the Christ" instead of "Thou art Christ," as it stood in 1611. The marginal dates found in most King James Bibles were first introduced in 1701; they are taken from Archbishop Ussher's work on Biblical chronology (1650–54); many of these dates are now known to be far from correct.

The King James Bible did not immediately win its way to popular favor. For a long time the Geneva version remained the favorite with people of Puritan sympathies. Yet the King James version steadily won its way to a complete ascendancy over all other versions. So strong was its hold upon the people of English tongue that for two and a half centuries there was no concerted movement of

a widely representative sort looking toward a new version
of the Scriptures.

16. *English Versions between 1611 and 1881.*—In the
long interval between 1611 and 1881 there were, as one
must recognize as a thing inevitable, many private ventures in Bible translation.   One such was The New
Testament translated by William Mace, 1729; another
A Liberal Translation by Dr. Edward Harwood, 1768.
These were attempts to render the New Testament in the
language of the day.   From Mace's translation we might
cite such expressions as this: "When ye fast, don't put
on a dismal air as the hyprocrites do" (Matt. 6: 16).
Harwood declared it to be his desire "to diffuse over the
sacred page the elegance of modern English."   His
efforts produced such results as these: "The daughter of
Herodias . . . a young lady who danced with inimitable
grace and elegance" (Matt. 14: 6) ; and "A gentleman of
splendid family and opulent fortune had two sons" (Matt.
21 : 28).   Our common version has, for the latter passage,
simply: "A certain man had two sons."   Of the other
private ventures in the way of Bible revision or new
translation mention may be made of four.   The first is a
version of the whole Bible made by Charles Thompson,
once Secretary to the Congress of the United States.
This was published in Philadelphia in 1808.   It is a
work of considerable merit, but its historical interest lies
in the fact that it is the first version of the Bible produced
in America.   Some years before the great "Revision" was
undertaken, some American Baptist scholars made a version of the New Testament designed to give clear expression to their views of baptism.   Also Professor Noyes of
the Harvard Divinity School made a version of the New
Testament.   Of more value than these was a translation

of the New Testament by Dr. Henry Alford, Dean of Canterbury (London, 1862, second edition 1867). Dr. Alford was one of the ablest Biblical scholars of his time, and his work is of high merit. Later he became an important member of the Committee of Revisers for the Revision (of 1881-1885).

17. *The Anglo-American Revision.*—When we reflect upon the felicity, beauty and power of the King James Bible, upon the honor and dignity that have been accorded it, upon the measure of its influence in shaping the thought and language of all that speak the English tongue, we naturally ask, What considerations were deemed sufficient to require a fresh revision of that great translation of the Sacred Scriptures? The answer is clear and simple: It was the new knowledge of the languages and text of the Bible.

In the earlier decades of the nineteenth century such scholars as Gesenius and Winer made a new epoch in the grammar of the Old and New Testaments. Further grammatical and lexical discoveries and improvements were made in no small number from time to time. In this respect Biblical science was simply keeping step with the advance in philological science generally. Many faulty renderings were pointed out in the modern commentaries on the Biblical books, and improvements suggested. Of at least equal interest and importance was the rapid advance in the knowledge of the text. A great many valuable manuscripts, especially of the New Testament, had come to light in the long interval. Not one of the five best manuscripts of the New Testament was known to the King James translators. Through the labors of a long line of scholars, from Bengel and Griesbach to Westcott and Hort, the multitudes of texts had been carefully compared. An improved text, especially of the New Testament, was already in the possession of the scholars, therefore there arose a general demand for a revision that should give the people the benefit of the new knowledge, both of the text and of the languages of the Scriptures. In addition to this major consideration it was pointed out that here and there the language of the King James Bible had become almost obsolete.

The first positive step looking toward revision was taken in the Upper House of the Convocation of Canterbury on February 10, 1870, when it was voted to appoint a committee to report upon the advisability of a revision. Accordingly, within a few months a Joint Committee of both houses of Convocation was elected and duly instructed and empowered for their task. The fundamental Resolutions pertaining to the Revision were adopted by the Convocation of Canterbury on the third and fifth days of May, 1870. They comprised five points, of which the last three are in brief as follows: That a new translation is not contemplated, nor any alteration in language except where competent scholars deemed such change necessary; that in the changes the style of the existing version be closely followed; that Convocation should nominate a body of its own members to undertake the work of revision, "who shall be at liberty to invite the coöperation of any eminent for scholarship to whatever nation or religious body they may belong." The Committee formed in pursuance of this action then on the 25th day of May, 1870, agreed to certain Principles and Rules, chief among which are those limiting the number of changes as closely as possible and those guaranteeing the amplest discussion and fullest inquiry on all disputed points.

The Committee proper was entirely British; but from the beginning of the enterprise it was felt that the co-operation of American scholars was desirable and necessary. Accordingly an American Committee of Revision was appointed. This Committee was to be consulted on all matters of text and translation, but the British Committee was to have the right of final decision as to all renderings. The American Committee, however, was to have the privilege of recording in an Appendix a list of readings and renderings preferred by them; and further, after the lapse of twenty years from the publication of the Revised New Testament, they should be at liberty to publish an edition embodying their preferences in the text. These privileges the American Committee used; the final result was "The American Standard Edition" of the Revised Version (Thomas Nelson & Sons, 1901).

The British Committee divided itself into two Companies, the one for the Old Testament, the other for the New. These Companies numbered about 27 members each at the beginning. The New Testament Company suffered the loss of four by death; there were ten deaths in the Old Testament Company, but in the earlier years new members were added to fill vacancies. The New Testament Company began its work on June 22, 1870, and finished it on November 11, 1880. The Old Testament Company met for the first time on June 30, 1870, and concluded its work on June 20, 1884. The publication took place on May 17, 1881, and May 19, 1885, respectively. (For a fuller account of the Revision see the highly instructive Prefaces to the New and Old Testaments, also the Preface to the American Standard Edition.)

The work of revision was carried on with the greatest

patience, thoroughness and impartiality. In the matter of faithfulness to the original text the Revision is deserving of all praise. Its clearness and exactness of rendering are everywhere recognized. And yet the reception of the work has been disappointing. By universal consent it is far inferior to the King James Version in rhythm and in literary charm generally. Then, too, it continually reminds one of the study—the version is a bit pedantic. If in addition to the flower of British and American Biblical scholars the Committee had invited such men as Tennyson, Ruskin and Matthew Arnold, and such as Lowell, Longfellow and Holmes to coöperate with them, we might have had a version that would have satisfied every just demand.

In spite of its faults, however, the Revised Version has been gradually winning its way. Its greatly superior correctness is forcing general recognition. The defenders of the Revision have been many, and they have wielded strong weapons. The best brief discussion of the practical merits of the work is that by Dr. George Milligan, "The Expository Value of the Revised Version." In addition to this, one may well consult the fuller discussions of Westcott ("Some Lessons of the Revised Version of the New Testament," 1897) and Ellicott ("Addresses on the Revised Version of Holy Scripture," 1901). The use of a Parallel Bible or Parallel New Testament is indispensable for those who would make a real comparison of the two versions.

The revision of the New Testament has given less satisfaction than that of the Old, but, at all events, the Revised Version sheds great light upon the meaning of the text. Perhaps this great revision will prove to have been only a necessary preliminary step toward a real triumph of scholarship united with literary grace. A version which is thoroughly critical and yet done into idiomatic English of high literary skill would be welcomed by multitudes.

18. *Recent Versions of the Bible in English and other Tongues.*—Since the publication of the Revision (1881, 1885, and 1901) several modern English versions have appeared. Perhaps the most important of these are the following: (1) *"The Modern Speech New Testament,"* translated by R. F. Weymouth. The work is described on the title-page as "an idiomatic translation into everyday English." It was published in London in 1902, and has found a multitude of appreciative readers. Of course it was not designed to supplant the Revised or the Authorized version. (2) *"The New Testament,* a New Translation by James Moffatt, D. D., D. Litt., Yates Professor of New Testament Greek and Exegesis, Mansfield College, Oxford, 1913."* This also is a modern speech version, and it shows even finer insight and power of expression than Weymouth. It is specially useful to the Bible student. (3) *"The Holy Scriptures,* according to the Masoretic Text, a New Translation, with the aid of previous Versions and with constant consultation of Jewish Authorities. Philadelphia. The Jewish Publication Society of America, 5677–1917."* (The term "Holy Scriptures" means in this instance only the Old Testament.) The work has been well done, and is of interest to Christian scholars as showing the best Jewish critical thought upon the text of the Old Testament.

In Germany several modern versions have been offered to the public. A revision of Luther's version (1883–1890) has proved comparatively unsuccessful. The people still cling fondly to the old version of Luther.

Since that date several excellent critical translations have appeared, and also a few designed for more popular use. Weizsäcker's translation of the New Testament is a marvel of scholarship and literary skill. The translation of the Old Testament edited by Kautzsch (a fourth edition, thoroughly revised, under the editorship of Bertholet, is now complete 1923), though of less literary merit, is equally scholarly. The 400th anniversary of the Luther New Testament in 1922 has awakened a pretty extensive demand for a really adequate revision of the Luther Bible.

The modern French translation by Louis Segond was published in 1873 and has won no little praise.

The history of Bible versions represents an amazing measure of devotion and scholarly research. It represents also in the main a general progress in the understanding of the text. Not that a final version is to be thought of! Every living tongue undergoes inevitable changes and this tends in time to antiquate any version, however excellent. But scholarship, too, advances as time passes. New light upon the text demands expression in our versions. The Bible student will find it abundantly worth while to compare the versions and, if possible, to study them, along with the original texts. It is of particular interest to read a "modern speech translation" in comparison with the standard versions.

There is one lesson which, above others, should be taken to heart in connection with the study of the versions, namely, that God has not made the understanding of the mind of the Spirit dependent upon the faultless scholarship of translators. The word of God is a free and living thing, and is not bound by the letter of Scripture.

PART IV: THE BIBLE IN THE CHURCH

We have traced in outline the history of the Bible in the making and of its transmission through the centuries, and have seen how it has been given to the peoples of the earth in their own tongues. We come now to consider the significance of the Bible for the faith and life of the church.

PART IV: THE BIBLE IN THE CHURCH

Chapter XIX

THE HISTORIC PLACE OF THE BIBLE IN THE CHURCH

While multitudes of books have been written on the Bible in the making, the history of "the finished Bible" has been strangely neglected. Indeed, no book as yet gives an adequate treatment of the subject.[1] Yet the finished Bible has had a history of immense interest and significance.

1. *Biblical authority an historic fact.*

So long as the church has had the Bible she has ascribed to it a divine authority. Whatever the reason or ground for it, the fact itself is beyond question. No religious body calling itself Christian has ever thought of repudiating the Bible. Not that the attitude toward the Bible has been always and everywhere the same in Christendom. All branches of the church agree indeed in acknowledging the divine authority of the Bible, but there

---

[1] Ernst von Dobschütz has made it known that he hopes to supply the deficiency. Already he has made an important contribution to this end in his article on "The Bible in the Church" in Hastings' Encyclopædia of Religion and Ethics. The design of von Dobschütz was inspired by Kähler's brief sketch, "Die Geschichte der Bibel," incorporated in his volume "Zur Bibelfrage," 1907.

are important differences of opinion regarding the nature and scope of its authority.

2. *Biblical authority antedates the written word.*

The authority of the word was acknowledged in the church even while as yet it was but a spoken word. In due time the word, which "at the first was spoken by the Lord himself and was confirmed unto us by those who heard him," became also a written word; but it gained no new authority by being written. The authority which the church recognized and acknowledged was the authority of God himself speaking through his chosen messengers. Whether the word came in spoken or in written form was felt to make no difference in its authority.

When Jesus appeared, the Jewish people had a Bible, a written word. And they held this Bible to be finished and closed for all time. Its authority was for them unimpeachable. "It is written!" A clear appeal to Scripture was held to be sufficient to end all controversy. But the written word even of the Old Testament had first been—at least in the main—a spoken word.

Jesus himself stood firmly upon the Old Testament as the word of God. Yet his knowledge of the Father was such that he could not regard the Old Testament revelation as complete. He therefore came "to fulfill," that is, to supply what was lacking both in the Law and in the Prophets. He spoke also "as one having authority, and not as the scribes." With supreme authority he could say: "Of old time it hath been said unto you . . . but I say unto you." He brought the new wine that could not but burst the old wineskins. The new and larger message at length found expression in a literature, which eventually gained official recognition as "Holy Scripture" along with the Old Testament.

3. *The church is founded upon the word.*

Not upon the written as over against the spoken word, nor upon the spoken as over against the written word. The church was living and growing before there were any New Testament scriptures. Moreover, the New Testament, viewed historically, was manifestly brought forth by the church. It is not the words as particular forms of language but the word as pointing to the divine truth and reality that is the foundation of the church. It is Jesus Christ himself, the supreme revealer of God, the living word, who is the church's one foundation; but it is through the word of Biblical testimony to him that the church is begotten and lives and grows. No one can create the Christ or reach him in the realm of fancy. No man can reasonably hope to discover the real Christ without the aid of those who knew him as he lived among men. No apostolic preaching, no church.

4. *Historical phases of the church's attitude toward the Bible.*

So long as any of the apostles lived, the church everywhere accorded them peculiar honor and held their word in the highest respect. Not that the apostles were thought of as having any authority of their own. Even Jesus came not in his own name, but in the name of the Father, who had sent him. And the apostles, for their part, laid no claim to either personal or official authority. "Ministers through whom ye became believers," "your servants for Jesus' sake," "not lords over your faith, but helpers of your joy"—such is Paul's thought of the apostolic office. And the churches honored the apostles, at the first, solely as bearers of a heavenly message, certainly not because of any authority lodged in an office. Yet neither did the apostles themselves fail to assert, nor did the Christian people fail to recognize, that the word preached came with the highest possible authority. It was the authority of the truth itself; the word "came with power," with the power to convince and to gain that divine mastery over the spirit of man which is perfect liberty.

So long as this free and inward relation to the earliest witnesses to the gospel prevailed, nothing but good could come from honoring the apostolic word. Very early, however, the leaven of secularism began to work in the church. It was, of course, right and necessary that the church should develop some sort of outward organization; for in order to accomplish her work in the world she must have a body as well as a spirit. But the movement toward an ever firmer and more complex organization brought with it many a subtle temptation to try the use of worldly means for the accomplishment of spiritual ends. And so it came about that an external ecclesiastical authority more and more displaced the free spiritual relation to the gospel.

During the period in which the church was moving toward a firm general organization the watchword was *apostolicity*. That is to say, whatever is apostolic is true and binding. And at the close of this period the church was persuaded that she had a threefold standard and warrant of apostolic teaching and practice: (1) the apostolic scriptures canonized along with the Old Testament; (2) the bishops, the successors of the apostles and continuators of their teaching and practice; (3) the dogma of the

"Catholic" (universal) Church, especially as set forth in the Nicene Creed (A. D. 325).

Of these three institutions whose authority was acknowledged by the ancient Catholic Church, the first has stood the test of time and criticism far better than the others. The episcopate has not proved a sure safeguard of apostolic teaching and practice. The very assumption of security from substantial error really made an unconscious drift away from the original direction a most likely thing. And as for the ancient dogma, however excellent it may be in its main substance, it has lost its hold upon many modern Christians. But the New Testament is a living fountain to which the church joyfully turns ever and again.

That phase of the history of the Bible in the church, which began with the formation of the ancient Catholic Church, lasted with no very marked change until the Reformation. In all this period the increasing emphasis upon the divine authority of the hierarchy forced the Bible more and more into the background. Since the living successors of the apostles were guiding the church, why should anyone trouble himself about the Scriptures? In all the Middle Ages no recognized leader of church thought seriously raised the question of squaring the church's doctrine with the teaching of the New Testament. The identity of the two was simply taken for granted.

At length, however, certain souls, whose longing for religious certainty the dogma of the church had failed to satisfy, found their way back to the New Testament and there found light and peace. The new light brought about the Reformation; and since it sprang from a new insight into the New Testament, the Reformation brought about a fundamental change of attitude toward Scripture and church tradition. Popes and Councils, Luther declared, might err and indeed had erred, but the Scriptures could be unconditionally relied on. According to the principles of the Reformation, church doctrine and practice are to be strictly controlled by the teachings of the New Testament, while in the Roman Catholic Church the Scriptures continue to be subordinate to ecclesiastical tradition.

But the Reformers did not appeal, as some suppose, to the mere letter of Scripture, but rather to its spirit and substance. If they had appealed from the external authority of a contemporary pope to the mere word of a Paul or a John as another external authority, nothing would have been gained for faith. If a contemporary pope might err, why not also an apostle in his day? Perceiving this possibility, the Reformers sought to probe to the very heart of the matter. They recognized that even an apostle's word could give no assurance of a gracious God, unless God himself by his Spirit should confirm the word by an inward testimony. To know the Scripture promises true, one must find them attested by the Holy Spirit himself (testimonium Spiritus sancti internum), or, as we commonly express it to-day, by experience. The standpoint of Luther and the other Reformers was, therefore, not a slavish subjection to the letter of Scripture. According to Luther the Bible is Holy Scripture because and in so far as it has to do with Christ. Whatever in the Bible does not concern Christ and our relation to him was for Luther irrelevant to faith.

Later phases of the Protestant attitude toward the Bible represent a considerable variety. The simple and genuinely religious conception of the function of the Scriptures that we have seen in the Reformers soon gave way to a rigid doctrine of verbal inspiration and complete inerrancy that has proved a hindrance to the free religious operation of the word. This conception of the Bible in the older Protestant orthodoxy was the seed of a harvest of distress and uncertainty which the church has been reaping in more recent times. For when modern inquiry showed the untenableness of the dogma of the miraculous inerrancy of the letter of Scripture, multitudes of falsely instructed Christians felt that the very foundations were being removed. But in some quarters a very different tendency of thought in relation to the Bible has been manifest. A rather negative inference as to the supremacy of the Bible has been drawn by many from the results of historical criticism. The present situation is such as to force upon the church a careful reconsideration of the whole Bible question. Clear and satisfying answers to certain fundamental questions are demanded. What is the real function of the Bible? Does it bring a revelation from God? What are we to think of the relation between the divine and the human element in it? For these and other like questions many modern Christians have no answer.

5. *The nature and scope of the authority of the Bible.*

The variation in Christian opinion regarding the nature and scope of the Bible's authority may be largely referred to a want of clearness as to the *function* of the Bible. It is universally agreed that the *chief* function of the Bible is religious—to acquaint men with God. But it is necessary to go further and say: The *sole* function of the Bible, *as Bible,* is religious. The Bible has, it is true, a multitude of incidental uses and values. It has great interest and significance as literature, it is an important historical source-book, it has unusual value for ethical instruction. But the Bible *as Bible* has but the one function—to bring man into fellowship with God.

Since the special function of the Bible is purely religious, it follows that its authority for the church is a purely *religious authority*. The sufficiency of the Bible in the domain of religion is established by the fact that it actually does bring men into conscious fellowship with God. Its excellences or its defects in matters of world-knowledge are irrelevant to faith. In respect of knowledge of history and nature the Biblical writers were children of their time. Their religious significance for us depends solely upon their knowledge of God. No amount of mere world-knowledge could give the Bible religious authority, and its scientific limitations can take away nothing from the force of its religious message.

Just as the scope of the Bible's authority is the domain of religion and nothing else, so *the nature of its authority is inward and spiritual*. There is no place for outward constraint in matters of the spirit. No human power can have the right to compel or require assent to any teaching, for God himself does not deal so with men and therefore he has committed no such authority to men. Besides, absolutely nothing is gained for religion by a formal assent or an outward conformity. No man, not even an apostle, can believe for another. I must have personal access to the truth by which I am to live. Although the New Testament is the testimony of those who had every opportunity to know the mind of Christ and were so sure of the truth that they were ready to die for it, and although their testimony stands before us with all the sanctions of Christian history and experience, yet that New Testament demands of us no blind submission to its word. It only asks that we open our eyes to see the truth and obey it as we see it. We need the witness of the apostles, but not in order that they may do our knowing and believing for us. We need the witness of the earliest believers in order that, by their aid, we, too, may find and share the treasures that made them rich.

Many people take offense at the word authority; it seems to smack of outward constraint, and they will have none of it. But the mightiest constraint in the world is that of truth and love. He who in his inmost soul yields conscience, heart and will to the mastery of the truth of God will know himself held fast and yet in perfect liberty.

The question of the relation of the Bible to the church as an organization and to the individual member of the church is of much historic and present interest. Catholicism emphasizes the claim of the church to control the use of the Bible; Protestantism asserts the individual's full right to an open Bible. Doubtless a certain element of truth lies back of the Catholic claim, while the thought of the Bible as the individual's book is liable to abuse. For the Bible is the church's book, and also the individual's book.

Roman Catholicism prizes the Bible and even encourages the reading of it under the strict control of the church. But in subordinating the Bible to church tradition the whole tendency is to take the Bible out of the hands of the laity; and in any event ecclesiastical control of Bible reading means the placing of restrictions upon the understanding of the Bible. The extreme opposite is the attitude of some fanatical sects, who fancy that they can go straight to the Bible and find the will of God without the help of the full body of believers. But he who despises history and severs the cord of fellowship with the great company of the good and wise in the church of the present or the past, cannot understand and appropriate the full message of the Bible. Christianity is expressing itself ever anew and in fresh forms throughout history. Present-day Christianity must be interpreted and its tendencies corrected in the light of primitive Christianity, and primitive Christianity must be interpreted in the light of history and present experience.

The Bible is in the first instance the *church's book*. It grew out of the fellowship; it was made to serve the fellowship. It cannot be made the basis of a purely individualistic piety. It is the fountain and the standard of the church's teaching and practice. And yet it is *a book for the individual,* in so far as the individual recognizes himself as a member of Christ's body, and seeks to serve others and at the same time to be helped by others.

To acknowledge the authority of the Bible is something vastly more than to ascribe to the book an inapproachable dignity. Biblical authority is through and through a practical thing. The question is not what dignity we ascribe to the Bible, but what influence and control the Bible actually exerts, or of right should exert, in the church.

The Bible is the chief means of grace, and it has been so since it came into being. Because God is in it, because it is "God-breathing," the Scriptures have been found "profitable for teaching, for reproof, for correction, for instruction in righteousness." An historic but secondary use of the Scriptures is to draw upon it and appeal to it for the establishment of dogma. Fundamentally the principle is right, yet many evils entered in with it. In the first place, too much stress was laid upon the formal wording of the dogma, and that tended to enslave men's minds. Also the Scripture was in many instances perverted in order to lend support to dogma. If the dogma had been conceived as nothing more than an approximation to a perfect summary of the truth of the gospel, to which believers gave spontaneous consent, yet with the understanding that the formula was subject to revision and improvement from time to time or perhaps might be allowed to fall into disuse, then there would be nothing objectionable in the use of dogma, or in the appeal to Scripture to confirm it. But there was a general tendency to hold dogma to be essentially perfect for all time. This holds true not only in respect to the Greek and the Roman Catholic Churches but in no small measure also in respect to Protestantism. And wherever dogma is so exalted, the Bible is almost sure to be subordinated to it. It was the Reformation which again restored the Bible to its rightful place and use; and yet nothing could exceed the violence done to the sense of the Bible by some Protestants, who have used it chiefly as a storehouse of proof-texts.

The most significant aspect of the Bible's place in the church is its settled use in public worship and instruction. In Catholicism the public reading of the Scriptures has been sacrificed to the magnifying of ritual, but it has never been wholly discontinued. Aside from liturgical formulas, the Holy Scriptures are the only writings that have ever been honored by being regularly read in the public worship of Christendom. Again, the church's preaching as a part of stated public worship has been almost universally based upon the Bible. The same is true of the largest part of the regular systems of religious instruction in Christendom. The Bible formed the most important element in ancient and modern catechetical instruction and is the chief textbook in the modern Sunday school. And no one can fail to be impressed by the fact that the church's songs—her hymns, psalms and anthems—are directly or indirectly Biblical. Even the adornments of the churches—the paintings, the mosaics, the sculptures—for the most part represent Biblical subjects. Then there is the Bible in the private use of Christians. In every great forward movement of Protestantism the private use of the Bible has been immensely increased. Indeed, the greatest advances in religious life from the beginning have been associated with a revival of Bible reading.

What the church thinks of her Bible is shown by the fact that in the great missionary enterprises of the Church the Bible was given to the people at the earliest moment. In those missions in which the Bible was not given to the people (as in some Catholic missions), the work has not stood.

CHAPTER XX

THE BIBLE AND REVELATION

The impressive history of the influence of the Bible upon the church presupposes a sufficient cause. The church is sure that the preëminence of the Bible is not due to her voice but to the power of God. For the Bible, she is persuaded, brings a real revelation of God himself. Does the Bible truly disclose God? This is the fundamental question as to the Bible's significance. Is the Bible in the last analysis a record of men's thoughts and experience in the course of a long but unsuccessful search after God? Or is it a true witness to the self-revealing God? If it is the former, it would have a certain dubious and pathetic interest for us, but it could be no guiding light. If it is the latter, it is of priceless value.

The church has never assumed to lend authority to the Bible, but only to recognize the divine authority inherent in it. And the authority which she acknowledges is the authority of divine revelation. This, the church is persuaded, is the book which above all others bears true witness of God. Jesus Christ the supreme personal revelation of God and the Bible the witness to that revelation—this is the standpoint of the Christian church.

Taken in its widest sense, revelation means the unveiling or disclosing of anything that was hidden. In the domain of religion, however, revelation can properly mean only the self-manifestation and self-imparting of God. If

God has disclosed himself—if he has given us to know his heart, his purpose, his personal attitude toward us—then we have a revelation indeed. But if God himself remains hidden, then—no matter what else may be made known— we have nothing that deserves to be called a revelation. Let it be supposed, for the sake of illustration, that God has miraculously imparted to some man a wealth of information concerning Methuselah, or concerning the inhabitants of Mars, or has indicated to him the exact number of the stars, or has shown some long-buried chamber in which were to be found the lost dramas of Æschylus and Sophocles, would such "revelations" be—REVELATION? Unless, beside all that, God has also disclosed himself, then man is in the same spiritual darkness as before.

God is not naturally known to man, is not an object to be discovered, handled and examined by our scientific processes. God is known only as he gives himself to be known by coming into personal self-revealing relations with men. Not that God forces the knowledge of himself upon men. We on our part must look, if we would see; we must seek God, if we would find him. But we should not be seeking him at all, if he had not somehow already touched us and stirred us up to seek him. Moreover, all our seeking would be forever futile, if God did not more and more disclose himself to us as we follow on to know him.

The theme "Bible and Revelation" presents two fundamental questions: (1) Has God revealed himself? and, if he has revealed himself, (2) What is the relation of the Bible to the revelation that he has made? Or the whole main issue may be stated in one simple question: Does the Bible truly show us God?

It is not within the scope of our present study to enter into a detailed examination of the proofs of a divine revelation. What is here offered presupposes both the possibility and the fact of a self-revelation of God to men and is especially designed to point out the relation of the Bible to the revelation which the Christian church claims to possess.

It is the firm persuasion of Christian believers that God has indeed revealed himself. He has revealed himself in nature, but in nature he does not reveal himself as moral Ruler, much less as loving Father. God has revealed himself in history; here as moral Governor, as the "Power, not ourselves, making for righteousness." But God has also revealed himself in the hearts of men, giving them his Spirit. If this direct gift of personal fellowship were no reality, then neither history nor nature would afford any real revelation at all. He who thinks he sees God in nature, but not in history nor in the inner self, has not known him. On the other hand, he who fancies that he finds God in his heart, but can find no trace of him in nature and especially in history, cannot be sure he is not the victim of an illusion.

The Biblical revelation is, above all, historical. Always God has been working out his purpose among men. Prophetic souls, men to whom God gave a larger measure of his Spirit, were his interpreters. At length he sent into the world Jesus Christ, who was the supreme Prophet, but also much more than that. He was in his own person the supreme revelation of God. Henceforth those who really know Jesus Christ and are overmastered by the conviction that he knew the Father, both believe and know "the Christlike God." Jesus knows God and teaches us to know him.

Three broad, fundamental thoughts regarding revelation are involved in the Christian view. (1) Jesus Christ is the supreme revelation of God. (2) Revelation was progressive from the beginning until Christ. (3) Revelation is an affair of the present as truly as of the past.

Jesus reveals the Father, and that suffices. And yet he did not come to bring the first knowledge of God. He came not as innovator but as fulfiller. Those who believe in him are sure that in the glory of God that shines in the face of Jesus Christ there is no darkness at all. But the assurance that Jesus brought the full personal revelation of the Father does not imply that revelation ceases with the historical Christ. Each real believer throughout the ages finds anew the revelation of the Father in Jesus Christ. Moreover, the understanding of the mind of Christ may and should increase and broaden through the ages. Yet in all this we are only increasingly appropriating the truth that Jesus brought to light.

The Christian faith does not imply that God has revealed himself only in the events recorded in the Bible. It appears rather that God has nowhere "left himself without witness." But Christianity does hold that in Jesus Christ God is revealed with an all-sufficient clearness and fulness, that in him are summed up all the "broken lights" of men's knowledge of God.

Two propositions may fairly express the fundamental relation of the Bible to the Christian revelation. (1) The Bible is the witness to a progressive revelation that finds its perfect consummation in Jesus Christ. (2) The Biblical testimony is then in turn the effectual means of bringing the reader or hearer to the place where he too may gain the same knowledge of God as the writers possessed. In other words, the Bible issued from revelation and it leads to revelation. The Bible is not itself the revelation, but is the witness to the revelation. It is God that is revealed.

Not every utterance of the Bible has to do with revelation. The Bible contains numberless references to matters open to common observation or inquiry. It brings only confusion to speak of such things as "revealed."

The Christian standpoint is simply this: the message of the Bible is based upon the knowledge of God. In its quintessence the Bible is not the record of man's ideas and experiences in his search after God, but rather God's disclosure of himself in and through the experiences of men. True enough, men made the record; and yet the Bible is not a mere record of a human adventure but rather a record of God's progressive self-revelation. Take the Bible as a whole—above all take the Christ of the Bible—and it is impossible to deny that in it and back of it lies the sure knowledge of God.

Is the Bible, then, altogether true? We must unlearn the tendency to vain quibbling over matters that can have no significance for faith. If the Bible's message is true, then the Bible is true. More specifically, if the Christ of the Bible is true, then the Bible is true. If we unlearn the old disposition to seek for signs and wonders in the structure of the Bible, and learn to read it with the sole aim of understanding God's workings, we shall not be disappointed. Prophets, psalmists, apostles knew God. Above all, Jesus knew God, and he can teach us to know him.

Chapter XXI

THE BIBLE AND INSPIRATION

To those who recognize in the Bible the witness to the supreme self-revelation of God the question naturally arises: Is not then the writing itself divinely given or controlled? Must not the God who gave the revelation have also provided for it a perfect and superhuman expression in language? And indeed it is the universal belief of the Christian church that in some way the Bible is the gift of God, that its writers somehow wrote "as they were moved by the Holy Spirit." The nature of that inspiration we are to consider briefly.

The use of the term "inspiration" has long been unsettled. In its broadest sense inspiration means an "inbreathing" of the Divine Spirit into man. In this sense all fellowship with God is inspiration. But the term is most commonly used to indicate specifically the divine origin of the Scriptures. Ordinarily when one says, "I believe the Bible is inspired," the hearer will probably take him to mean that he believes that somehow God caused the words to be written just as they stand. In dealing with the subject of the inspiration of the Bible it is very important that we distinguish carefully between what the word inspiration *might* mean and what sense it actually bore as used by this or that thinker in the course of church history. For the understanding of the term has been extremely varied.

In general it may be asserted that the Christian church is well persuaded (1) that God and not man is the ultimate source of the Christian message; and (2) that God enabled his witnesses to deliver their message with adequate clearness and force. But this is a pretty broad statement. Multitudes of Christians would not be content without the fullest assertion of a complete and exact miraculous suggestion of the very words of the Bible. Such an extreme position is natural enough, but it is quite unnecessary. It is natural because those who believe that God gave the message, can so easily be led to infer that he must have given it in a wholly miraculous manner. But even a rather superficial examination of the Bible shows that it has not the mechanical perfection once ascribed to it. Our second better thought, however, assures us that the Bible is a mightier and more effective book with its human limitations than it could have been, if it had only superhuman qualities.

The older views of inspiration rest upon a fundamental misconception of the relation between the Spirit of God and the spirit of man. The supernatural agency of God was separated by a wide gulf from the natural functions of man. If then God inspired men to write or speak, he would lift them out of their human plane into a plane of superhuman freedom from error of every sort. In inspiration God would suggest the very words to be used. The Biblical writers were often called "the penmen of the Holy Ghost." Sometimes they were even likened to the pen in the hand of a writer. Thus the books of the Bible were, in the last analysis, God's writings and not man's. What was written was often represented as being in part quite beyond the grasp even of the writer himself. He wrote not from his own experience and assurance; he wrote mechanically what he was bidden to write.

Now inspiration so conceived is not real inspiration at all. The agent is depersonalized—is turned into a machine. But genuine inspiration signifies the illumination and exaltation of one's personality. He who is inspired is thereby rendered not less but rather more himself. Fellowship with God sets human personality free. We are made for fellowship with our Creator, and this fellowship does not cancel but enhances our individuality and personality.

In the old conception of inspiration there lies a further misconception. It is false to regard the sphere of the natural and that of the supernatural as separated by a gulf. Natural and supernatural constitute one system. Therefore, the marks of inspiration could never be found in the removal of the human factor with its limitations, but simply in the presence of a divine element of light and power. The Scriptures constitute a "superhuman book" only in the sense that their message is from God and not from man apart from God. In every other sense the Bible is human, thoroughly and intensely human. No truer characterization of the Bible as a whole can be given than this: The Bible is the witness of believing men as to their experience of God. This term "witness" goes to the heart of the matter. It presupposes the Divine Reality, for this is that to which witness is borne. If the Bible were merely a testimony as to men's vain seeking after God, it would be a purely human book. But since it is the testimony of men to whom God had revealed himself, we rightly acknowledge their message as the word of God.

Evidently inspiration and revelation belong together.

An inspiration without revelation would be empty, and a revelation without inspiration would be unthinkable.

In claiming inspiration for the Bible we have no reason to assert that inspiration is confined to the Bible. When we declare that the Bible is inspired, we do by implication deny that anything that *contradicts* its message is of God; but certainly the Christian estimate of the Bible does not involve the assertion that nothing outside the Bible, even though perchance bearing the same message, can be inspired. Surely inspiration has been continuous in the church. For wherever the Biblical faith is a reality, there must be also the Biblical inspiration, else the word would be without power and life. But this continuous inspiration holds us fast to the Biblical Christ. It cannot lead us away from Christ, but must ever lead us to him. Unless we have something of inspiration when we are reading the Bible we shall not be able to understand it spiritually.

The question of Biblical inspiration as related to poetical and æsthetic inspiration is often raised. Poets, musicians, painters and the like are often spoken of as inspired. The idea is a very natural one, and there is a sense in which it is to be accepted. The gifts of genius are from God, and all insight into truth and beauty comes somehow from our Maker. But religious inspiration is something other than the inspiration of genius. A man religiously inspired utters divine truth as he has learned it through fellowship with the living God. The inspiration of genius is possible without conscious personal communion with God. The prophet, however, may be a poet too, and the poet a prophet. Æsthetic gifts and religion are often joined in one person, but they are not the same thing. When we hear people say, "The Bible is inspired because it inspires me," we should not fail to recognize how vague the statement is. If our meaning were only that the Bible gives us æsthetic inspiration, surely the statement would have no special significance. But if we mean, "I know the Bible is inspired, because it brings me into fellowship with God," then we have got to the root of the matter. The claim for the writers of the Bible is not that they had genius—though some of them surely had it—but that they wrote out of their communion with God.

When men tell us that there is inspiration in all the world's "Bibles" and that the difference is only one of degree, not of kind, we must reply: The real issue does not lie at this point. We may grant that in all of the books of the world's great religions there may be truths which could only come from God. The real issue respecting the claims of the several "Bibles" does not appear when we ask: Which is inspired and which is not? The issue is brought out only when we ask: Where is the way to the true and living God clearly pointed out? Now, only our Bible shows the true God so clearly that men may have sure and satisfying fellowship with Him. This our Bible can do, and does, because it has Christ. We pass by all quibbling over the presence or absence of inspiration in all the books of other religions. We may even frankly grant a measure of inspiration in them all. Nevertheless, one supreme fact stands for us above dispute: only our Bible has Jesus Christ, and only Jesus Christ shows us the Father.

Thus we see that our estimate of the Bible does not stand or fall with any theory as to the miraculous origin of the writings. We do not need a doctrine of a special or exclusive inspiration for our Bible in order to esteem it as the supreme means of grace, the means by which we come into fellowship with the living God. We need the testimony of those who have found the treasure of eternal life, in order that we, too, may go and find it for ourselves. We are not expected to be Christians of a secondary or tertiary rank. We are to know for ourselves. This knowledge, to be sure, we obtain through the word of faithful witnesses, but it is through their word only as it is attested and proved true in our own lives.

The claim of complete inerrancy in the Scriptures is not only unnecessary, but even injurious. Men do not need to be omniscient in order to be true and adequate witnesses. God could have given us a mechanically flawless book, but it pleased him to give us the "treasure in earthen vessels"; and doubtless "the excellency of the power" is far more clearly manifest in a Bible that is a genuine reflection of human experience than it could have been in a purely superhuman book. It is hard to see how a purely miraculous book could have penetrated the hearts of men, for it would have only the qualities that belong to another world. There are in the Bible discrepancies in matters of history and the like. But that is not all. The Bible shows also, here and there, moral and religious ideas which are not on the level of the revelation of God in Jesus Christ. To teach children that God was really well pleased with all that the ancient Israelites did in his name, is to make genuine Christian faith hard for them. The glory of the Bible is not in a flawless superhuman structure, but in its power to bring men into fellowship with God.

Chapter XXII

WRITTEN WORD AND LIVING VOICE

What is the relation between the written word and the living voice of the gospel in the church to-day? For Protestant Christianity the Bible is the rule of faith. Its sufficiency and finality are consistently acknowledged. This emphasis upon what is written has led many to infer an immeasurable superiority of Scripture over the living voice of the gospel. A little reflection, however, must show that it is quite unnecessary to affirm a fundamental difference here. The peculiar significance of the written as related to the spoken word lies in two facts: the Bible testimony is *primary,* and it is *unchangeable.* The written word alone is available for use as a standard or court of last resort. For such a use the spoken word is too fleeting, too unstable. Yet the church, in all its branches and in every age, has used, as the chief and direct means of propagating its principles, the spoken word. Besides this, she has constantly used other Christian writings of many sorts along with the Bible. The church has never attempted to evangelize the world or instruct and edify believers by merely putting the written testimony of the primitive church into the hands of unbelievers, while living Christians kept silence. The Christian faith is a living and present thing. Its object is the living God, and the living witnesses of the faith continue to cry, "Come and see."

But not all words spoken in the name of the Christian

faith are genuinely Christian. Only the word that acquaints men with God as revealed in Jesus Christ is purely Christian. This was the substance of primitive Christian preaching, and it is the substance of genuine Christian preaching to-day. But the preaching of each age and of each individual has its peculiar characteristics. The expression of the same fundamental reality is illimitable in variety. No believer, not even an apostle, has exhausted the truth that is in Jesus Christ, and as ages come and go, the church meets new problems and is destined to receive deeper insight into the meaning of the gospel for human life. The essential gospel of Jesus Christ must be given to each age in the language and modes of thought that belong to that age. The spoken word in each age may be as genuine and purely Christian as the primitive testimony of the apostles. But this is possible only as men hold fast the revelation in the Biblical Christ. Yet we are not bound to the letter of Scripture, but only to the reality of Christ as the revealer of the living God. The problem for the church in every age, and for each individual teacher or preacher of the gospel, is to hold firmly the essence of the historical revelation, and to interpret its meaning for each time and occasion as it comes.

The Christian faith lives and grows because its Divine Object is living. It is impossible that faith should have anything else for its object than a living person. Jesus Christ himself is the living Word of God. In his own person he expresses what God is in his relation to men. Now human words may be mere words; God's word is reality, actuality. That which makes scripture Holy Scripture is that it directly or indirectly preaches the living God and the Christ.

Jesus himself taught the true nature and function of

Scripture when he said to the Jews: "Ye search the scriptures, because ye think that in *them* ye have eternal life, and they are they that testify of *me;* but ye will not come to me that ye might have life." The Bible is a means of grace, not an end in itself. The church holds forth the word of life, but it is only in order to point to Christ. She cherishes the Bible, not as having a value apart from God, but as showing the way to God. The whole truth of the matter is finely summed up in a hymn by Bishop W. W. How, a part of which we quote.

> O Word of God incarnate,
>   O Wisdom from on high
> O Truth unchanged, unchanging.
>   O Light of our dark sky:
> We praise Thee for the radiance
>   That from the hallowed page,
> A lantern to our footsteps,
>   Shines on from age to age.
>
> The Church from Thee, her Master,
>   Received the gift divine;
> And still that light she lifteth
>   O'er all the earth to shine.
> It is the golden casket
>   Where gems of truth are stored;
> It is the heaven-drawn picture
>   Of Thee, the living Word.
>
> It floateth like a banner
>   Before God's hosts unfurled;
> It shineth like a beacon
>   Above the darkling world;
> It is the chart and compass
>   That o'er life's surging sea
> 'Mid mists and rocks and quicksands,
>   Still guides, O Christ, to Thee.

But there are many thinkers who, while recognizing that the divine light shines for us in the Bible, yet refuse to acknowledge its finality. A classical example of this view are the lines of Lowell:

> Slowly the Bible of the race is writ
> And not on paper leaves nor leaves of stone;
> Each age, each kindred, adds to it,
> Texts of despair or hope, of joy or moan.
> While swings the sea, while mists the
>   mountains shroud,
> While thunder's surges burst on cliffs
>   of cloud,
> Still at the prophets' feet the nations sit.

Others, too, have proposed an enlargement of the idea of a Bible for mankind. H. G. Wells, for example, proposes a Bible of civilization, an anthology of the most inspiring books from all human sources. That there is a large element of truth in the thought of Lowell and in that of Wells cannot be denied. There are immensely important and helpful writings for the spiritual life of man outside of the Bible. But such critics seem to overlook a matter of fundamental significance. The supremacy of the Bible in the world's literature does not imply any exclusion from our thought of any book that has truth and power. Its supremacy still lies in this: that it alone affords full and clear knowledge of the Christ. No speculation and no superhistorical inspiration can be a substitute for the knowledge of the historic Christ. If he be lifted up, he will draw all men unto himself; and he is lifted up in the Scriptures that center in him. The church is a living organism whose duty it is to interpret its Christ, "who is the same yesterday, to-day, yea, and forever." If the church should confine herself to the recitation of the New Testament, she would be denying the faith in the living Lord who operates to-day through his Spirit. Christianity, therefore, unites, as no other religion does, the origins and the present life of faith; and, moreover, the church looks forward to the consummation of all things in Christ. Other religions are chained to a dead past or they merely drift. Christianity has in itself the principle of progress and freedom, because it is the religion of the Spirit—the Spirit that was given by Christ and that breathes in the Holy Scriptures.

PART V: THE BIBLE IN THE WORLD

PART V: THE BIBLE IN THE WORLD

CHAPTER XXIII

THE BIBLE THE BOOK OF MANKIND

The celebration of the hundredth anniversary of the founding of the British and Foreign Bible Society occurred in 1904. The centenary of the American Bible Society was celebrated in 1916. In connection with these events a wealth of literature appeared bearing upon the history of the Bible among the nations. Among the writings called forth by the centenary of the British and Foreign Bible Society, special mention may be made of William Canton's "The Bible and the Anglo-Saxon People." Another is an essay by the late Martin Kaehler in Halle on the theme, "The Book of Mankind" (Das Buch der Menschheit). This essay was frankly taken by Dr. Warfield of Princeton as the basis of a paper read at the World's Bible Congress at the Panama-Pacific Exposition in San Francisco in 1915, and afterwards (1916) published by the American Bible Society as the first of its Centennial Pamphlets. The paper is entitled: "The Bible the Book of Mankind." Kaehler had made a twofold division of his essay: "1. The Bible is becoming the book of mankind. 2. The Bible is becoming the book of mankind, because it *is* the book of mankind."

If one inquires concerning the extent of the spread of the Bible among the nations, it is impossible to give a report that is not in a measure already antiquated before it falls under the eye of the reader. At its centenary in 1904 the greatest of the world's Bible societies (the British and Foreign) could announce that it alone furnished the Bible—either the whole or portions of it—in 370 languages and dialects. Versions represented by other Bible societies in various countries brought the total to nearly 500. In a recent issue of *The Bible in the World,* the organ of the British Society, the question as to the number of languages and issues of the Bible is answered (revised for year 1923).

"The question is often asked, 'Into how many languages and dialects has the Bible been translated and published?' In order to arrive at an answer which shall be approximately accurate, we will limit ourselves to printed editions which contain, as a rule, at least one complete book of Scripture. Moreover, we must solve the standing problem, 'When is a dialect not a dialect?' by assuming that two kindred forms of speech are sufficiently unlike to be classed separately when Christian missionaries find it necessary for their purpose to make a distinct version of the gospel in each of the two forms.

"The Bible House to-day contains records of editions of the Scriptures in about 785 languages and dialects. This total, however, includes (1) a few obsolete languages which are represented only by printed texts of early manuscript translations, and also (2) as many as sixty-five modern dialects in which versions have been published merely for philological purposes. When we deduct these, there remain about 700 languages and dialects in which at least one complete book of Scripture has been printed for religious use. This total includes the complete Bible in about 140 different forms of speech."

As to the number of Bibles, Testaments and portions circulated throughout the world, complete statistics are, of course, impossible. The regular Bible societies keep a careful record, but the many great houses whose Bibles are on a commercial basis publish no statistics of sales. Shortly before the war, careful computations showed that the annual output of Bibles and portions of the Bible was at least 30,000,000, and now again it stands at about the same figure. Following are the statistics of the three largest distributors of Bibles for the year 1917. The Bible societies represented are the British and Foreign, the American, and the National Bible Society of Scotland.

	Bibles	Test's	Portions	Total Issues
B. F. B. S.....	837,168	1,903,315	6,798,752	9,539,235
A. B. S.......	244,515	1,556,385	3,417,664	4,818,564
N. B. S. S.....	49,095	304,084	3,385,270	3,738,413
TOTALS.....	1,130,778	3,363,748	13,601,686	18,096,212

It will be of interest to many to have the complete statistics of these societies up to the end of 1917:

	Years	Bibles	Tests and Portions	Total Issues
B. F. B. S..	1807–1917	60,767,274	223,397,079	284,164,353
A. B. S....	1816–1917	24,359,006	103,751,917	128,110,923
N. B. S. S..	1861–1917	7,175,045	51,665,708	58,840,753
TOTALS..........		92,301,325	378,814,704	481,116,209

Aside from a number of minor societies that are in affiliation with the larger ones, there are twenty-one general Bible societies in the Protestant world. The design of all alike is to further the distribution of the Scriptures without pecuniary profit. Indeed, a large part of their output is distributed gratis. At least thirteen of these societies were founded in the years between 1804 and 1818. The Bible Society of Belgium was founded as late as 1909. The American Bible Society in its report for 1921 gave the latest available statistics of the output of all the twenty-one societies—for the year 1920 where possible. The total circulation for one year as thus reported was more than 16,000,000 copies of the Bible or portions of it. But it must be remembered that there are also scores of houses publishing Bibles on a purely commercial basis.

But the Bible is not merely translated into so very many languages; it has also been made the people's book in every land where Christianity or, at least, Protestantism has prevailed. Even before the time of Christ the Old Testament became an active influence in large circles of Gentiles through the Septuagint version. But it was not possible for it to become a world book without the New Testament, for only the New Testament has a purely universal message. Only when taken up into that Evangel which was "to course and range through all the world" could the Old Testament become a portion of the book of mankind. The Old Testament has been universalized only as Christianity put into the background the temporary and merely national aspects of it and has read the whole in the light of its fulfillment and spiritualization in Christ. Thus the Old Testament, read in the light of the New, has become a power in the world that it never was in the time before Christ.

When the gospel of Jesus Christ began to be preached, Greek was the almost universal language of the civilized world.   The oldest extant Christian scriptures were written in Greek.   As the gospel was carried from land to land and penetrated every stratum of society, its literature began to be the book of the nations.   Wherever the gospel went, the book was carried, and it went as the people's book.   Where Greek was not the language of the people, the New Testament, and sometimes the Old, appeared also in vernacular versions.   The West had its Latin Bible, though in Rome itself for some centuries the Christian circles chiefly used Greek.   In the East we find the Syriac Bible, in the South the Coptic version.   In the North, in the course of time, Ulfilas gave the people of his tongue the Gothic version.   In short, the Bible was never the clergy's book alone, but the people's book.   In our day the Bible may be read by more than three-fourths of the human family in their own tongue.

Manifestly it would not be enough that the Bible has become a book of many peoples, if it did not everywhere become also the book of the people.   Of course the Bible could become the book of the people generally only as it was first the book of the people in the church.   In the earliest Christian centuries the Bible was the individual Christian's book quite as much as it was the book of the organized church.   Bible reading was everywhere recommended.   "The deepest and ultimate reason why every Christian should read the Bible lies in this, that, just as everyone should *speak* to God as often as possible, so also everyone should *listen* to God as often as possible.   *Oratio* and *lectio* belong together; so we read in countless passages from the later Fathers, but Cyprian had already said it quite clearly.   He wrote to Donatus: 'Be assiduous in both prayer and reading; in the one you speak to God, in the other God speaks to you.' "

The early conquests of the Bible were, however, not consistently pushed forward to the end. The Middle Ages were characterized by an exaltation of ecclesiastical tradition at the expense of the Bible. Besides this, there came the long-enduring and growing cleft between church and people—a Latin church and an ever-increasingly non-Latin people. And the church, with new and selfish interests, came to think that the people could not be trusted with the Scriptures. The foolish and unbelieving notion actually prevailed in ecclesiastical circles that the uncouth language of the people could not express the sacred contents of the gospel.

The art of printing was introduced about the middle of the fifteenth century. The first entire book to be printed was a Latin Bible (known as Cardinal Mazarin's Bible). W. A. Copinger catalogues 144 editions of the Latin Bible for the first half-century of printing, and for the sixteenth century no fewer than 438. In the period before the invention of printing a country priest could hardly afford a Bible. The size of the mediæval Bibles was immense, literally deserving the name which they were known by—Bibliotheca. They consisted ordinarily of four or five—in one instance of fourteen—large folio volumes. The price would range from about $75 for the plainest to $2,000 for the finest copies. The introduction of printing happily brought the Bible within the reach of all but the really poor.

It was the Reformation which restored the Bible to its rightful place in the church and among the people. It became the people's book in every country where the Reformation really prevailed. What the Bible in the vernacular has meant to the Anglo-Saxon people can never be told. In Germany, Holland, Switzerland and the Scandinavian countries the Bible became almost as much the people's book as it did in England. "The German language is moulded by this Bible (Luther's). . . . In Luther's time the dialects still prevailed. . . . It is unquestionably due to Luther's Bible that the Germans have one language for all literary purposes" (E. von Dobschütz).

But the most marvelous triumph of the Bible is not its mere translation into the language of all sorts of races, but the way in which it has come to seem to be native in each race. Thus it has become the greatest unifying force in the world, for it binds all Christians together as the people of the Book. As the Bible becomes the book of people after people, it assimilates them to one another in modes of thought, expression and feeling. The missionary has often felt the difficulty of translation into the language of a pagan people to be enormous. Yet the difficulty is never insurmountable. In the end the Bible lifts up and glorifies every language. "The Malay is the most eloquent language in the world," said an inhabitant of the Archipelago; "look at our translation of the Bible." "White people have many advantages," said a Zulu— "railways, telegraphs, breech-loaders; they are skillful, they are rich, they are well dressed; but there is one advantage which they have not, and we have—the Gospels in Zulu."

Now, the Bible could not thus become the book of mankind unless in its very nature there were inherent in it something essentially universal. It becomes the book of mankind in fact, because it is the book of mankind in spirit. No other ancient book shows such a view of the unity and common destiny of the race. Even the Old Testament, in spite of the narrow nationalism that it often manifests, clearly recognizes the one universal God and the universality of his purpose. It affords us a clear insight into the struggle between the particularism of the mass of the people of Israel and the universalism of the great prophets. The nature of that conflict can be appreciated if we compare the spirit of Deutero-Isaiah, Jonah, and other like utterances with the intense nationalism of the Book of Esther. The New Testament is the grandest possible testimony to the power of the faith that takes in all mankind as over against the selfishness of the husbandmen who were ready to kill the prophets, and even the Son, in order that the inheritance might be theirs.

Chapter XXIV

THE BIBLE AND CIVILIZATION

Mankind has achieved much that is great and wonderful in the struggle for knowledge and power. And yet the course of human history is strewn with the wrecks of nations and civilizations. In many ways glorious progress has been made, but there have also been many fearful lapses. Progress is not an unconditional necessity, and we do *not* see the "steady gain of man." The fond optimism that fancies it sees in human history nothing but steady progress cannot maintain itself. And at present men generally recognize that not always and everywhere does man show progress. Still we have a right to our confidence that God is working out his purpose for the human race. The fearful declines of various civilizations may even help to show the way of real progress, in so far as these catastrophes show that only the civilization that is rooted and grounded in the eternal truth can withstand the strains and shocks that come to all. For God shakes from time to time the things that are, in order that the things that cannot be shaken may remain. It is an historical fact of stupendous import that when the ancient civilizations suffered some overwhelming catastrophe, they showed no power of recovery, while the great upheavals within the bounds of Christendom have never yet broken the power of Christian civilization. The fall of the Western Roman Empire revealed the impotency of heathen culture, but the forces of Christianity were not overcome by the inroads of barbarism. The recent World War has brought a fearful disorganization of public morals, so that a vast lawlessness displays itself in many quarters; and yet we have no cause to fear that the fundamental principles of Christian civilization will yield to the spirit of Antichrist. Even though the world-spirit should seem for a time to conquer, we may be sure that the spirit of Christian faith and life will reassert itself in undiminished power. Some of the historic forms of ecclesiastical life may be broken, and some of the institutions which men have called Christian may yet be set aside. This, however, does not mean that Christianity is in danger of overthrow. The life that is produced by the teaching and the spirit of Jesus Christ cannot but survive and grow. Since Christianity must work out its heavenly vocation in the world, it inevitably assumes forms and organizations which are outward and temporal. The vital spirit of the church strives to control these forms and make them subject to itself, yet the church as a visible institution in the world ever feels the pressure of the world striving to control its life. There is in the church the struggle between the spiritual and the secular elements, just as in the individual there is a struggle between the spirit and the body—the spirit striving after the eternal and heavenly, the body tending to conform itself to the present world. If, then, the organized church seems sometimes to suppress the truth and to hinder progress, this cannot be laid to the charge of the spirit of Christianity and the Bible. The free spirit of truth in the Bible is the very principle of progress.

Our present theme is the influence of the Bible upon civilization, not the broader one of influence of the church, nor even of Christianity in general. The influence of the

Christian faith extends beyond the limits of the influence of the book, and yet the book in its turn has exerted an influence even beyond the limits of the church's life. Christianity's book has been an educative and civilizing force wherever it has touched the life of humanity.

The idea of civilization includes two primary elements, the intellectual and the social. We call men civilized when they know how to live together with a sense of the values which history has bequeathed and with a conscious purpose to conserve and enhance those values. Civilization may be defined as the holding of the past in the present. But it is also a recognition of the truth that the future is implicit in the present. A civilization that looks only at the past is futile and dying. Genuine civilization is progressive. But it is a matter of immeasurable importance what sort of principles and aims control the movements of society as men look toward the future. Not all movement is progress. When, therefore, we ask concerning the influence of the Bible on civilization, we should not merely have an eye for the quantity of its influence, but also should judge of its quality. We must ask concerning the solidity of the structure of Christian civilization and concerning its ideals for further building.

Civilization is the more or less complete organization of all the phases of the intelligent social life of mankind. It shows itself in the ability to make the knowledge, accomplishment and art of the individual available for the whole community. It has to do, accordingly, with art and industry and trade, with literature and education, with religious institutions, and with the maintenance of social rights and redress of social wrongs. In all these human relations and interests, religion has ever been an important—generally the dominant—factor. In the long run a people's civilization will show itself to be as that people's religion. Moreover, it is apt to be true that the religion makes civilization rather than the civilization makes the religion. The intellectual progress of a people sometimes unmakes a given religion, but philosophy and science have never succeeded in making a new religion to take the place of a dying superstition. "Pagan religion is full on one side, but empty on the other." In the end pagan religion turns out to be comparatively futile, and generally it is degrading. Idolatry, at least, is necessarily degrading: "they that make them (the idols) are like unto them." The life of a people will be controlled by the people's conception of God.

In the earlier years of the reign of Queen Victoria, an African embassy came to London to pay her homage. They presented gifts and with them a question from their prince. He desired to know the secret of England's greatness. In reply the Queen delivered to them a splendid copy of the Bible to be brought to their prince with this word: "Tell the prince that this Book is the secret of England's greatness." Now, this holds true respecting the moral greatness of England or any Christian nation. Whether the earthly power of a people is due to the same cause is another question. Yet surely the real greatness of any people is moral and religious.

The relation of the Bible to civilization is a vast theme; only a very summary sketch of it can be offered here. We begin with an inquiry into the secret of the Bible's unique influence upon the life of mankind.

The Bible is at once the most radical and the most conservative of books. It is the most conservative, because it continually points to the eternal reality of God himself and his historical self-revelation in Jesus Christ.

Thus the Bible shows where the good and the true are to be found, and forbids mere drifting. It is, at the same time, the most radical of books, because it goes to the root of every matter, and cuts away the rubbish of falsehood and dissolves useless and obstructive customs. Thus it makes impossible the perpetual idolizing of the formal aspects of human life and institutions, and at the same time forbids the casting away of the essential truth established in human history. The Bible is so tremendously progressive a book because it is at once the book of God and the book of mankind.

1. *The Bible and Social Morality.*—The effect of the Bible upon the life of mankind has its roots in the Christian conception of the *Fatherhood of God.* It is a conception of his universal love and goodness joined with an inexorable righteousness in his government and his requirement of like righteousness on the part of his children. As a corollary of God's Fatherhood the thought of the *brotherhood of man* asserts itself. Out of this twofold unity of the Christian view of life have grown fruits of social love and righteousness of which the non-Christian world scarcely dreamed.

Christianity sets an immense value upon the individual. No other system of thought and life approaches it in this respect. At the same time Christianity quite eclipses all other systems in its *emphasis upon the social principle.* The Bible alone recognizes and honors all men as men, and it alone seeks to realize a genuine universal brotherhood. It is a brotherhood of mutual reverence and love, and of positive mutual service. It would be most interesting and rewarding if we might here trace out the historical effects of the Biblical conception of the sacredness and value of human life. We could go back to the divine lesson to Abraham that he should not, after the manner of the surrounding peoples, sacrifice his son. We should note the immense significance of the commandment, "Thou shalt not kill." We should then dwell upon Jesus' works of mercy, who "came not to destroy life but to save it." We should mark the way in which Christian sentiment abolished infanticide in the Roman world, and then in turn the cruel gladiatorial shows. Furthermore, we should show how in Christian lands alone the care of the weak and sick became a settled principle expressing itself in hospitals and asylums. Also the abolition of slavery, though it came tardily, is clearly the outgrowth of the Biblical estimate of man.

The Bible alone affords an adequate conception of the *worth of woman as the equal of man,* and a true basis for a *sound family life.* We need not trace the steps of the Christian revolution in this regard—the main facts will be patent to the reader.

Again the Bible has proved the profoundest humanizing and socializing agency in that it recognizes the *dignity of labor* and of *humble service.* However crying the wrongs of "labor" are and have been within the bounds of Christian civilization, these wrongs are recognized as altogether opposed to Christianity; moreover, Christianity has wonderfully lessened them, and it can never rest until they are all removed. It is impossible to affirm that the church in its organized character has consistently championed the rights of the common people. The church as a visible institution has never been the perfect expression of its own innermost spirit, which is the spirit of righteousness. The laws of the Hebrews were a Magna Charta of the rights of men. The prophets were fearless champions of social righteousness. Jesus above all effectually taught and actually inspired the practice of brotherly love toward all men. This spirit cannot possibly be repudiated by his followers. And indeed Christianity has already wrought great things in the reformation of the industrial and economic life of mankind.

2. *The Bible and Civil Institutions.*—The Bible does not predetermine for us what form of government we shall adopt. It does not specifically or directly sanction any mere form of government as such, whether it be monarchy or democracy. Nevertheless, the inner principles of the Bible's teachings have had a great deal to do with shaping the constitutions and laws of states. These principles are broad and simple, but they are fundamental and unyielding. At the same time the modes in which the principles express themselves may and do differ very widely. Moreover, we must recognize it as a fact that a government monarchical in form may effectually guarantee the rights of man, while a so-called democracy may be a grievous tyranny. In its relation to the civil life of man, as in every other relation, the Bible is not a book of rules but a book of principles.

Modern civilization is rooted chiefly in the life of three nations of antiquity: Israel, Greece and Rome. It is often said that from Greece we have derived our chief conceptions of art, philosophy and intellectual culture in general, from Rome we have received the greatest lessons in law and political organization, while from Israel we have our religion. But let us not fail to see that even in the matter of law the Mosaic legislation has been of enormous influence upon modern civilization—some authorities maintain that it has been no less powerful than that of Rome. That influence has been exerted in two ways, the indirect and the direct. How great the influence of the Hebrew laws was upon the ancient systems of Greece we cannot easily determine. Various ancient authorities and modern scholars have asserted that the philosophers Plato and Aristotle were acquainted with the laws of Moses and derived many of their ideas from them. While the philosophers were not lawgivers they exerted a strong influence upon the course of practical affairs. The Hebrew influence upon Greece was, however, largely an unconscious one—it must have come about through commerce and travel more than through books. It must be admitted that that influence, while considerable, was not really so marked as some writers fondly maintain. On the other hand, it is clear that the *spirit*—rather than the form—of Hebrew legislation was a real factor in the legislation of the Roman Empire in the period following the nominal Christianization of the Empire. Here that influence is more direct than it could be in the pre-Christian era. So far as English law is concerned, Alfred the Great drew directly and largely upon the Mosaic legislation. Another period in which the Old Testament law and the teaching of the New Testament were of mighty influence in England was that of the Puritan domination under Cromwell. At a still earlier period the phase of the Reformation that centered in Geneva and about the person of John Calvin was marked by essentially the same features. The same was true of the Reformation in Scotland under John Knox. When later the Puritans settled in New England, they earnestly strove to establish a government, under the sanction or permission of the English crown, that should be as Biblical as possible. It had, however, too much of the character of the Old Testament law, which did not, of course, rise to the level of the liberty of the New Testament.

A full exposition of the dependence of modern civil law upon the Bible cannot be attempted here. A few statements of eminent authorities may be added to what has been said, and the details of the matter be left for the interested reader's further inquiry. Kent, in his Commentaries, declares that the ideas of right and justice that largely prevail in Western civilization depend in the main upon Christianity. Dr. D. O. Mears has said: "The vital principles given at Sinai appear alike in the code of Theodosius, the laws of Charlemagne and of Alfred, wending their way from the wilderness around Sinai to the very smallest New England town; making the words of Dean Milman literally true: 'The Hebrew Lawgiver has exercised a more extensive and permanent influence over the destinies of mankind than any other individual in the annals of the world.'" Sir Matthew Hale, in a certain decision, declared that "Christianity is parcel of the common law." Many other jurists, English and American, have enunciated the same doctrine. Daniel Webster, for example, declared: "The Christian religion, in its general principles, must ever be regarded among us as the foundation of civil society." Another writer says: "The Christian system is the moral source of an undetermined but very large part of our common as well as of our statute law."

3. *The Bible in its relation to exploration and commerce.*—In a considerable measure it is self-interest that has dominated exploration and commerce. Nevertheless, the religion of the Bible has in many an instance shown itself to be the effectual motive in both; and certainly Christianity has opened up doors for commerce which mere business enterprise was powerless to move. The most impressive missionary figure of the nineteenth cen-

tury was the great explorer, David Livingstone. His attitude toward the task of exploration is shown in the words: "The end of the exploration is the beginning of the enterprise." His contributions to geographical knowledge were immense, and they were purchased at tremendous cost and with wonderful heroism. But many another missionary has in some measure shared in such work as Livingstone did. In view of it all, R. N. Cust, Esq., once Honorary Secretary of the Royal Asiatic Society, made this statement: "The missionary appears to me to be the highest type of human excellence in the nineteenth century, and his profession to be the noblest. He has the enterprise of the merchant, without the narrow desire of the gain; the dauntlessness of the soldier, without the necessity of shedding blood; the zeal of the geographical explorer, but for a higher motive than science." Early in the nineteenth century the directors of the East India Company expressed the following judgment: "The sending of Christian missionaries into our Eastern possessions is the maddest, most expensive, most unwarrantable project that was ever proposed by a lunatic enthusiast." And yet subsequent history has made it clear that not only in India but everywhere in the Orient and in the Islands of the Pacific it is the missionaries that have done more than all other agencies in opening up commerce. As to India, Sir Rivers Thompson, formerly Lieutenant-Governor of Bengal, declared: "In my judgment, Christian missionaries have done more real and lasting good to the people of India than all other agencies combined."

4. *The Bible and Art.*—The influence of the Bible on the development of art has confessedly been immense; yet it must be acknowledged that that influence belongs chiefly to the Christian era and not to Old Testament times. The

art of most peoples of antiquity developed largely by means of their efforts worthily to represent their gods by images. But Israel was forbidden to make images either of Jehovah himself or of anything on the land or in the sea. That is, images for religious uses; but the people came to think that they must make no image of any living thing for any purpose whatsoever. This misconception was an effectual check upon the artistic spirit of the people. Yet it is clear that such art as the people of Israel did develop in ancient times was largely inspired by their religious conceptions. This is manifest in the account of the building of Solomon's temple with its ornamentation, and in the descriptions of the vestments of the priests, and other matters. The coming of Christ and the triumph of the free spirit of the gospel broke down the barriers to the right exercise of the artistic instinct.

The domain of art in which religion finds its most characteristic expression is *architecture*. Ruskin said: "Every great national architecture has been the result and exponent of a great national religion." But Christianity has inspired architectural ideals that are as universal as the race. Mohammedan art is not universally adaptable; neither, of course, is the art of the modern pagan religions. The art of ancient Greece undoubtedly has the elements of truth which fit it for the widest uses and for all time. Yet even the art of Greece was not adequate for the use of the church without very marked modifications. The church gradually evolved its own type of architecture, or rather several types. The crown of the development is the Gothic type. The spiritual suggestiveness of the Gothic architecture is felt by all. It is a noteworthy fact that, just as the classical style prevails in edifices for civil government, so the Gothic style prevails in church architecture. It would, however, be unfair to fail to recognize the glories of other styles, as they are represented in certain great churches: the Byzantine (Sancta Sophia and the new Westminster Roman Catholic Cathedral); churches of the Italian Renaissance, based largely on classical models (the Cathedral at Florence and St. Peter's Church at Rome); and churches of still other types —Romanesque, Norman, and composite.

The churches and chapels of Christendom—especially in Catholic countries—have been filled with pictures and images either realistic or symbolical. The practical significance of these pictures and images is splendidly set forth by Ruskin ("Stones of Venice"). He is describing St. Mark's, which he aptly calls "The Book Temple." Its "walls," he says, "necessarily became the poor man's Bible, and a picture was more easily read upon the walls than a chapter."

A brief survey of the history of *painting* clearly reveals the enormous influence of the Bible and the Christian religion upon its development. From the Roman catacombs we learn how early painting was brought into the service of religion and how the Biblical history, especially the life of Christ, furnished a wealth of material for the artist. Early Italian painting just preceding the Renaissance was intensely and impressively Christian. And from that time to this a very large part of the best of the world's paintings owes its idea and inspiration to the Bible. When one thinks of the most impressive and powerful paintings in the world, our minds immediately turn—not forgetful of the equal technical merits of other creations—to such pictures as Da Vinci's "Last Supper," Raphael's "Sistine Madonna" and "Transfiguration," Rubens' "Descent from the Cross," and various Biblical paintings and etchings by Rembrandt. And if we glance over the art of our own day (and of the period recently closed) we cannot pass by "The Prophets" by Sargent nor the religious subjects of the Pre-Raphaelites, of Gebhardt, and of Steinhausen.

The influence of the Bible upon *music* has been no less mighty than upon architecture and painting. Indeed, it sometimes seems to have been profounder here than anywhere else. For from the beginning there was no barrier to the expression of the religious feeling in "making a joyful noise unto the Lord," with all manner of instruments of music to lend their voices to the chorus of praise. It was only in a period of unhealthy reaction that the use of music in worship was curtailed in modern Protestantism.

The Bible has furnished the themes for an immense variety and wealth of song—hymns, anthems, cantatas, oratorios. Also much noble organ music has been inspired by the Christian religion and dedicated to use in Christian worship. It must suffice here merely to remind the reader of the vast religious import of the works of Palestrina, Bach, Handel, Haydn, Mandelssohn and other masters. Their best work was inspired by the Christian faith and their grandest themes are derived from the Bible. A certain writer has said that not so much the land of Palestine, but rather the passion music of Bach, deserves to be called the fifth Gospel. But the same thing applies, in varying measure, to many another great composer—to Mozart and Beethoven and César Franck. Perhaps, however, the inspiring power of the Bible and the Christian faith in the realm of music is nowhere so convincingly manifested as in the wealth of noble—in some instances unsurpassable—strains, produced by relatively

obscure men, to voice the praises of the people in their
public worship. While much congregational psalmody is
unworthy of its lofty theme, it is universally acknowledged that the best chorales, psalm- and hymn-tunes show
a depth of feeling, and a dignity of expression not easily
surpassed.

5. *The Bible and Learning.*—Not in spirit only, but
also in the most direct practical way the Bible has been a
wonderful educator of the mind of man. It has the principle of progress at its very core. It teaches that it is the
will of God that men should adore him in his works.
Therefore God gave the earth into the dominion of men,
while he himself rules over all. It cannot be denied that
ecclesiastical authority has often stood in the way of the
progress of science. The opposition of church tradition to the new knowledge in the realm of nature has
been no more bitter—probably it has been even less bitter
—than that in relation to historical and Biblical science.
But the force that has been continually overcoming the
fear of the light has been the very spirit of the Bible itself.
No doubt the general desire of the human mind "to learn
some new thing" has been a constant factor; yet it is in
Christian lands that the spirit of learning has chiefly
flourished. "The learning of the Egyptians" died out
and was buried. The glorious intellectual life of ancient
Greece might have been swept away—after it had suffered
a long period of decay—but for the saving grace of Christianity. Certainly it is Christianity that—in spite of the
Church's shortcomings—kept alive the seeds of learning
in the Middle Ages. And it is an obvious fact that nearly
all the universities of the Middle Ages and of the modern
world owe their origin to the spirit of the Christian religion. Down to the present time the same spirit of faith

continues to show itself in according the largest possible freedom to the intellectual life. It must, of course, be acknowledged that in the name of the Christian religion some men have continually sought to set limits to free inquiry. Yet wherever this tendency has appeared, there have arisen champions of intellectual freedom and progress, who clearly drew their inspiration from the Bible. And it is these that have continually carried off the palm. One might almost say that the Bible has been the charter of intellectual as well as civil liberty for the modern world. We hear much concerning the conflict between science and dogma, but it is a remarkable fact that the spirit of progress continually bursts forth wherever there is a free use of the Scriptures, and it is the Bible itself which proves the deadliest foe to the spirit that would fix religious thought in a scheme of unalterable dogma.

CHAPTER XXV

THE BIBLE AND THE WORLD'S LITERATURE

Whatever the influence of the Bible upon the subsequent development of literature, it is itself a rich and marvelous literature. The narrative art displayed in large portions of the Old Testament, notably Genesis and the books of Samuel and the Kings, is of the very highest order. The poetry of the Psalter, of Job and Isaiah is in its way unequaled. Also the New Testament has a literary merit, especially in the record of the discourses of Jesus, that is beyond praise. Many competent critics have given the book of Job the first place among the world's great poems. And as for the prophecies of Isaiah of Jerusalem, these show a brilliancy, energy and imaginative power that reveal their author as the equal of any poet-orator that the world has known.

The so-called Bibles of the non-Christian world are by no means void of literary excellences. These, however, are, by comparison with the literature of our Bible, relatively few and slight. The Vedas are good literature, also the Zend-Avesta; but what are these in comparison with our Bible? As for the Koran, it is an unspeakably dreary book. At least it seems so to us; Mohammedan scholars would have us believe there are great beauties in it.

We are here concerned, however, not so much in according to the Bible its rightful place as a body of literature as in recognizing the measure of *the Bible's influence upon the literature of the nations of Christendom*. This influence has been immense in all Christian countries, but perhaps greatest among English-speaking peoples. For obvious reasons we shall dwell chiefly upon the influence of the Bible in English literature. At the same time we must not overlook the relevant facts that pertain to other countries. Let one but mention the names of Dante, Tasso, Pascal, Fénélon, Goethe, Schiller, Tolstoy, and the fact of the breadth and depth of that influence is at once apparent. Not that all these writers were in full accord with the Biblical doctrine. Goethe, for example, declared himself to be "a decided non-Christian"; and yet his writings manifest a very intimate acquaintance with the Bible in a wealth of interesting allusion.

The beginnings of modern literature in Anglo-Saxon England were Biblical. We have already had a glimpse of the work of Caedmon in his "Bible Paraphrases." Following this inspired though unlettered poet we come to two other great names, the names of men of genius and learning: Bede and Alcuin. The Venerable Bede has been called "the father of English learning." Alcuin, also a Bible translator, became the adviser of Charlemagne, and as such he had the honor of founding the University of Paris and giving a mighty impulse to Christian learning in Charlemagne's vast realm. We have seen, moreover, how King Alfred was himself either Bible translator or the procurer of the work by the hands of others. To him England owes, if tradition may be relied on, not only the founding of Oxford University, but the beginnings of England's prose literature. And we know that for Alfred the Bible was the one supreme book.

Now the influence of the Bible upon English literature is by no means confined to the work which consciously represents the spirit of the Bible. Chaucer's debt to the

Bible, for example, is far greater than one might infer from his rather worldly view of life. The same remark must be applied also to many a later writer, for even those writers who are more or less indifferent to the Biblical faith are nowise free from the spell of the literary idiom of the Bible.

We are considering the influence of the English Bible, in any or all of its versions, upon English literature. Manifestly the extent of that influence will be found to vary in different periods and with different individuals more or less in the measure of their interest in and occupation with its contents. The influence of Wicklif's Bible upon literature was less than it might have been, if the language had not been rather rapidly altering in the century between him and Tindale. But we have seen that Tindale's memory retained and unconsciously reproduced much of Wicklif's phraseology. With Tindale's New Testament the influence of the Bible upon literature begins to be more marked.

The three who rank perhaps highest in the Elizabethan and the next following age—Spenser, Shakespeare and Milton—drew immensely from the Bible. Of very particular interest is the study of the theme, "The Bible in Shakespeare," to which more than one writer has devoted an entire volume. Milton's great yet unpretentious contemporary, John Bunyan, was simply saturated with the thought and language of the Bible. "The Pilgrim's Progress" has been the object of an immense admiration, except in those times or in those circles where so-called "fine writing" was affected. Bunyan, this most Biblical of English writers, is also a model of pure and vigorous English.

Between the age of the Puritan movement of the seventeenth century and the revival of evangelical religion in the eighteenth century the use of the Bible among the English people lapsed considerably. In this period, also, Biblical language and Biblical allusions are less in evidence than formerly. It is true, Pope is very fond of Biblical allusions, and he uses them very aptly. This, however, is with him rather superficial. In this period the models of classical antiquity are more in evidence than those furnished by the Biblical writers. From about the middle of the eighteenth century, however, a religious awakening sent men back to their Bible, with the result of a great deepening of feeling and a great gain in the simplicity and sincerity of expression. From the time of Cowper to the present day the influence of the Bible upon English thought and literary style has been exceedingly great.

The Biblical element in Byron is an impressive and significant phenomenon. Byron was no Christian saint, but he knew his Bible, and was fond of Biblical themes and Biblical language. And there is Sir Walter Scott. The attentive reader cannot but note how wonderfully apt and how frequent are his Biblical allusions.

We might call the roster of the great names in English literature in the nineteenth century, and should find that in nearly every instance their indebtedness to the Bible is very great. This applies in a very special measure to Ruskin, regarded by many as the supreme master of English prose in his time. He tells us how he learned to use his mother tongue. As a boy he was strictly required to read and know his Bible. His mother was his teacher. She began "with the first verse of Genesis, and went straight through to the last verse of the Apocalypse—hard names, numbers, Levitical law and all; and began again at Genesis next day. If a name was hard, the better the exercise in pronunciation; if a chapter was tiresome, the better the lesson in patience; if loathsome, the better the lesson in faith that there was some use in its being so outspoken." Besides the daily reading, the boy was required to learn by heart a considerable number of passages in the Bible. The extent of Ruskin's use of the Bible in his writings may be seen—yet only in part—in a book of 300 pages entitled "The Bible References of John Ruskin" (London: George Allen, 1898). The collection is doubtless relatively complete, but only in so far as Ruskin's *direct references* to the Bible are concerned. If one would collect all the passages in the works of Ruskin which contain mere allusions to the Bible in addition to these specific references, the book would be a much larger one—to say nothing of the countless places in which the language of the Bible has influenced his expression.

Aside from Ruskin the two English writers of the first order whose use of the Bible is most abundant and impressive are Tennyson and Browning. The former has borne testimony to his appreciation of the style of the English Bible in the following words: "The Bible ought to be read, were it only for the sake of the grand English in which it is written, an education in itself." The most accessible and convenient study of Tennyson's use of the Bible is to be found in Henry van Dyke's "The Poetry of Tennyson," in the chapter entitled "The Bible in Tennyson." A more minute study of the subject is Edna Moore Robinson's "Tennyson's Use of the Bible" (a Johns Hopkins University doctor's dissertation, 1917). The author has noted about 2,000 Biblical allusions in Tennyson, and she does not pretend to have exhausted them.

Browning's use of the Bible is even richer than Tennyson's. Biblical allusions are particularly abundant in "The Ring and the Book." In Browning's use of the Bible one is frequently struck by a certain originality of interpretation—he gives the reader no whimsical view of the passage, but often he sets it in a very clear and novel light. For a fuller study of the subject the reader is referred to "The Bible in Browning, with particular reference to The Ring and the Book," by Minnie Gresham Machen, Macmillan, 1903.

England had no finer literary critic in the nineteenth century than Matthew Arnold. His estimate of the English of our Bible is therefore of great weight. When the English Bible was made, good English, he says, "was in the air." In that period, "get a body of learned divines and set them down to translate, the right meaning they might often have difficulty with, but the right style was pretty well sure to come of itself." Writing on the same general theme, Professor A. S. Cook expresses a similar judgment: "When a writer, with a native vigor, lightness and rapidity of his own, has become wholly permeated, as it were, with the thought and diction of the Bible, . . . we have from him such a clear, simple and picturesque style as that of Bunyan."

PART VI: HOW TO READ THE BIBLE

PART VI: HOW TO READ THE BIBLE

Chapter XXVI

THE APPROACH TO THE BIBLE

(a) *The Aim.*—"Understandest thou what thou readest?" Like every other book, the Bible wants to be understood. It claims no honor for itself except as the vehicle of a divine message. And there is no honor that can be bestowed upon it comparable with understanding it. Yet for any one of us its meaning can remain a hidden treasure. The treasure is most rich, but it has only a potential, not an actual, value, until it is brought to the light. The true object of Bible reading is to understand what is written.

But what is it to understand the Bible? The force of this question will be clearer if we make it universal and ask: What is it to understand *any* book? The answer is plain: We have understood a book, when, through the medium of the given words, we have penetrated to the author's own thought and intention.

Doubtless the ultimate aim of all serious Bible reading is to discover what message of truth it may have for men to-day, but the immediate task is to ascertain what the words meant when first written.

In the reading of books there are, of course, various levels and degrees of understanding. A child and a man may be reading the same book: ordinarily the man will see more in the book than the child can see; and yet the child's understanding is real as far as it goes. We understand a writing in the measure in which we enter into the writer's situation and share in his experiences. If he is dealing with matters wholly inaccessible to our experience, we shall be able to understand nothing. Where, on the other hand, we are able to enter fully into a situation like that of the writer, our understanding can be relatively complete. Between these extremes lie all the various degrees of understanding.

(b) *The Problem*.—Here, then, lies our problem: How may we overcome the distance that separates writer from reader? How may we put ourselves in the place of the writer, see with his eyes, hear with his ears, feel with his heart? For the measure in which we are able to do this will be the measure of our understanding.

All human speech, whether spoken or written, is an effort at communication. The speaker or writer desires to share with others his thought, feeling and purpose. But human communication is a mutual affair; it involves a *mutual approach*. On the one side, the speaker or writer must find the way of approach to hearer or reader. He needs to be acquainted with his situation and to understand his idiom of thought and speech. On the other, the hearer or reader must do his part; he, too, must find a way to meet the one who is seeking to communicate something. Neither part of the affair proceeds automatically. The task of the first party is self-expression in relation to given hearers or readers. This is sometimes exceedingly difficult and is never quite effortless. The task of the hearer or reader also may be pretty strenuous, and, at best, understanding never comes without sympathetic attention. The speaker has at his command certain means of expression which the writer lacks. Moreover, when a speaker's meaning is not quite clear to us, we are sometimes at liberty to ask for further elucidation. But when it is a book we have before us— at all events, if it is a book whose author is no longer with us—the issue, whether the author is to be understood or not, lies wholly with us. The writer has done what he could, he has made his "approach." Well for him, if he clearly understood the mind, temper and special situation of those whom he addressed. But having once delivered himself, he is at the mercy of the reader. If even the original readers of a Biblical author could not understand him without effort and attention, it is manifest that for readers like ourselves, so remote in time and place, there must have sprung up difficulties, which the original readers did not have to reckon with.

The problem of Biblical interpretation is primarily a problem of *the right approach*. Secondarily, there come also certain technical questions, especially questions of method. These are important; and yet method and all that goes with it will prove futile, if the first principles are not sound. Given the right approach, and the application of the principles will tend to be right also.

The problem of the right approach to the Bible is twofold. *First,* we must find means to overcome, as completely as possible, the distance that separates us from the Biblical writers; we must, that is to say, put ourselves, as nearly as may be, in the situation of the original readers of a given book. This is a matter of immense consequence for our understanding of the Bible, and the thing is not easy to accomplish; yet it is after all only a preliminary work. It is merely the clearing away of the obstructions that time has placed in the way, hindering our coming into the immediate presence of the author. But if we have succeeded in this, there lies still before us the *second part* of our task. Just as it was with the original readers, so we have now to penetrate to the real meaning of the writer, to apprehend and understand the truth, the spirit, the life, that is in the words and behind them.——The first part of our problem is to find the true *historical approach;* the second is to find the right *personal approach.* The first is a matter of philological and historical research; the second is a matter of spiritual intuition.

The Bible lies open before us; it is there to be read and understood. Not all its treasures, however, are easily accessible. There are many parts which, without patient scholarly research, must remain obscure. Yet, happily, God has not made our communion with him and our vital understanding of his word dependent upon the researches of scholars. The heart of the Bible—above all, the revelation of God in Jesus Christ—stands out as something so simple, so immediate, so universal, so timeless, that it can become clear to all men in any age. But even the unlearned Christian shares in the benefits of the researches of the scholars. True to his vocation in the church, the scholar points out to others the things which he himself has discovered, and so the insight which he has gained becomes more and more the common possession of the whole community of believers. No unlearned man, who stands in living fellowship with the Christian brotherhood, can read his Bible without enjoying, consciously or unconsciously, many of the fruits of the labors of Biblical scholars. Indeed, the two ways of approaching the Bible —the historical-scientific and the spiritual-intuitive—can never be wholly separated. No man is a mere thinking machine and none is a purely intuitional soul, utterly devoid of scientific interest and independent of the technique of language. The Bible is really interpreted only in so far as the approach to it is both historical and spiritual.

(c) *The Historical Approach.*—Whatever has a place in history is to be viewed and understood historically. This is, to be sure, an obvious truism, and yet the principle is one which we often forget. No phenomenon of history is an isolated occurrence; every event stands in organic relation to a given situation and to a chain of antecedents. This holds true of the Bible as of everything else in history. Nothing in it is to be fully understood unless viewed in its true historical relation. All this, in a general way, we recognize, and yet too often we lose sight of it. One of the two great essentials in the art of Bible reading is that we learn to read it historically.

To read the Bible historically means two things: we must have a clear *historical aim* and a sound *historical method*.

The historical aim in Bible reading, though so often lost from view, is in principle very clear. It is simply this: to see the given words just as their author meant them.

If anyone should object that such a goal is unattainable, that we can never recover the original situation perfectly, let it be once more observed that even present situations and current utterances cannot be known by us absolutely. We know in part; and yet we can and do attain to a wonderfully clear and rich knowledge of things at hand and of things remote. An adequate historical understanding of the Bible is attainable.

And if it should be objected further, that what we really require, when we read our Bible, is to lay hold of its present message, its abiding truth, the plain answer must be: We cannot expect to gain the end without the use of the obvious means. Doubtless the really significant thing in the Bible is its abiding truth; the original circumstantial setting of the message is not the vital thing. And yet the road for us into the abiding truth of the Bible lies through the writings as historically given. We shall hardly apprehend the present force of the words if we neglect the original meaning.

What, then, are the things that must be done in order that we may come at a Biblical author with the greatest possible immediacy? What hindrances are to be overcome?

(1) We have to do with books written *in other tongues* than our own. By an immense amount of labor on the part of many scholars this natural obstacle has been very effectually overcome for us. Not, however, completely; many translations are altogether admirable, but none can be ideally perfect. Besides, every translation, no matter how adequate when first put forth, tends gradually to become obsolete. As readers of the English Bible, we have been made to realize that the stream of time has been surely, if slowly, carrying us away from that grand landmark, the familiar King James Version. There is need of continuous labor on the part of Biblical scholars to give us the most intelligible rendering of the text in our own speech. And every Bible reader who is able to do so will do well to familiarize himself with the Scriptures in the original tongues.

(2) The Biblical books are *ancient literature* and we are moderns. Those writings are the outgrowth of a long

history, all of which is ancient to us. The essence of the Bible we believe to be timeless, eternal; but that eternal essence we find there clothed in modes of thought belonging to ages very unlike our own time. Yet this ancient book must be so read and interpreted as to speak clearly to the men of to-day. Here again the ordinary Bible reader is largely dependent upon the illumination that comes from the researches of men of special learning. Left to himself he would find much of the Bible hopelessly obscure. Progress in the knowledge of the Bible is the outcome of the fellowship and coöperation of many laborers in this field. What we might not have been able to discover for ourselves we may, perhaps, both see and appreciate, when another points it out to us. Earnest Biblical research has cleared away many obstructions in the way to the temple of Holy Scripture.

(3) We need to gain a clear view of the *special situation* that forms the historical background of each several writing. Each book came into existence as a result of a particular set of influences and in relation to a particular set of circumstances. Everything, therefore, that can be learned concerning the author's personality and history, concerning the occasion of the writing, and concerning the persons addressed, will shed light upon the meaning of the words. In many instances the book itself reveals a large part of all we need to know of its historical and psychological background, but in every instance we may be able to discover valuable sidelights. This holds true in an eminent degree in the study of prophetic literature and most of the apostolic Epistles, for these writings sprang directly out of lively concrete situations.

(4) The historical approach to the Bible assumes that its modes of thought and expression are *genuinely* human.

The most thorough examination of the phenomena of Biblical authorship confirms this assumption. Therefore (in the words of Dr. Benjamin Jowett) : "Interpret the Bible like any other book!" The incomparable significance of its message lifts the Bible, in this respect, out of the company of all other books, yet that message has come to us in an utterly human manner. There is nothing abnormal, nothing extra-human, in the Bible writers' approach to their readers; therefore our approach to them should be normally human. We should read the Bible in the well-grounded assurance that the writers meant to make their meaning plain and that we are bound to be equally straightforward in our dealings with them. All strange, artificial and fantastic schemes of interpretation are to be utterly avoided.

From the ancient Jewish rabbis there passed into the Christian Church an inclination to seek for some spiritual mystery beneath the literal sense of Scripture. It was supposed that the meaning of the inspired word could not possibly exhaust itself in the mere literal sense. And so it came about that many of the Church Fathers held that almost every text had a *twofold sense,* the literal and the spiritual. Some (as Origen) found a *threefold sense* in Scripture. This was later extended to a *fourfold* sense, so that every text or story had to be interpreted "literally, allegorically, tropologically, and anagogically." A mediæval couplet sets forth the theory :

> Littera gesta docet ; quid credas Allegoria ;
> Moralis quid agas ; quo tendas Anagogia.

Manifestly such a method of "interpretation" is loose enough to give play to all sorts of capricious fancies; it ceases to be interpretation and becomes a method of injecting one's own notions into the text rather than drawing forth the meaning of the writer.

Fortunately there were many Church Fathers who did not accept the allegorizing method. The leading advocates of the principle that Scripture had one plain meaning belonged to Antioch, so that the advocates of a common-sense interpretation were known as "the Antiochian School" in distinction from "the Alexandrian School" of Origen. But in a later period church dogma checked both the allegorists and the common-sense interpreters. The authority of the Church settled once for all what was the sense of Scripture. The Reformers repudiated the dogmatic control of interpretation as well as the allegorizing method. The Protestant churches, however, soon drifted into a more or less dogmatic groove or bias, interpreting the Bible in support of their special doctrines.

"Interpret the Bible like any other book." This represents the standpoint of modern Biblical scholarship. Scripture has one plain sense, and it is our business to understand it. The literal sense of Scripture may have to do with the most spiritual matters, but the language does not bear a double meaning. "The literal sense," said Frederick Maurice, "is the spiritual sense."

A few specimens of the "spiritualizing" of Scripture should prove useful. The Rabbi Akiba said that there was a mystic meaning in every letter and even every tittle and flourish of every letter in Scripture. Philo, a Jewish philosopher of the Platonic stamp, held that the whole or the greatest part of the Hebrew legislation is allegorical. Origen, who was specially given to a spiritualizing interpretation, fancied he had solid support for this in the well-known verse: "The letter killeth, but the Spirit giveth life." But he certainly misunderstood his text. Read in connection with the whole argument of which it is a sort of conclusion, the text simply teaches that the letter of the law threatened death to those who disobeyed it, while the Spirit promises life to all who will believe. But Origen, minded to "spiritualize" everything, had no trouble in explaining away whatever in the Old Testament seemed to him unreasonable or unworthy of God. In multitudes of passages he finds the literal story meaningless and unedifying, and so he seeks a meaning worthy of the mind of God. How, he asks, could the hearers be edified by the trivialities of Leviticus and Numbers? God cannot be thought of as having given minute regulations about fat and leaven. Of what advantage could it be to read of the drunkenness of Noah, or of other foul stories in the Bible? And so, because he was determined to find something "spiritual" in every passage, whether such a thing was really there or not, he either denied or ignored the literal sense of many passages. A curious example of his fantastic method is seen in his explanation of the words of John the Baptist: "whose shoe's latchet I am not worthy to unloose." "I think," says Origen, "that one of the shoes is the incarnation, when the Son of God assumes flesh and blood, and (the other) the descent into Hades."

Now all this is not only fanciful, subjective, and arbitrary, but it is also unspiritual. For it is imposing our thoughts upon the Scriptures, it is not waiting upon God.

The recognition of the genuine human aspects of the Bible must include the largest possible appreciation of the literary species and types represented in the Bible. An acquaintance with the dominant characteristics of the Hebrew literary genius will help greatly in the interpretation of many passages. Is it a bit of folk-lore that we have before us? Or perhaps a traditional narrative? Or a prophetic oracle? Or a psalm for the temple service? In each instance inquiry will show that the Hebrews had developed a special characteristic manner suited to the purpose. Poetry in the Bible must be read not merely as poetry, but as Hebrew poetry, a narrative as a Hebrew narrative, and so forth. The historical approach to the Bible includes the æsthetic-literary appreciation and understanding. Such, then, is the problem of the historical approach to the Bible. In order to reach the point where we can enjoy the clearest view of the Bible, we need to avail ourselves of the help of those who have learned more than we. But after all it is our own attitude and effort that must signify most. No one can look and listen and understand for us. All that "Helps" and helpers can do is to make access easier for us. "The true use of interpretation," as Dr. Benjamin Jowett has well said, "is to get rid of interpretation, and to leave us alone in the company of the author."

(d) *The Personal Approach.*—Unless the Bible is studied historically it cannot be understood fully; unless it is read with a personal touch and intuition it cannot be understood at all. Much of the Bible can be understood without scholarship, none of it without a certain spiritual intelligence. The same is true, of course, in relation to every book that has to do with human life. To the reading of any such book one must bring "the hearing ear and the understanding heart."

(1) He who would read the Bible understandingly, must come with *the largest possible openness of mind and freedom from bias.* Now an open mind is not the same thing as a doubtful mind. The doubter may, indeed, have

an open mind, but no less may the Christian believer. The open-minded Christian does not "wake up every morning with the thought that everything is an open question." The Christian has at least one great certainty: that God has revealed himself in the Christ of the Bible. Hence he is sure of the truth of the Bible's essential message, which is the word concerning Christ. But this practical, religious certainty regarding the Bible settles no question as to the sense of any passage or the correctness of mere details.

If the Christian believer in reading his Bible is inclined to take it for granted that everything in it is absolutely correct and right, the reader who is not yet a believer needs to guard against an adverse prejudice and a spirit of unfairness. The reader of the Bible must learn to listen, to be intelligently receptive. It is not for him to judge or guess what the writer should be saying, but to note precisely what he does say.

(2) The reader of the Bible should use and honor his own *common sense*. There is no sphere of life where common sense is a means of such blessing as just in religion and especially in the reading of the Bible. In the Whitsunday prayer for the gifts of the Spirit, in the Book of Common Prayer, there is this most wholesome petition: "Grant us by the same Spirit to have a right judgment in all things." We honor our Creator when we faithfully use our understanding. It is mere fanaticism that holds it to be unspiritual so to do.

(3) To read the Bible aright it is necessary also that we use our *moral sense*. Now our conscience can never determine what a Bible writer actually said in any given passage. That is a question for intelligent historical inquiry to settle. But our moral sense, enlightened by

the revelation of Jesus Christ, is competent to distinguish between that which is in keeping with that revelation and that which belongs to a lower level. In the Old Testament there are passages which ascribe thoughts and purposes to God, which are incompatible with his revelation of himself in Jesus Christ. When dealing with such passages the Bible reader is in danger of falling into a snare. He is tempted either to explain away the limitation of the writer's moral insight or else he feels himself forced to call something good in God which he would call evil in man. Infinitely better is it frankly to recognize the moral imperfections of the Old Testament religion. Jesus recognized them. "Of old time it hath been said unto you . . . but I say unto you." To sum up the thought: Our moral sense has nothing to say as to what a Bible writer actually said or meant, but an enlightened Christian conscience refuses to be blind to the presence of religious ideas in the Bible that fall below the level of Christ's supreme revelation of God. Such things are not the mind of the Spirit, but the thoughts of men.

(4) We must read the Bible in the spirit of *loyalty to the truth and freedom from all human authority in spiritual things*. Wherever we find truth we have not merely to recognize but also to obey it. And indeed it is only in the practice of it that our knowledge of the truth can grow and become ever surer and clearer. Nothing but condemnation and shame can come from seeing the light and then refusing to walk in it. But the truth, once perceived, absolutely binds the conscience. There is no escape.

Yet the conscience which freely acknowledges itself bound by the truth and the right enters into perfect freedom. By virtue of its truth—a truth which each man

may know for himself—the Bible sets the loyal soul free
from every other authority. The church has no right to
enslave our consciences or our understanding. "The
right of private judgment," which the Reformers so
strongly asserted, is a fundamental principle in the
spiritual realm. The right of private judgment is not
the fancied right to be deaf to the voice of testimony.
The individual cannot discover the gospel for himself;
he needs the testimony of those who can show him where
the priceless treasure is to be found. Yet the church's
ministry to the individual is not to believe for him, but
to guide him into the truth, so that he may see, judge
and believe for himself. The right to see the light for
oneself—this is the right of private judgment.

The danger of ecclesiastical or dogmatic control of our
Bible reading is a very real one. The Roman Church has
its well-defined dogmatic interpretation of Scripture. This
we reject and condemn; and yet the Protestant denomina-
tions generally have their traditional, semi-official interpretations. We must rise above all sectarian exegesis,
proving all things and holding fast that which is good.
In the rich and free fellowship with the thought and life
of Christendom we shall be able to escape the tyranny of
ecclesiastical authority on the one hand and the vagaries
of fanatical eccentrics on the other.

What the Bible can and does mean to individual souls
can never be told. It has been the book of light and
strength and consolation to countless millions. To Augustine, after hearing a most appealing sermon by Ambrose
at Milan, there seemed to come the unspoken words, *Tolle
lege, tolle lege.* In the reading of the Gospels he found
the light. It was the study of the Bible that brought
Luther into the liberty of a son of God and made him a

Reformer. And it as while listening to Luther's preface to his commentary on the Epistle to the Romans that Wesley "felt his heart strangely warmed." It was with words of the Bible on their lips—words that had brought daily comfort to their hearts—that the martyrs met their death. It was so even of our Lord himself. Surely the Bible, the church's book, is also the individual's book.

Chapter XXVII

PRACTICAL SUGGESTIONS ON HOW TO READ THE BIBLE

The fundamental principles of Biblical interpretation have been set forth. Their quintessence is this: We must read the Bible in the light of all our knowledge of its history and nature and with a sincere effort to enter into its innermost spirit. Some suggestions as to the application of these principles are here offered.

(a) *Read the Bible in a Correct Text.*—We have learned that the translation of the Bible text has not been free from errors. Modern scholarship has accomplished very much in the correction of the text. So far as the New Testament is concerned, the recent critical editions doubtless represent a very close approximation to the original form of the writings. The text of the Old Testament seems to contain errors that can never be removed. Now while the errors of the text are in very few instances of serious import, some of them do occasion more or less confusion. Therefore, if reading the Bible in the original tongue, let the student avail himself of the results of the best criticism; and if he reads in a translation, let him use, along with the older version, the best recent translations, since these are based upon a critical text.

(b) *Read the Bible with Constant Reference to Its Own Literary History.*

The principle with which we have here to do has already

been pointed out; it remains for us now to add some elucidations and illustrations.

The literary history is one phase of the general history of the people of Israel, which includes the whole complex of the nation's life, outward and inward. As the literature is an organic part of the whole, the whole must be kept in view when we view the part. But we are here concerned specially with the literary history. A literary history involves, among other things, a temporal sequence of writings, the influence of earlier upon later writings, and a history of the ideas even before they are embodied in the given books. Each writing has its place in the stream of intellectual and literary development.

(1) Therefore, in dealing with any writing, we should take full account of *its relative age*. Earlier and later writings do not move in just the same plane or sphere of ideas. Ideas have a history. Their first appearance in literature is seldom their first appearance in life. Their roots may perhaps be traced back very far indeed. It will, however, never do to assume that, because we find an idea clearly expressed in a certain book, the same idea, at least in germ, must be present in all the earlier Biblical writings. Nothing is more sure to distort the Scriptures than, for example, the disposition to read the ideas of the New Testament into every book of the Old. And yet this very thing has been much in evidence. Doubtless the germs of much of Jesus' teaching are clearly to be seen in the Old Testament, but it is no less clear that he brought something that was new. If everything that Jesus taught and wrought was already in the Old Testament, then we are in error in fancying that we have a New Testament. There are ideas in the later Prophets that are not seen in Amos and Hosea. In like manner the

later Psalms show, as related to the earlier ones, a development of ideas. Between the Synoptics and the Fourth Gospel lies no little space of time, and in that interval the development of thought was rapid. Paul's later Epistles as compared with his earlier ones reveal important changes in the life of the churches and even some interesting changes in his own mode of thinking.

(2) *We should read the Bible with a full recognition of all that is involved in the diversity of authorship.* Biblical writers show as much individuality as any others. They do not cast their thoughts in a single mold; their utterances throughout bear the stamp of their individual personalities. They sometimes differ in opinion even respecting serious matters. The larger unity of their testimony is a harmony that somehow rises above many minor dissonances. We have no right to seek to reduce these differences to a mechanical uniformity or mere monotone. The thought and temper of Amos and the writer of the Priestly Code are not the same. There is a vast difference between the attitude of the authors of the books of Ruth and Jonah on the one hand, and that of the book of Esther on the other. Paul and James, and again Paul and John, although in profound agreement in what is really essential, represent quite divergent types of thought. The Evangelists will be found to show a number of discrepancies in details. Such facts are to be frankly recognized. They enhance the interest of the Bible and they do not diminish its value.

Some books of the Old Testament clearly fall below the standard of the higher levels of religion in Israel. This is true especially of Esther and the Song of Solomon, but also—though in another way—of Ecclesiastes. The Song of Solomon has to do with earthly love, and of its kind it is admirable. But let it be read as it is. The attempt to make it symbolize the mutual love of Christ and the Church is unwarranted. For the writer of the book of Ecclesiastes one must have great respect. He was struggling for a victorious faith, and that fact gives the book great value; only we must not fail to recognize its limitations. Its author was "a gentle cynic," who found faith difficult. That these two last-named books gained a place in the Canon was doubtless due to their association with the name of Solomon. But the fact that they are in the Canon affords no excuse for reading into them what is not there.

(3) Intelligent readers of the Bible will duly reckon with the fact that some books of the Old Testament are *compilations* (Psalms, Proverbs) and others (the Hexateuch and others) are of *composite authorship*. It is confusing and misleading not to recognize the Psalter as the hymn-book of the nation, having many authors. The book of Proverbs, too, must have come from many sources; it contains the proverbs of the people, even though Solomon may have been the source of many of the sayings. Now, not all the Psalms and not all the Proverbs are in perfect mutual accord. Some Psalms have a priestly, and others a prophetic, spirit. Some are on a very high plane of spirituality, while others—as the imprecatory Psalms—fall below the usual Old Testament level. All these facts are to be seen as they are.

(4) *The manifoldness of the literary forms of the Bible* must not be disregarded by the Bible reader. The Bible is to be read *as literature,* albeit a literature rich in eternal truth. However many and important the statements of truth that may fairly be based upon the Bible, the Bible itself is literature and not dogma. It is, more-

over, an Oriental—specifically, a Semitic—literature; the Oriental idioms of thought and expression are not those of the Occident. Besides, as we have seen, the Bible exhibits all the different species of Semitic literature. This state of things is really obvious enough, yet many readers of the Bible have failed to give it practical recognition. They refuse to read poetry as poetry, because everything in the Bible must be "just so." Now there are in the Bible just as unmistakable examples of frank fiction as one may find anywhere. It is probable that the author of Jonah would be distressed, if he were alive to-day, to find many persons insisting upon a literal interpretation of his wonderful narrative. Then there are passages of poetry in which the imagery is amazingly bold. Must one feel bound to take songs about the sun and moon standing still and the little hills skipping like lambs as having been intended to be taken literally? Biblical writers exercised the poet's license as freely as others.

(c) The application of the principle *that each book is to be read with reference to its historical background* requires some illustration. Every book, as we have seen, sprang from a particular historical and psychological situation. In respect of its origin, no book is timeless—though in respect of their destiny some are timeless, because they are for all time. As to the books of the Bible, in some instances the historical setting is relatively unimportant, while in others an adequate understanding is quite impossible without a pretty clear knowledge of the historical background. The book of Job is an example of the first class, Isaiah or Jeremiah of the other. We shall never be able to know much about the historical relations of the book of Job or of a large number of the

Psalms, but these, because they move in the realm of the inner life and are not intimately related with outward events, are still richly intelligible. When, however, we turn to a book of prophecy in the Old Testament or an Epistle of Paul in the New, we begin to realize how indispensable historical insight is. And, happily, an adequate historical insight is generally attainable.

But what means have we of gaining this necessary historical insight? There are three means available. The first—and generally the most important—is the given writing itself. Since it sprang from a given historical and psychological situation, it necessarily reflects it. Use the writing as a glass, through which you are to look in order to understand and vividly realize the life from which the writing sprang. This every intelligent reader can do in a greater or smaller measure, but of course the finished art of historical interpretation is not learned in a day. The second means of help is the historical insight and perspective afforded by the other Biblical writers. One would not think of gaining a clear understanding of the apostolic Epistles without studying them in the light of the narrative of the Acts. The book of Jeremiah must be read in the light of the history as reflected in the book of Kings, the writings of earlier prophets, and the book of Deuteronomy. The last source of light is the extra-Biblical history. This throws much light upon Bible history. The records of Assyria and Babylonia are very important for certain periods of Old Testament history and literature, especially for the books of Isaiah, Jeremiah and Ezekiel. For the last centuries of the Old Testament times and for the New Testament times extra-Biblical sidelights are relatively abundant.

Now it is not to be supposed that the beginner in the

study of the Bible can at once become a master in this vast field. But even the beginner can have the right method. Even from the beginning one can understand what historical interpretation means, and can set himself about the practice of it.

(d) *Some further implications of the historical view of the Bible.*

(1) Observe the *principle of unity* in a writing. Let the structure of a book be clearly noted. If it is a book in the stricter sense, a writing with some organic unity as distinguished from a compilation, then the reader should keep the book as a whole in view. Now every literary unity has some fundamental aim, some controlling purpose. Therefore the parts must be viewed in relation to the whole and the whole in relation to the parts. We must, of course, take in a book or a discourse word by word, we cannot take in the whole at once; nevertheless, the competent reader or listener will bear in mind that he has not got the full meaning until he has followed to the end. Therefore, *interpret a book as a whole.*

(2) *Read a text in connection with its context.* This is, of course, only a corollary of the principle of unity. The atomistic method—the wresting of texts from their surroundings—is a most fruitful source of misunderstandings and perversions of the sense of Scripture. The Bible is not a congeries of atoms, a string of sayings to be understood and used one by one. The Scripture is discourse, an organism of thought and speech. Sometimes the wresting of texts is more comical and irreverent than misleading, as when Lorenzo Dow preached upon the text (as he announced it) : "Top-knot, come down!" (It was a sermon against the fanciful headgear of the women of his time.) The words are a perversion of a

fragment of the solemn passage: "Let him that is upon the housetop not come down to take anything out of his house." But unfortunately many texts are handled in a much more injurious—if less irreverent—fashion. When in all solemnity a text is wrested from its surroundings and made to say what the writer never dreamed of, that is confusing and misleading. The whole "proof-text method" in theology must be repudiated. Not that there are no texts which stand forth in a grand completeness, so that it seems as if the whole gospel were contained in them. The repudiation of the proof-text method means only that one must view every part in relation to the whole. If, then, a part seems or proves to be an epitome of the whole, it is eminently proper to appreciate it accordingly. But the rich significance of the part appears only as we know the whole. We see clearly that John 3:16 ("God so loved the world," etc.) is an epitome of the whole gospel, but we discover this when we have known the whole message, and not before.

Some sects have been built about some perverted text. Indeed, most sects have had their "favorite texts," which they have either more or less perverted or at least brought into an unnatural prominence, thus destroying the true perspective of Scripture.

The proof-text method is such that, if its validity be unquestioned, "you can prove anything by the Bible." St. Augustine hit the truth of the matter when he wrote: "The *sense* of Scripture is Scripture." When one simply says, "The Bible says" this or that, it behooves us to inquire whether *the words* are there merely, or whether the Bible *really teaches* the thing. There are many statements in the Bible which a writer sets up only in order to refute them.

Examples of wrested texts are countless. An interesting one is "Touch not, taste not, handle not" (Col. 2:21). It is often applied to the use of alcoholic beverages. But Paul made no reference to drink in this passage; he was rebuking some of his readers for yielding to the slavery of external ordinances. The good cause of temperance has a solid enough foundation without resorting to a foolish perversion of Scripture. More often, however, it is an unworthy cause that appeals to some favorite text.

> "In religion
> What error is there but some sober brow
> Will bless it and approve it with a text?"

> "The Devil can cite Scripture for his purpose."

To put the matter briefly: Reading a text according to its context is to inquire, not what these words might mean if taken apart from the context, but what they actually do mean in the given connection.

From what has been said, one will rightly infer the necessity of disregarding the traditional chapter-and-verse divisions in the Bible. In many instances these correspond in a measure to the logical structure of the writings, but very often they seriously disturb the sense. The writings fall logically into sentences and paragraphs, and these are to be determined by an analysis of the structure of the given passages.

(3) *Compare Scripture with Scripture.* But do it intelligently! It is obviously desirable to compare the several writings of a single author in order to get a better perspective of his world of thought. This will save one from a too partial and restricted application of any particular expression. But also compare one part of

Scripture with all other parts. This, however, should not be done without the fullest recognition of the contrasts as well as the similarities in the modes of thought (e.g., Esther in comparison with Jonah). The uncritical assembling of passages that chance to contain the same word or phrase often leads to confusion.

(e) *The Use and Misuse of the Bible.* We have recognized that the Bible is to be *read and understood* as it is, and not as we might wish or fancy it to be. The same principle of sincerity requires that we *use* the Bible in accordance with its real nature and purpose. Not every fraction of Scripture has its separate use. The sense, the soul of Scripture, this and this only has a use in religion. In connection with our consideration of the right uses of the Scriptures it may be well to notice some of the radical misuses to which the Bible is sometimes subjected.

It is a radical misuse of the Bible to regard it as a talisman, or to use its words as magic. Equally unwarranted and superstitious is the practice of opening the Bible at random and placing the finger upon a certain spot and then taking those words—usually with some arbitrary perversion of their sense—as the determining factor in some matter of conduct.

It is a radical misuse of the Bible to claim its sanction for whatever institutions or practices are mentioned in it without being specifically condemned. Polygamy, slavery, and many other evils have been defended by such unwarranted appeals to the Bible.

It is a radical misuse of the Bible to appeal to it as the last resort in any matter of natural or historical science.

(f) *The Right Use of the Bible.*

(1) *The Devotional and Practical Reading of the*

Bible. It is clearly the main intention of the writers of the Biblical books to help men to a knowledge of the living God. It is equally clear that the reason why the Christian world cherishes the Bible above all other books is the certainty that in it and through it God is really found. The supreme function and use of the Bible is religious. But the Scriptures, being a collection of rich and varied literature, are susceptible of a variety of uses. The Bible may be read merely as literature : its contents will then be found marvelously rich and impressive. Or it may be used as a field of philological study : the languages of the Bible are highly interesting and important, and they have had an interesting history. Or, again, one may study the Bible as a source-book of history—the history of peoples and manners and intellectual culture : from this point of view the Bible is an exceedingly rich mine. One may also study the Bible critically in order to learn all that may be known of its origin and transmission and all its historical relations. All these uses of the Bible are merely incidental to its main use. As such they are absolutely legitimate, but they are not the use of the Bible *as Bible.* All uses but one belong to its outer court. But it is possible to enter into its inner sanctuary. The heart of the Bible is God himself as revealed in Jesus Christ. All literary and historical appreciation of the Bible should serve as a help to the higher, spiritual appreciation of its message; but also these may prove a barrier, if we lose our sense of perspective.

Especially Biblical criticism may so absorb one's interest that he fail to pass beyond the sphere of the external into the heart of the Bible. The real function of criticism, as we have previously seen, is to keep open the way into the sanctuary of Scripture. If, however, we so

occupy ourselves with the external aspects of the Bible
that we forget to penetrate into the sanctuary, criticism
becomes a hindrance to religion.   Criticism is in itself
lawful and good, but like all good things, it may be perverted from its true ends.   Recognizing both the use and
the abuse of criticism, some pious scholars have coun-
selled us to keep our *critical* and our *devotional* reading
of the Bible quite separate.   Rightly understood, there
is wisdom in this counsel.   Otherwise understood, it
involves a serious fallacy.   When the scholar reads his
Bible devotionally, he need not cast aside the knowledge
that he has gained from critical study.   Indeed, he cannot
and must not do this; it would be hypocrisy to try to do it.
If his critical study has been done as becomes a Christian,
the criticism has been hallowed, it has helped to keep open
for him the way into the sanctuary.   At the same time
the critical scholar needs to feed upon the word just as
truly—yes, and just as simply—as the plainest believer.
It is not necessary to be a babe in understanding in order
to have a simple faith.   Yet the scholar needs to give
earnest heed to the art of dwelling chiefly upon the things
that pertain to the essence of religion—the contemplation
of God's works and ways, and the spirit of loyal service.
Certain well-known lines of George Herbert may, without
violence, be very well applied to our study of the Bible:

> A man that looks on glass,
>   On it may stay his eye;
> Or, if he pleaseth, through it pass,
>   And then the heavens espy.

It is only where we stay the eye upon the external aspects
of the Bible, that criticism becomes vain and unfruitful.
  The practical design of the Bible is not best served by

a desultory reading of it.   If we confine our reading of
the Bible to certain favorite portions, we shall fail to get
the instruction and inspiration that come from the larger
perspective.   At the same time it is not only natural but
also eminently fitting that we should exalt some portions
above some others.   It may be good, at times, to read the
Bible through in course.   Yet if one gives to Leviticus as
much time and thought as to Luke, the true balance and
perspective are lost.   Jesus Christ is the center and ruling
personality of Scripture.   Therefore the four Gospels
should have the chief place in any scheme of Bible reading.   It would be well to read from the Gospels daily.
Next in order of importance come the most of the remaining New Testament writings.   In the reading of the Old
Testament the religious instinct will naturally give the
preëminence to many of the Psalms, to Job, and to the
mightiest books of prophecy—Amos, Hosea, Isaiah,
Jeremiah and others.   Large portions of the Pentateuch
and of the books of Samuel and Kings are full of religious
inspiration.   On these and other peculiarly rich portions
of Scripture we should chiefly feed.   But while we
naturally read the great and deep portions with a greater
frequency and ardor, we should not utterly neglect those
portions that have less to say to the men of to-day.

Since it is the supreme end of the Bible to bring men
into fellowship with God, the book is to be read with
prayer and with the sincere desire to know the mind of
the Spirit, and, knowing, to obey.

(2) *The Use of the Bible as the Source of Teaching
in the Church.*—The universal Christian recognition of
the Bible as the supreme book of revelation is immensely
significant, yet obviously the mere formal recognition of
its authority is no guarantee that in actual practice the

Bible will be rightly used as the source and standard of the church's teaching. The wide diversity of views as to "what the Bible teaches" is a sufficient proof of this statement.

Some of the differences of opinion as to the substance of the Bible's teachings and as to the right way to use the Bible in Christian instruction are due to dogmatic prepossessions. Many people go to the Bible, not to learn what it teaches, but to find support for their own dogmas. A famous Latin couplet, some centuries old, refers to the Bible as "the book in which each man seeks and finds his own dogmas." Only a radical change of mind can help people who are in the grip of dogmatic prejudice. But there are people who are of an honest and teachable spirit and yet miss the right way in their use of the Bible. Certain general misconceptions vitiate their method.

(a) *The Use of the Bible in Theology.*—The organized church has never been wholly without something in the way of dogma (a platform, or consensus as to first principles). For a long time, however, the early church had no official statement of its creed, only a free general consensus. And in modern times some Protestant bodies have sought to return to the primitive order in this regard and be free from all official formulations of creed. Yet all are agreed in this, that the community of believers must have a general consensus respecting first principles as a platform or basis of coöperation. The question then arises as to the relation of the Bible to the church's creed.

Historically the creeds of Christendom have taken shape under the influence of two general factors: first, the primitive Christian tradition, which we find embodied in the New Testament, and secondly, the various modifying

forces comprehended by the term "historical evolution."
Now the *forms* of Christian thought are under the inevi-
table law of change and development. Moreover, the
conception of the meaning of Christianity should be enlarged, enriched and clarified in the course of history.
And yet in its *essential substance* it is what it was from
the beginning: the fellowship with God through Jesus
Christ and service in his kingdom. For this reason
Christianity must be true to its original principles. This
means that the church must be securely anchored in the
New Testament. The Christian creed must be faithfully
Biblical. It is not bound to the Biblical forms of expression, but only to the substance of the Biblical truth.
For this is eternal. There are many ideas in the Bible
which are but the shell of the truth; these fall away; but
the Christian faith cannot let go anything of the real
revelation of God that is given through the Christ of
the Gospels, neither can it introduce elements from foreign
sources without threatening the very life of the faith.
In its innermost essence the Christian creed must remain
the confession to the Lordship of the Christ of the Bible.
And it is a significant fact that no branch of the church
has ever put forth a dogma without claiming that it was
Biblical.

Theology is not the same thing as dogma, although
there is theology in dogma. That is to say, theology
helped to shape the dogma. Theology is the attempt to
give a reasoned statement of the faith; as such it is
more or less the affair of individuals, even though it cannot flourish without large coöperation. Dogma, on the
other hand, is a positive statement of the basis of church
fellowship; as such it is the affair of the whole communion. All conscious members of the communion have

a creed (dogma), but only thinking Christians have any theology to speak of.

It might be inferred from this, that it would be best to leave theology to a select class. What use (people often ask) has the ordinary Christian with theology? Now it must be granted that the church does not need a vast multitude of professional theologians. Yet every thinking Christian should be and is something of a theologian. And it is of immense practical consequence that the "lay theology" should be sane and helpful. For the great issues of Christian thinking are always determined in the end by the experience and common sense of the laity. It is above all important that the laity should read the Bible with a sure touch and intuition as to what it really means and teaches. For to the laity—in the homes, Bible schools and so forth—falls the larger part of the task of Christian instruction.

In this connection little more than a mere reference to principles already set forth can be offered. The Bible reader must bear in mind that what "the Bible says" (or seems to say) in a given passage is not always "what the Bible teaches." The teaching of the Bible is not everything that is in the Bible; its teaching is its revelation of God. Since Christ is the center and sum of the Biblical revelation, everything in the Bible should be read and judged from this high standpoint. That which is imperfect and merely preparatory should be seen and judged in its actual relations to the whole Biblical movement. Jesus Christ himself is the criterion of what is truly "scriptural."

(b) *The Use of the Bible in the Church's Program of Instruction.*—Once the church's public instruction depended—aside from Christian literature—upon two means: the pulpit and catechetical classes. The growth of the modern Bible school and its ramifications in the religious day school and other features are highly significant. We are now in a new era of religious education. And since the Bible is sure to be the great source-book and manual of religious instruction even in the new era, it is of the greatest consequence that we learn how to handle it aright.

In the Protestant churches the pulpit was once the great teaching agency. The growth of the modern Sunday school, together with other influences, has tended to minimize the teaching function of the pulpit. In some quarters there is now a decided movement toward "a teaching ministry." It is particularly important that the handling of the Bible in the pulpit should be fitted to the needs of the present day.

In its handling of the Bible the pulpit must be absolutely frank. Not that it is necessary to "preach criticism." Indeed, it is, strictly speaking, impossible to *preach* criticism; it is only a positive message that can be preached. Criticism belongs to the school and the study. But the preaching should at least assume a form that is in keeping with the results of the scientific study of the Bible. Moreover, the people, in one way or another, should be made acquainted with the true state of inquiry as to the nature and growth of the Bible. Especially they should be made to see that faith is not and cannot be jeopardized by honest criticism. On such matters the pulpit should not be silent. The believing church should be absolutely positive in her message, but her very certainty should make her fearless regarding the historical study of the Bible. No man who is wholly given to the proclamation of the Biblical message will find anything really embarrassing in Biblical science.

A notorious evil in the handling of the Bible in some pulpits is the frequent violation of the sense of the text. The custom of "taking a text" from the Bible is a good one, for Christian preaching must hold fast to the Christian sources. But it is far better to preach without a text than to take one and then pervert it.

In the present day there is a crying need for competent lay instructors in the field of religion. The teachers in our Bible schools must learn, above everything else, how to read their Bible aright, so that they may rightly use it in their instruction. Assuming that the necessary knowledge of the Bible has been acquired, several general and a multitude of particular questions of method will arise. The first question relates to the question of the selection of material for study and illustration. The material of the Bible cannot be used indiscriminately. Some portions have little or no direct interest for the life of our time; and some have only a subordinate place. A well-considered purpose must control in the selection of material. The teacher, however, should avoid becoming too individual in his point of view; the common judgment of Christian teachers will help to enlarge his outlook. Then comes the problem of what to do with certain so-called "Bible difficulties." Many teachers are embarrassed by the pupils' questions as to the literalness of such stories as those of the creation of woman, of the Garden of Eden, of the immense age of the patriarchs, of the Flood, of the fish that swallowed Jonah, and the like. On such matters two simple remarks must suffice. In the first place, fearless honesty must be practised; in the long run this is the surer and safer way. In the second place, the teacher, who is aglow with the certainty that God is revealed in the Bible, will find a way to make the human aspects of the Bible to be as little embarrassing to his pupils as they are to himself.   In the light of God himself these difficulties become as nothing.

BIBLIOGRAPHY AND SUGGESTIONS FOR FURTHER STUDY

THE TEXT

The Bible student should first of all provide himself with the best texts and versions. Besides the King James Version he should have the Revised Version, especially the American Standard Bible (Thomas Nelson and Sons, 1901). To these should be added one or more of the "modern speech" versions of the New Testament. Of these, Moffatt's enjoys the highest repute; next to this, Weymouth's. Very recently Ballantine and Goodspeed have each put forth a translation.

For the intelligent reading of the Bible one of the best of helps is Moulton's *Modern Reader's Bible,* issued both in a single volume and in parts. In this edition the text is so printed as to bring out the varieties of literary form.

If one is able to read the Bible in the original tongues, critical texts should be procured: for the Old Testament, Kittel's; for the New, Westcott and Hort's or Nestle's. The latter is issued in a convenient and inexpensive form by the British and Foreign Bible Society. It is further important that one should have a good edition of the Apocrypha, especially the Old Testament Apocrypha. The Clarendon Press, Oxford, puts out an excellent edition of the text in English, and R. H. Charles has edited the Apocrypha and Pseudepigrapha of the Old Testament in almost ideal fashion with introduction and notes (2 large volumes).

BIBLE DICTIONARIES

Access to a modern Bible Dictionary is indispensable. The two best of those confined within the limits of a single volume are *The Standard Dictionary of the Bible,* edited by Jacobus (Funk and Wagnalls, New York), and *A One-Volume Bible Dictionary,* edited by Hastings (Edinburgh and New York). Of still greater value are the ampler works, especially Hastings' *Dictionary of the Bible,* 5 volumes (including the Extra Volume). In addition to these, the *Encyclopædia Biblica,* edited by Cheyne, and the *International Bible Encyclopædia* (Chicago), are of real value.

Dr. Hastings edited also a *Dictionary of Christ and the Gospels* and a *Dictionary of the Apostolic Age,* each in 2 large volumes. These are no less admirable than the main Dictionary. Mention should be made of the valuable *Jewish Encyclopædia* and to the splendid Biblical articles in the *Encyclopædia Britannica.*

GENERAL INTRODUCTORY GUIDES TO BIBLE STUDY

Of such there are many; but of the large number, some are very unsystematic, some are thoroughly antiquated, and some are too dogmatic. A few really helpful ones may be mentioned—and the list could be very greatly extended. H. L. Willett, *Our Bible,* Chicago, 1917; George Hodges, *How to know the Bible,* Indianapolis, 1918; H. B. Hunting, *The Story of our Bible,* 1915; J. H. Penniman, *A Book about the English Bible,* New

York, 1919; Smyth, a series of little volumes, *The Bible in the Making; How we got our Bible; The Old Documents and the New Bible; How God inspired the Bible;* Sunderland, *The Origin and Character of the Bible;* Peake, *The Bible: its Origin, its Significance, and its Abiding Worth;* also his briefer work, *The Nature of Scripture,* 1922; Dods, *The Bible, its Origin and Nature;* Briggs, *A General Introduction to the Study of Holy Scripture.*— The books named represent various degrees of difficulty. That by Hunting is designed for those just entering upon serious study. Then the books by Willett, Hodges, Penniman and Smyth are designed for popular use. For those who desire to inquire into the deeper aspects of the Bible question, the books by Peake are among the best. For those interested in the bearing of Biblical criticism upon the fundamental question of faith the following books may be further recommended: G. A. Smith, *Modern Criticism and the Preaching of the Old Testament;* Eiselen, *The Christian View of the Old Testament;* Bade, *The Old Testament in the Light of To-day;* W. N. Clarke, *Sixty Years With the Bible.* As a guide to the principles of interpretation: Gilbert, *A Short History of Interpretation.*

THE ORIGIN OF THE BOOKS OF THE BIBLE

Introductions to the Old Testament by Driver, Cornill, Moore, McFadyen, Gray, Fowler, and Sellin (1923).

Introductions to the New Testament by Jülicher, Moffatt, and Bacon, and *Story of the New Testament* by Goodspeed.

Also for the Old Testament, W. R. Smith's *Old Testament in the Jewish Church* is very valuable.

BIBLICAL HISTORY AND ARCHÆOLOGY

The general text-books on Old Testament History by H. P. Smith, Wade, and Peritz are excellent. *The Historical Bible Series* by Kent is very useful. For the New Testament the *New Testament History* by Rall will afford an excellent introduction. McGiffert's *Christianity in the Apostolic Age* is a standard work. As an introduction to Biblical archæology perhaps the most convenient book is Barton, *Archæology and the Bible.* See also Price, *Monuments and the Old Testament;* Jeremias, *The Old Testament in the Light of the Ancient East;* Ball, *Light from the East;* Rogers, *Cuneiform Parallels to the Old Testament.* For the bearing of the discoveries of papyri upon the knowledge of the New Testament, consult Deissmann, *Light from the Ancient East,* rewritten edition 1923, and Cobern, *The New Archæological Discoveries.*

BIBLICAL GEOGRAPHY

The most convenient first introduction to the study of Biblical geography is afforded by Kent, *Biblical History and Geography.* For a fuller study one must go to G. A. Smith's great books, *Historical Geography of the Holy Land,* and *Jerusalem.* An admirable little book in this field is Laura H. Wild's *Geographic Influences in Old Testament Masterpieces.*

THE RELIGION AND THEOLOGY OF THE BIBLE

From the wealth of books in this field only a few will be named, for these will afford guidance for further research. Robinson, *The Religious Ideas of the Old Testament;* Schultz, *Old Testament Theology;* Davidson, *Old*

Testament Theology, and *Old Testament Prophecy;* Cornill, *The Prophets of Israel;* Knudson, *Beacon Lights of Prophecy,* and *The Religious Teaching of the Old Testament;* Stevens, *The Theology of the New Testament;* Beyschlag, *New Testament Theology;* Wendt, *The Teaching of Jesus.* There are many other works on these themes, especially on the teaching of Jesus. Also Paul and John are amply treated in many books.

HISTORY OF THE ENGLISH BIBLE

Price, *Ancestry of Our English Bible;* Westcott, *History of the English Bible,* 3d edition by W. A. Wright, 1905.

THE BIBLE AS LITERATURE

Gardiner, *The Bible as Literature,* 1912; R. G. Moulton, *The Literary Study of the Bible,* 1895; Wood and Grant, *The Bible as Literature,* 1914; Eckman, *The Literary Primacy of the Bible;* Works, *The Bible in English Literature;* a book by Burgess and one by Wordsworth on Shakespeare's use of the Bible. Genung, *A Guide to the Literature of the Bible;* L. H. Wild, *A Literary Guide to the Bible;* Gordon, *The Poetry of the Old Testament.*

THE BIBLE AND CIVILIZATION

Ernst von Dobschütz, *The Influence of the Bible on Civilization;* D. O. Mears, *The Book of Books;* William Canton, *The Bible and the Anglo-Saxon People.*

COMMENTARIES

Commentaries of the older type were generally too exclusively grammatical and philological, too atomistic.

Some of them, however, were dogmatic and sectarian in spirit and tendency. The typical modern commentary is not less thorough in respect to grammatical details, but it is incomparably more historical, seeking to discover and show the historical background and occasion of writing and to exhibit its standpoint and reproduce its argument. Among the best commentaries are the following:

A Commentary on the Bible, ed. by A. S. Peake (one volume), *The Oxford Bible for Schools, The Cambridge Bible for Schools and Colleges, The New Century Bible* (Macmillan), *The Temple Bible, The International Critical Commentary, The Westminster Commentary.*

The last two are very exhaustive in their treatment. For the average Bible student the other (much briefer) works will be found more available.

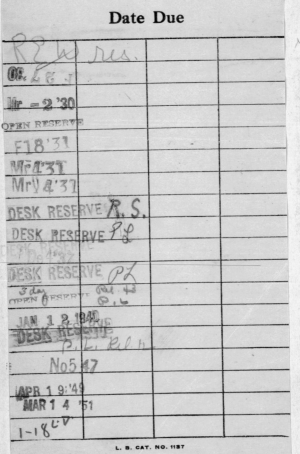

Date Due